THE BATTLE OF
LONG TAN

Lex McAulay was born in 1939 in Innisfail, Queensland, and grew up there. His background knowledge for *The Battle of Long Tan* comes from 22 years of service in the army, much of it in intelligence, and 3 tours of duty in Vietnam. Under the pseudonym David Alexander he is the author of *When the Buffalo Fight,* a highly acclaimed novel of the Vietnam war; and under his own name wrote *Into the Dragon's Jaws,* the story of the bombing of Rabaul in 1943. He is married and now lives in Canberra.

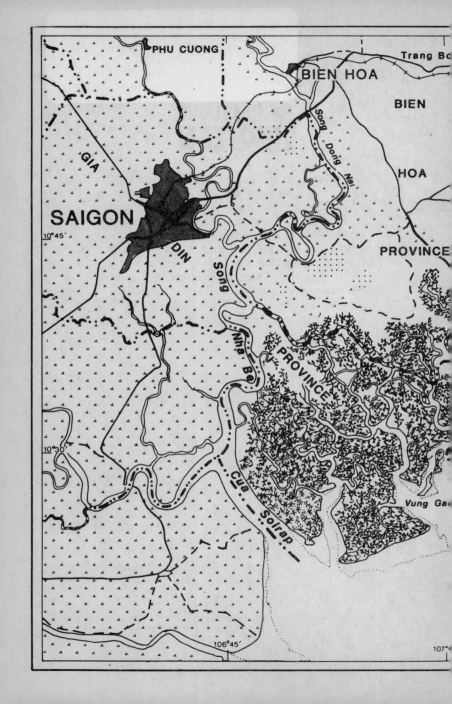

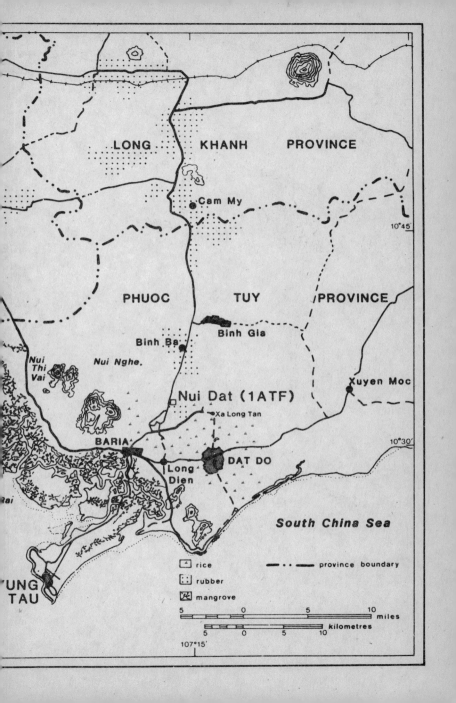

LONG   KHANH   PROVINCE

● Cam My

10°45'

PHUOC   TUY   PROVINCE

Binh Gia

Binh Ba ●

Nui Thi Vai   Nui Nghe.

Nui Dat (1ATF)

▲Xa Long Tan

Xuyen Moc ●

BARIA

10°30'

Long Dien   DAT DO

Rai

UNG TAU

South China Sea

▢ rice   ● ● ● ■ province boundary
⦂ rubber
▨ mangrove

5   0   5   10
├──────┼──────────┤ miles

5   0   5   10
├──┼──────┤ kilometres

107°15'

THE BATTLE OF
LONG TAN

Lex McAulay

ARROW BOOKS

Arrow Books Limited
62–65 Chandos Place, London WC2N 4NW

An imprint of Century Hutchinson Limited

London Melbourne Sydney Auckland
Johannesburg and agencies throughout
the world

First published in Great Britain 1987

© Lex McAulay 1986

Printed and bound in Great Britain by
Anchor Brendon Limited, Tiptree, Essex

ISBN 0 09 952530 5

Contents

Acknowledgements

THE STORY OF the Battle of Long Tan would have been impossible to present without the willing assistance, and patience, of those listed below. They gave their time, lent photos and documents, and put up with many questions about that long-ago afternoon; and deserve credit for so doing. At the same time, any shortcomings in the book are mine.

My own acknowledgement must go to Dr Bruce Horsfield, of the Centre for the Study of Educational Communication and Media, La Trobe University, Melbourne, whose primary research brought me into the all-important interviews and document searches, initially to locate what was available from the VC side. Bruce's aim was to see a film or television programme made about the action at Long Tan. When I commented that there was a book straining to leap out of all the material gathered, he selflessly offered it to me for that purpose.

Like many others, I had thought that D Company was ambushed on that day and then carried along to salvation by other people's efforts. However, Bruce, comparing survivors' accounts, convincingly argued that the Vietcong were as surprised at the contact as D Company. His scholarly documentation of this argument is worthy of praise.

It is hoped that this book will help to ensure that credit is given to all those to whom it is due for their part in the battle on 18 August 1966, in Phuoc Tuy Province, Republic of Vietnam.

Some of the following were interviewed by Bruce, and some by me. In the interests of brevity, the only ranks included are those of people who were, or have risen to become, of one-star rank — that is, Brigadier or its equivalent.

Ian Affleck, Peter Ainslie, 'Yank' Akell, Frank Alcorta, Patti Amphlett, Rod Armstrong, Geoff Banfield, Peter Bennett, George Bindley, Kevin Branch, Bob Buick, John Bullen, Barry Campton, Nick Cater, Phil Cooke, Steve Corvini, Helen Creagh, Richmond Cubis, Ian Darlington, Alan Deller, John Dermody, Peter Dinham, Cliff Dohle, Peter Doyle, Laurie Drinkwater, Harry Esler, Alan Evans, Brig. David Ferguson, Richard Fisher, Bill

Fogarty, Gavin Fry, Neville Gair, Kevin Graham, Bob Grandin, Brian Halls, Richard Hannigan, David Harris, Brig. Harry Honner, Maj. Gen. R.N.L. Hopkins, Brig. O.D. Jackson, Col Joye, Geoff Kendall, Leo Kucks, Bruce Lane, Brig. Paul Lipscombe, I.E.R. ('Black Mac') McDonald, Barry Meller, John Murphy, Russ Perandis, Bob Piper, Neil Rankin, Air Cdre Peter Raw, Brian Reilly, 'Pom' Rencher, Adrian Roberts, Chris Roughley, John Rowe, David Sabben, Ian Savage, Air Cdre Ray Scott, Peter Short, Harry Smith, Ross Smith, Ernie Sparahan, Maury Stanley, Peter Tedder, 'Paddy' Todd, Colin Townsend, Ken Tronk, Dave Wells, Brian Wickens.

Acknowledgement must also go to Army Office and RAAF Historical Office, Department of Defence, for their assistance in giving us access to relevant documents; and to the Australian War Memorial for its, as always, unstinting help when asked. The people with whom we had personal contact are in the list above, but the assistance given by the organizations with which they are connected is also gratefully acknowledged.

The photographs that appear in this book came from a variety of sources: the Australian War Memorial (which supplied nearly half of them), Peter Dinham, Peter Doyle, Harry Honner, 'Pom' Rencher, Adrian Roberts, Ian Savage, Harry Smith, Ross Smith, Maury Stanley, Mike Wells, Brian Wickens, and the Royal Australian Army Medical Corps. Again, the cooperation of all concerned is gratefully acknowledged. Finally, my thanks also to Wendy Gorton, who drew the maps.

Introduction

ON 18 AUGUST 1966, the most intense battle ever to involve Australian soldiers and forces of the National Liberation Front (NLF), commonly called the Vietcong (VC), was fought in a rubber plantation at a place called Long Tan, Phuoc Tuy Province, in the Republic of Vietnam (RVN). Although battles involving larger Australian units were fought before and after Long Tan, on no other occasion was so small an Australian force engaged for so long, and so intensely, by so large an enemy.

It is often said that truth is stranger than fiction, and this seems to be the case with Long Tan. Any fictional presentation of 100 inexperienced young soldiers fighting at least ten and probably fifteen or twenty times their own number, in a rubber plantation providing little cover, in a blinding rainstorm; killing and wounding at least one-third of their opponents; then being relieved by a force arriving just as the enemy is massing for the final unstoppable charge — any such scenario would be ridiculed as the worst type of Hollywood glorification of war.

Yet this is what did happen on that August afternoon.

Unfortunately, almost no documents allowing a view of the VC side are known to have been taken by the Australians, either at the battle or later. This is regrettable, as it was the intention of the author to give specific rather than anonymous recognition to the Vietnamese participants, who, though defeated, performed as they so often did in the face of Allied firepower, and went into the attack again and again; and then removed as many men and weapons as they could from the battlefield, to the extent that only three wounded VC were left to be captured the next day.

The performance of the VC on the scene should be rated highly, and the Australian feat of arms can be appreciated only when the mettle of their enemy is taken into account.

It is to the young men of both sides who fought that day at Long Tan that this book is dedicated.

The Setting

In peace there's nothing so becomes a man
As modest stillness and humility:
But when the blast of war blows in our ears,
Then imitate the action of the tiger;
Stiffen the sinews, summon up the blood,
Disguise fair nature with hard-favour'd rage;
Then lend the eye a terrible aspect...

King Henry V (III. i.)

THE VIETNAMESE are the most dynamic race in Indo-China, and many of their neighbours live in fear of them. The history of Vietnam can be traced back for several thousand years, to kingdoms in the Red River area in the north. Gradually the Vietnamese moved south, overwhelming the peoples before them, and were actively colonizing the Mekong region not long before the arrival of the Europeans in the same area. It was only the colonizing activities of the French which halted — temporarily — Vietnamese expansion into the giant rice-paddy that is Kampuchea.

The Vietnamese hold the unique distinction of having been a Chinese colony for a thousand years and yet thrown off the Chinese yoke and re-established their nation; and then defeated a further Chinese invasion. This would be the equivalent today of pre-Norman England emerging as a Saxon nation again.

Despite a typically Asian respect for learning and culture, the Vietnamese have always been warlike, and their history includes many revolts and rebellions, overthrows of dynasties, and campaigns both of expansion and of resistance to invaders.

In the 1850s, the French began colonizing in Indo-China by force of arms, after more peaceful methods had failed to gain them preferential treatment at court. They were never undisputed masters, and the flame of Vietnamese resistance always remained alive — though it often subsided to not much more than an ember.

European technological superiority was negated by the arrival of the Japanese, who encouraged anti-French Vietnamese. As in other parts of Asia, when it was clear that the war was lost and the Japanese concept of a Co-prosperity Sphere similarly defeated, 'Independence' was given to the Vietnamese, in August 1945.

This opportunity was seized by Ho chi Minh and his Vietminh forces, the best-organized, most disciplined and most dynamic of the anti-French groups. On 2 September 1945, in Hanoi, accompanied by a small unit of the American OSS, Ho declared the independence of Vietnam.

Despite, or perhaps because of, the humiliation of German occupation during the years 1940−44 and liberation by US-British armies, the French would not agree to an independent Vietnam. A nine-year war ensued.

The overconfident Vietminh suffered heavily in some of the early battles when the French could bring to bear mechanized forces, air power and artillery power. Learning quickly, the Vietnamese fought whenever possible at times and places of their own choosing, while year after year the French tried to bring about more of the set-piece battles they were sure of winning.

The Vietminh not only waged a military and political struggle against the French, but simultaneously set about dismantling and rebuilding society in the areas under their control — and, as much as possible, in those under French control as well. Notable in this struggle were concerted campaigns of terror, ostensibly to eliminate the wealthy peasants and urban businessmen. The first was in 1953 and others followed, through to 1956. After the aims for each had been achieved, Ho chi Minh would apologize deeply, another member of the hierarchy would resign (but retain his Politburo position), and the process would continue.

Ho was seen as the gentle nationalist, whose subordinates were responsible for the repeated excesses. About 100 000 people are estimated to have been murdered in these campaigns, and eventually (after the French had gone) the people of Ho's own home province revolted against the Hanoi regime.

As well as the general population, the Party itself was purged. No figures were given for the total number of people imprisoned or executed, but it was later stated that 12 000 had been released from jail.

The Vietminh finally obliged the French and gave them their set-piece battle, at Dienbienphu. After its defeat there, France had had enough; and in July 1954 Vietnam became independent, though split up into a North and a South Vietnam.

At the Geneva Conference that ended the war, separate accords were signed for Cambodia, Laos and Vietnam. Article 14 of the Vietnam agreement referred in passing to 'general elections which will bring about the unification of Vietnam'. A fourth unsigned 'Final Declaration' set the deadline for the elections as July 1956.

However, nothing was specified for these elections — such as exactly what the people were to vote for, or who would be represented. Like the signed ceasefire agreements, the Final Declaration was intended to help France to leave Indo-China as quickly as possible.

In the North, which was given to the Vietminh, the customary Communist eradication of differing political views soon resulted in a totalitarian state. The situation in the South was very different, with an influx of northern refugees, and with many political parties and religious groups combining forces, dispersing and realigning themselves in an effort to win government power.

About 900 000 people fled the North, and an estimated 400 000 more would have gone but were not allowed to do so by the Vietminh — in contravention of the ceasefire agreement. This exodus was embarrassing for the Vietminh, and for the myth of universal love for 'Uncle Ho'.

Only some 50 000 went north.

Ngo Dinh Diem, devout Catholic and strongly anti-Communist and anti-colonial, was brought from exile in the United States to head the fledgling South. Diem quickly realized that any election would see the fragmented South easily outvoted by the controlled North, and rejected the idea of Vietnam-wide elections.

Diem began governing a newly created nation that had almost no experienced people in government at any level, no competent public service, and an Army flung together by the French — but with some units more akin to feudal armies in their loyalties, based on religion, locale or the sheer charisma of the leader.

The French, despite their self-proclaimed mission of bringing civilization, had generally regarded Vietnam as a source of profits. All decision-making was by Frenchmen, for France. Unless a Vietnamese became a Frenchman, he was unable to achieve positions of influence or power. When the colonial regime ended in mid-1954, Vietnam had none of the trained and experienced administrators so necessary for the successful operation of a modern democratic nation.

Despite the odds in these first crucial years, Diem succeeded in triumphing over his enemies, and over the situation at large. He smashed the armed gangs masquerading as military units (raised by the French to assist them in controlling areas of the country), kept the nation together, and began to make progress. Unfortunately, the early successes made him believe he was infallible, and he ceased listening to any advice except that of his brother Nhu, and Nhu's wife Madame Nhu, the 'Dragon Lady'.

The story of the decline and fall of the Diem regime has been well reported elsewhere, and it is sufficient here to state that by the time of Diem's overthrow and assassination in November 1963, his own inability to govern correctly and the machinations of his family had contributed to the growing power of the Communist-dominated National Liberation Front (NLF), popularly known inside and outside South Vietnam as the Vietcong (VC).

A skeleton Vietminh organization had remained, and those who had gone north in 1954 at the time of the partition into North and South were gradually infiltrated back, often to their home areas, to nurture and control the expanding resistance to Diem and his regime.

Corruption at all levels of the bureaucracy, governmental indifference to the people, police brutality, absentee landlords, religious repression, unpopular and unnecessary laws and regulations — all these, among other things, made the task of the VC propaganda and recruiting cadre relatively easy.

As early as January 1963, VC battalions discovered that they could stand and fight the Army of the Republic of Vietnam (ARVN) and win. By mid-1964, the ARVN controlled only the ground on which it stood at the time. In early 1965, a series of battles of regimental size across South Vietnam resulted in the systematic destruction of the ARVN Regular formations. By mid-1965, the Saigon regime had no units in reserve — everything was in the field, and being methodically annihilated by VC and North Vietnamese Army (NVA) units.

As the war dragged on, the ARVN found itself increasingly unable to provide capable commanders at all levels, burdened as it was with class divisions, religious differences between Buddhist and Catholic, corruption, nepotism and indifference to the needs of the junior ranks. Combat command was in general avoided; promotion and transfer were effected in a Byzantine world of intrigue, favours and feuds. Shining from all this like jewels were the honest, courageous, patriotic officers and men of the ARVN who led by example, upholding the honour of their country and people. It is one of the tragedies of our century that so many of their generals were unworthy of them.

The United States had been providing advisory assistance to the South Vietnamese government and forces since the departure

6

of the French, gradually increasing the size of this commitment as the war intensified. Australia had begun with a mere 30 advisers in 1962, and by 1965 their number had risen to 100. It was clear, despite these efforts, that South Vietnam was on the verge of collapse and absorption by force of arms into the Communist North.

American and Australian combat forces were sent to take the field and engage and destroy the rampant VC, providing time for the government in Saigon (GVN) to recover.

Australia sent the First Battalion, Royal Australian Regiment (1RAR), plus artillery, armour, engineers and logistics units suitable to support a battalion. These all came under control-for-operations of the US 173rd Airborne Brigade, and from June 1965 to June 1966 they operated in the provinces around Saigon, searching for and engaging VC and NVA units.

With guerrilla warfare, it should be remembered that if large battles are being fought, the guerrillas are winning — despite battlefield losses — because the population is providing the personnel for the big engagements; and, conversely, the government is losing popular support.

Meanwhile, an Australian Task Force of two infantry battalions and relevant supporting arms and services was being raised for duty in South Vietnam. It was decided that this force would operate somewhat independently, in an area to be allocated. The chosen location was Phuoc Tuy Province, to the south-east of Saigon, a long-time centre of resistance to the French and to the Saigon government.

The officer appointed to command the First Australian Task Force (1ATF) was Brigadier O.D. (David) Jackson, who had had active service experience in World War II (in the Middle East and New Guinea), and later in Korea. More recently, he had commanded the Australian Army Training Team Vietnam (AATTV) — generally called 'The Team' in the Australian Army — and the Australian Army Force Vietnam (AAFV), with the 1RAR Battalion Group its major component.

The only directive Jackson received, either verbally or in writing, as to his mission in the 1ATF area of operations was from General William Westmoreland, commander of all non-Vietnamese Allied forces: simply, 'Take over Phuoc Tuy'.

After some consideration it was decided to station the Task Force at Nui Dat, which was centrally located in the province, allowed a short supply-line from the logistics base at Vung Tau, and was literally within the most densely populated area. By being there, the Task Force would disrupt VC activity and control.

The way in which some of the units and individuals were more or less bundled into South Vietnam, with little logistical support — with even so simple a matter as the mail delivery being plagued by problems — was, for the 1960s, little short of scandalous. Fortunately, some items were held in storage to support SEATO operations if necessary, and if it had not been for these the situation would have been worse.

The physical conditions in Phuoc Tuy in mid-1966 were appalling. It was the wet season, and rainwater actually poured over the surface of the ground, unable to soak in. An entire military camp had to be built in the centre of an enemy-dominated region. Any construction activity became a mud-wallow.

Private Harry 'Horse' Esler, a first-intake National Serviceman, was in D Company 6RAR:

> They stuck us on a plane and flew us to Vietnam. We landed on a beach and I thought, *This is it. This is going to be great. A nice little beach at Vung Tau.* Then they whipped us up to Nui Dat into the middle of a rubber plantation. When we got there it was all mud. There was no machinery to help us, we had to do it all by hand, using entrenching tools.

The Protestant Chaplain of 6RAR was the Reverend Les Thompson, who had put his age up from 16 to 19 in order to join the AIF at the end of World War II, going to 67 Battalion and on to Japan with the Occupation Forces, and returning to Australia and discharge after one enlistment. In his own words, he 'became a Christian at the age of 28', and late in 1965, when already a clergyman, he was asked to join the Army's Chaplain's Department. He did so, and was pleased to find on arrival in 6RAR that he knew a few officers and Warrant Officers from his own days as a Digger.

Like many of the soldiers, he was 'pleased to leave the beach, a hot, horrible place in many ways, and to go into the bush, the rubber plantation at Nui Dat'.

Other soldiers also found Vung Tau unbearable. 'Even the South China Sea was warm and sticky', says 'Pom' Rencher, an Englishman who had joined the Australian Army and found himself in D Company, 6RAR (D/6RAR). He recalls: 'The D Company storeman, Tubby Campbell, decided he did not like it, and started swimming for home, clutching a bottle of gin. He was eventually shepherded back by a passing helicopter.'

Chaplain Thompson saw the early days as a period of 'shaking down and building up', and, although as unsure as the soldiers about the future, tried to provide a calm and human presence, and never lacked visitors around 'the Chaplain's tent'.

He could see little difference between the 'Nashos' and the 'Regs' — they were all young Aussies — and on one occasion asked a group of Nashos whether they would like to go home tomorrow. 'They all laughed and said the Regulars would never handle it!' In normal Australian fashion, they 'took shots' at one another in good fun.

The overriding priority was security, for it was realized from the beginning that the VC/NVA would not allow this intrusion to go quietly ahead.

Like commanders in most modern wars, Jackson could not get enough infantry for the many tasks necessary: to guard the developing base camp; to patrol close to and far from it; to carry out search operations for enemy in the nearby towns and villages; to be in readiness to move at once to engage located enemy; to be held ready to exploit any advantage from such an engagement; if needed, to guard the engineer and logistics activities; and to perform the thousand-and-one other tasks for which infantry are called.

But Jackson had only two battalions for all these jobs; what is more, they had to build their own part of the Task Force base. 'Pom' Rencher has vivid memories of cursing the unending work in camp, longing to be out on patrol; and when out there, cursing the endless walking under a pack in the rain, longing for camp.

One thing the Australians had in their favour, from the earliest days of 1RAR in 1965, was that only a few ARVN were allowed into the base, and absolutely no civilians. This was in contrast to the Vietnamese themselves, and to the US forces, who employed numerous local people as waiters, kitchen helpers, garbage removers, laundry maids, barbers, snackshop operators, and so on. With these hordes of local people entering and leaving bases daily, the gathering of intelligence was almost laughably easy for the VC. Security checks were little more than a formality, and the VC easily acquired the relevant documents and identity cards.

In addition, most US camps were constructed in an area first thoroughly cleared of all growth — thus allowing long-distance observation — while the Australians moved in under the rubber-trees in the plantation, gaining the double benefit of shade and cover from distant observers.

But despite these precautions, it was obvious to the VC where the Australians were. Their numbers were also easy to determine from what could be seen and deduced, and from the amount of information readily available from the media and the Australian forces' own Public Relations releases.

Jackson and his senior staff realized that the VC/NVA could not allow 1ATF to establish itself in this location. The VC had to retain control of the people, their food resources, the information they could provide, and the recruits they could supply, not to mention clothing, medicine, labour, money, and whatever else was requested or demanded of them. Without such access to the population, and such control, a guerrilla enemy is doomed to die of starvation and deprivation.

At the time 1ATF was struggling to establish a base camp, the enemy force in the neighbouring area was the VC 5th Division, comprising 274 and 275 Regiments plus supporting supply units. These formations were composed of well-trained and well-equipped troops who had progressed through the proven Communist guerrilla system of selection and training: from peasant youth to village guerrilla, to local platoon or company soldier, to member of a Main Force unit such as the 5th Division.

Promotion and selection for various duties in the VC was mainly on merit and, in the higher echelons, political reliability. Social class and religion, or 'connection', meant little.

Whereas in the ARVN only a token few officers were promoted from the lower classes of society, in the VC peasants could, if they had the ability, command battalions and regiments. The ARVN represented the distant Saigon government, tax-collectors, absentee landlords, corruption and political indifference, while the VC were often careful to be seen as modern Robin Hoods, protecting the people from all of that, made up (moreover) of local men and women, in an organization that needed only to promise a better life than that provided by the faraway regime in Saigon.

By claiming to be liberating the people from the harsh Saigon government, the VC were able selectively to destroy the local government presence, killing schoolteachers, village chiefs, minor officials, policemen, and sometimes the families of these — often as gruesomely as possible before an audience of the assembled villagers.

In addition, there was the naked use of terror to demonstrate their power to murder and destroy, as when mines were placed to detonate under cars and buses going to market, or bombs exploded in cinemas and busy parts of the towns and cities.

Despite denials from Hanoi, indisputable proof that the war in South Vietnam was controlled from Hanoi was provided by captured documents, prisoners and surrendered VC. During the war against the French, activities in the south had been directed by the Central Office for South Vietnam (COSVN), led by Le Duan, who later went on to senior positions in the North. With the defeat of the French, COSVN was deactivated, and activities were conducted by Party Committees at regional level.

In 1958, Le Duan toured and inspected the South, returning to Hanoi with a list of recommendations. The following year, the Central Committee of the Lao Dong Party in Hanoi determined on a military conquest of the South, and it was decided to reactivate COSVN. Le Duan's recommendations had been accepted, and were referred to as 'Resolution 15'. They mapped the course of the insurgency in the South: a 'National Front' was to be formed; it would be controlled by the southern branch of the Lao Dong Party; it would be supported by a southern 'liberation army'; and it would conduct a political struggle, with armed force to complement the political activity, to prepare the South to come under control of the North — that is, for unification.

In September 1960, Le Duan made a speech at the Third National Congress of the Lao Dong Party in which he stated that the Congress would define the line for the socialist revolution in the North and for the struggle to achieve reunification, and that a 'broad national united front' was needed in the South.

Accordingly, on 20 December 1960, the National Front for the Liberation of South Vietnam — commonly referred to as the National Liberation Front (NLF) — was created; in 1961 COSVN reappeared; and in 1962 the southern branch of the Lao Dong Party was formally dissolved, to be replaced immediately by the People's Revolutionary Party (PRP), acknowledged by the NLF as 'the highest organization'.

COSVN was superior to both the NLF and the PRP. Its leaders were members of the Lao Dong Politburo and Central Committee, and other chief members were selected by Hanoi. The role of COSVN was to coordinate and direct activities in the South, through directives and orders guided by policies established by the Lao Dong Party.

The organization of COSVN mirrored the structure extending down into the districts and villages of the regions and provinces for control of which the war was fought.

The National Representative Assembly of the PRP was theoretically the highest authority and supposedly elected the Central Executive Committee, which was the highest Party organization, conducted Party matters, and selected the Party Secretary and the members of the Current Affairs Committee.

The Current Affairs Committee, including the Party Secretary, deputies and officials of the Military Party Committee, was responsible for daily business, but all its directives were to be based on policies of the Central Executive Committee.

11

The Military Party Committee was the highest echelon of the military wing of the Party structure and was required to draft guidelines and plans for military and political activities, but these were decided by the Party Committee and the Current Affairs Committee. A Military Party Committee could be found in units of battalion size and higher, each being responsible to the next higher level, up to COSVN, and would be composed of the unit Commander, the Political Officer, and officers from subordinate units.

Along with these Committees were Sections for the NLF and its affiliated organizations: for Propaganda, Culture and Indoctrination; Postal Transportation and Communications; Military Proselyting; Finance and Economy; Public Health; and Forward Supply (i.e. logistics).

All of these, or their equivalents, were found in the regions and provinces, being repeated in some cases right down to villages and hamlets.

Because the battle was fought near the village of Long Tan, it would be convenient to use that village as an example. In 1966, Long Tan was one of 13 villages that comprised Long Dat District. Five Districts made up the Province, which was reorganized and renamed several times but was variously known as Ba Long, Ba Bien or Baria.

People in the village and district would have been involved, either voluntarily or not, in NLF organizations — such as Farmers', Women's, Youths', and so on — and contributed their time and activity, as well as their produce and money, to the Production Unit, the tax-collector, and the Forward Supply and Finance and Economy elements. As well as taxes, 'compulsory donations' were extracted. Receipts were given for all of the above.

Strangely, it was rare for tax-collectors ambushed by the Australians to be carrying much money, despite what their receipt books recorded on arrival at 1ATF.

After the decision in Hanoi to take the South by force, the thousands of Southerners who had gone north at the time of the 1954 partition were sent back to use their training in furthering the efforts of the NLF. Only a few hundred filtered south in 1959, but the number rose to 3000 in 1960 and 10000 in 1961. By late 1964 almost all of these had returned, and groups and formed units of NVA personnel were then sent.

The Southerners moving back to the land they had left five or more years before were not simply cannon-fodder, as the later NVA units were, but had been trained to take up duties as specialists, political officers, military commanders and committee members for the all-important political structure from village to region.

In Phuoc Tuy, the local men recruited into the combatant unit of the VC formed D445 Battalion, which had grown in traditional manner from a few squads to a platoon, to a company, to a battalion. Being born and bred in the area, they knew it intimately, and were generally able to come off best in ambushes and engagements as the guerrilla war evolved from mere resistance to Diem and his refusal to hold the promised elections.

In 1957, two 'companies' of the Binh Xuyen (river-pirates and gangsters in a private army recognized by the French but destroyed by Diem) moved into the Thi Vai area, west of Nui Dat. By the end of 1959 they had become a VC unit, reinforced by draft-dodgers, which was titled C40. Another company of draft-dodgers was formed, called C45.

In 1963 these two joined for a few minor operations, which produced little result and few casualties but provided experience. In December, with a total of about 100 men, they merged to form C445. Another group of 100 was called C445/40.

In September 1964, C445 joined with the Long Dat District Company for an attack on Phuoc Hai and an ambush, then operated with 1st Battalion, 274 Regiment for the Battle of Binh Gia.

In February 1965, the companies joined to form D445 Provincial Mobile Battalion. Before the Australian Task Force arrived, they had carried out several operations, including successful ambushes of ARVN Rangers and GVN Civic Action Teams, killing 40 men of the latter and taking their weapons.

Despite some losses, morale was high, for it was obvious that the NLF was gaining the upper hand. They were winning, and *seen* to be winning.

Reasons for joining the local VC were many. Few did so because of a belief in Communism. In fact, the VC were careful to present their NLF as such, a Front representing religious, political, professional, age, urban and rural, academic and student groups.

Chau, leader of D445's Reconnaissance Platoon for three years, claimed he joined because of disgust with the Diem regime and its refusal to hold unifying elections. He joined in 1961, and after experience in local actions was sent to Cambodia in 1963 for a course that enabled him to lead the reconnaissance element of D445, when it grew to battalion status.

Nam, who later commanded D445 Battalion and was killed in action in 1970, tried three times to join some part of the VC but was sent home as being an unknown and thus possibly a police spy. He and some friends considered joining the ARVN, but he did not want to be sent away from his home region. In this he was no different from tens of thousands of other young Vietnamese with a strong attachment to their home area. Nam was one of 14 children, and wanted to find some employment, no matter what, to relieve the burden on his parents. There was no land available, no possibility of education beyond the basic level, and no opportunity to learn a trade.

Another local was Hoa, who joined in 1964 during a recruiting drive by D445. The guerrillas were glamorous, and the deciding factor was hearing the bugler of D445 play. For an 18-year-old, in Vietnam as in many other countries around the world, the armed forces offered an obvious means of proving his manhood. But the reality was less palatable than the illusion. Hoa found the pay little and infrequent; living conditions were poor; visits to families were never unescorted; and medical supplies, always hard to get, had to be bought and delivered by parents or family members.

A third VC, not relevant to the action at Long Tan, told the author about his outrage when comparing the care and attention lavished on him by the Americans (when, dressed in ARVN uniform, he was injured in a traffic accident and taken to a US military hospital for recovery) with the scant treatment given him in the VC when he was ill. However, he soldiered on until the defeat of the Saigon regime.

The fear of being sent away from home by the ARVN was what also persuaded Long, another young man, to join the local VC unit in late 1961. At first he worked in a supply unit, later transferring to fully-armed status in D445. He too was disappointed to find that pay was lacking, as were food and medical attention. But at least he, like the others, was not far from home, and the GVN forces were beaten and seen to be so.

By mid-1966, D445 was composed of five companies, C1 to C5, totalling about 400 men, armed mostly with captured weapons of US origin.

For the North Vietnamese, there was no choice. The Party machinery ensured that all available males were supplied from town and village, with only one man left to carry on the family name. Those not needed in the North were put through the training camps and sent south, through all the hazards, to fight in the units there.

If the fighting units such as D445 and 274-275 Regiments can be imagined as the muscles of the Communist guerrilla movement, the supply and support organizations could be envisaged as the stomach and arteries, the Party apparatus as the skeleton

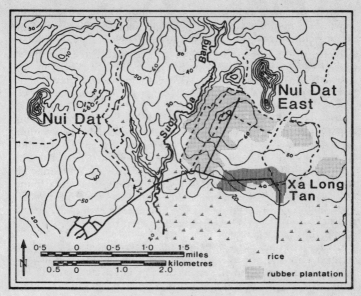

The Nui Dat and Long Tan area

and bones, and the highest level of the Party itself as the brain and nervous system. Trying to destroy a Communist guerrilla movement by fighting the 'muscles' was a long and ultimately self-defeating task. It was illnesses of the stomach or interruptions to the nervous system which promised results.

The VC in Phuoc Tuy were well aware of the threat to their stomach and nervous system posed by the arrival of 1ATF.

'We were angry at you from the start', explained Chau, the D445 Reconnaissance Platoon leader, 'because where you put your runway was exactly on the route we used when going from the western part of the province, past Nui Dat, to visit Long Tan and Long Phuoc villages.'

Off to the east, deep in the mountains, there would have been a conference of the VC regional leaders, both political and military. A résumé of the current situation in Vietnam, and in their regions, would have been presented. Their problems would have been discussed, solutions suggested, policy determined. The subject of the Australian mercenaries and their base would have been raised. After consideration of the military and political factors, including Australian politics, the committee decided to move against the base of 1ATF.

But as Brigadier Jackson was well aware, 1ATF was now at its weakest. Not only was the base camp in its beginnings, but most of the soldiers and officers were inexperienced. World War II, Korea, Malaya and Borneo notwithstanding, most of the junior ranks had no active service. A considerable number were National Servicemen called up for two years of military training and service where required.

The base camp being constructed by 1ATF at Nui Dat in Phuoc Tuy Province was the first since World War II that Australian forces had had to position in an area containing large formations of enemy, who could attack from any direction at any time or harass the supply-line from the coast.

In addition, certain peacetime policies, mostly concerning training safety in mainland Australia, hampered early activities and operations in the life of 1ATF. Infantry preparing for war were bound by the same safety rules for night firing as applied to the schoolboy Cadets. The artillery took far too long to get rounds onto a target, as at first they insisted on lengthy ranging procedures. The RAAF helicopter force had been used in Australia in the general support role, which did not include coming under fire. But the Army rapidly got accustomed to the American system: the pilot was in a combat zone, and not bound by the restrictions of peacetime civilian flight rules.

Brigadier Jackson initially used a US Army Iroquois helicopter provided on a daily basis — partly because, as a formation commander, he was entitled to its use; and also because he had arguments with RAAF pilots about flying where he wanted to go but they did not, for fear of endangering the aircraft. Bob Grandin, who flew on a crucial mission during the Battle of Long Tan, still recalls some of these occasions.

However, Ray Scott, then a Wing Commander and CO of 9 Squadron, denies this, claiming that it was clearly understood by all that the helicopter unit was going to war. But perhaps some individuals did not accept this fact as readily as others.

There are numerous anecdotes and examples quoted of RAAF reluctance to expose the aircraft to ground fire, generally by way of comparison with the US Army units with which the speaker had had experience. It was known to few, if any, that 9 Squadron had only six armoured seats, scrounged and on loan from the Americans. Officially, through the supply system, the first seats were not due to arrive until August 1966, and only then would two per month be supplied. Individual armour protection for the crews was not expected until December.

The RAAF in the early days of 1ATF was held in contempt by the Army because of this combination of lack of understanding and lack of preparedness for war in equipping the squadron. The Army, and initially the Special Air Service (SAS), much preferred to use the Americans — until the matter was resolved by both sides settling down to work together, and also in part by a visit from a senior RAAF officer from Canberra, the Chief of Air Staff, Sir Alistair Murdoch, to whom Brigadier Jackson explained the realities of life in Vietnam. Later, the SAS, which had exacting requirements, developed superior tactics and procedures with the RAAF, and would use no other.

It was during the Battle of Long Tan, on 18 August, that the matter would come to a head.

The RAAF force in Vietnam in August 1966 consisted mainly of 35 Squadron, with Caribou twin-engined transports; and 9 Squadron, with UH-1B Iroquois helicopters (generally nicknamed 'Hueys'). Both types of aircraft were used by the US forces, though the B-model Huey had been replaced by the D, and was used by the Americans mostly in the armed-helicopter (gunship) role.

The RAAF Commander at Vung Tau, and also the 1ATF air-element commander, was Group Captain Peter Raw, an experienced pilot and RAAF officer with service from World War II. Like other commanders in the Australian force in Vietnam, he had little time to prepare for his role: a bare two weeks to hand over command of 82 Wing at Amberley, go to Canberra for the necessary briefings and gain some experience of the problems of operating Caribou and Iroquois squadrons.

Raw's title of Task Force Air Commander was given him by the RAAF, and he gained the impression that this was done owing to 'friction' existing between the Army and the RAAF on the role of the Air Force in the type of war being fought in Vietnam. He thought his title should more properly have been Task Force Air Support Officer, as the Task Force itself had no aircraft to command (apart from the half-dozen Army Aviation machines — Cessnas and Sioux helicopters).

Very soon after arriving, Raw realized that the role of the helicopters of 9 Squadron was in reality support of the Army, despite the 'fright' of senior RAAF persons in Canberra that the Army might begin to control in detail the use of RAAF machines. The Canberra view was that the RAAF was to be 'completely and utterly independent'.

Experience was to show that the helicopters could not operate independently. The Caribou unit was another matter, and to all intents and purposes it became just another transport unit in the USAF presence, flying for the Australians only as tasked in their day-to-day operations.

The Department of Air's Organization Directive 8/66, dated 1 April 1966, clearly stated that the role of 9 Squadron was 'to provide helicopters in direct support of ATF for: −
  (i) troop positioning;
  (ii) troop extraction;
  (iii) logistic support; and
  (iv) aeromedical evacuation'.
However, the Department's Organization Directive 9/66, dated 18 April 1966, refined even further the way in which the helicopters would operate in the warzone. It was stated in paragraph 9 that:

> The function of No. 9 Squadron is to provide short-range transport support in the following roles: −
>   (a) the lift of troops from a secure staging area to a landing-zone that is relatively secure and when enemy resistance is not expected; i.e. troop positioning;
>   (b) the lift of troops from an operation area to a secure staging area when enemy resistance is anticipated on the last lift from the landing-zone; i.e. troop extraction;
>   (c) logistic support; and
>   (d) aeromedical evacuation.

Much of the friction between the Services was caused by use of the terms 'under command' and 'operational control', which allowed the Army to issue orders to the helicopters, to the point of interfering with Scott's command of his unit. An example was the order that door gunners be left out of the crews so that more infantry could be carried, which Scott refused to obey. He was vindicated when ground fire was received in the target area.

Scott had protested, suggesting that 'in direct support of' was a more applicable term and had been arrived at during the major wars of the preceding decades. This phrase was in fact used in Directive 8/66, as quoted above.

Living and working among the Army, Raw soon realized that it saw the RAAF as suppliers of transport to be called as and when needed, but without a complementary understanding of the limitations of the machines and crews. The Army made disparaging remarks about the RAAF personnel living in comfort at Vung Tau instead of living beside their planes in tents. As Raw recalls it:

> They had absolutely no understanding of the complexities of the maintenance requirement for the aeroplanes, of the crew rest and briefing that had to take place before the aeroplane could even be offered to the Army to do a day's work for them.

It was matters such as this that led to a lot of bad blood. But as operations progressed these matters tended to go out the window. There was ignorance on both sides of the house.

This lack of understanding on the part of the Army was put quite simply by Captain Barry Campton, Task Force Artillery Intelligence Officer: a Task Force is a combat formation, and the RAAF cannot be expected to set up a jet-engine maintenance shop in such a location.

Probably contributing to lack of sympathy from the Army was the fact that Vung Tau was where the soldiers went on leave, to let off steam and enjoy themselves, and that aspect of the town was associated with the RAAF living and working there. Also, the Huey was in everyday use by the Army, in all of its flying, and familiarity may have bred contempt. No one at 1ATF is likely to have thought that the four-engined C130 Hercules flying up from Australia should be based at Nui Dat; yet the everyday, common Huey was seen as a simple machine that should be close to hand.

The helicopter squadron arrived in Vietnam and became operational in June. Its first real mission was an urgent ammunition resupply, into what was found to be an unguarded and potentially lethal landing-zone. At the end of the month, Scott referred to the problems he could see arising — the inexperience of the RAAF Operations Room staff; the fact that the commanders of both 1ATF and the Australian Logistics unit (at Vung Tau) competed for the available helicopters; the Army tendency to use the Iroquois as a taxi; and the fact that the Army Operations staff were experienced in working with US units and 'do not or do not want to understand ARA/RAAF systems'.

On 4 July, however, 16 lightweight armoured seats arrived and the borrowed six were returned. On 28 July, 20 chest-protectors arrived.

At the end of July, Scott reported that tasking was still a problem, and warned that unless both Services understood the methods of tasking and operating the helicopters, inefficiency would result and 'bitterness and distrust between the Services will develop'.

In the time-honoured way, 9 Squadron's first door-mounts for machineguns were acquired by 'barter', one of Wing Commander Scott's crewmen having as a friend a US crew-chief. In the same time-honoured way, Scott wanted to know nothing about the matter, leaving the crewman to get on with it.

While 9 Squadron may have been lacking in items necessary for front-line flying, it was built around a core of experienced pilots and crews. Its operating policies and tactics had been carefully thought out, and practised as far as possible in Australia. Pilot and crew skills had been honed in New Guinea, arguably the worst flying area in the world.

In 1964 Ray Scott had visited almost every US aviation unit operating in Vietnam, and had spent time both observing and actually flying with them on missions. En route to Australia he had done the same in Malaysia, where British Commonwealth forces had been fighting against Sukarno's Indonesian units (the 'Confrontation' campaign).

Back in Australia, Scott had thought deeply about the US and British methods and evolved a basic doctrine for the RAAF helicopter units in the event of a similar war. Unable to afford the men and machines for US-style massed attacks, Australian forces would have to employ speed, stealth and deception, and Scott had devised helicopter tactics embodying these three principles.

However, when 9 Squadron arrived and prepared to operate, Scott encountered the Army attitude already described. Mostly as a result of 1RAR's experiences, the Army was intoxicated with the US helicopter operations. Starved of such lavish and powerful support on the Australian mainland, the Army, particularly the infantry and artillery, almost overnight came to expect it as the norm.

Furthermore, it was easy for the Army to adapt to this comparatively luxurious mode of operation: the Army did not have to contribute men, machines or units to the huge logistic base needed to provide the hundreds of helicopters of all sizes. These merely appeared out of the dawn, conjured up at a planning conference, and disappeared after the flight, when someone else prepared them for the next performance.

In addition, this was the heyday of the helicopter mystique. A generation before, in the US Army, the Airborne disciples had swept all before them. Now, it was the era of the rotary wing. Few who have experienced it will deny that there is interest, excitement and sheer exhilaration in participating — at whatever level, even as an observer — in the spectacle of 100 Hueys sweeping in at 100 knots, across rivers, mountains, jungles or swamps, to lift and deposit a battalion of infantry.

But despite the glamour and the adrenalin, massed helicopters and air power do not win counter-revolutionary campaigns. Peter Raw and Ray Scott had to wean the Army away from its champagne tastes, and back to the realities of beer.

On top of the early misunderstanding and dislike of the RAAF by many of his officers, Jackson had to face the realization that, except for a few who had not returned to Australia with 1RAR (and these were thinly scattered in Saigon and 1ATF), most of his staff were inexperienced. With longer service in Vietnam than almost any man under his command, and certainly longer than any of senior rank, Jackson was well aware of the problems and complexities of the war, the nature of the region in which 1ATF had arrived, and the uncertainties of the future.

He had been able to acquire the services of a few officers with prior experience in Vietnam, and brought in Major R.R. Hannigan as GSO2 (Operations). Dick Hannigan had been in Vietnam for about six months and worked with the US 1st Division, generally called 'The Big Red 1'.

Jackson's GSO2 (Intelligence) was Major John Rowe, who had arrived in October 1965 and been on the staff of HQ 173rd Airborne Brigade during the time of 1RAR's tour of duty. But Rowe contracted hepatitis, and before the Battle of Long Tan erupted he was in the Australian hospital at the logistics base near the coastal town of Vung Tau.

Like every other Allied formation in Vietnam, 1ATF needed accurate and timely information about the VC/NVA if it was to operate effectively. What information it was given on moving into Phuoc Tuy was not accepted as accurate, and virtually a complete beginning in this field was felt necessary. Of course, all this would take time; and time was what 1ATF did not have.

John Rowe felt that the unit commanders, with experience in warfare of a different kind, did not at first understand the difficulties of collecting, assessing and presenting reliable and timely information, or their own role in the process. 'They wanted', he recalls, 'to be told, "There are two VC behind that bush over there right now", and to be able to walk over and grab them.'

Few outside the Intelligence and Operations staffs in Vietnam knew of, or could envisage, the sheer volume of reports flooding in — all with differing assessments of accuracy — from the ARVN, from South Vietnamese government offices, and from US and other Allied units, as well as from the Australians themselves. Much of the information from Vietnamese sources was nonsense: useless figments of imagination, conjecture, exaggeration, or outright lies. Yet scattered through it all was the occasional pearl of truth and fact. It was in the plucking of these pearls from the sludge that the Intelligence staffs were inexperienced.

'We were always getting "wild and woolly" Int reports', says Dick Hannigan. 'There was nothing evident from them.'

To assist in the provision of better information from within Phuoc Tuy Province, Brigadier Jackson arranged for the transfer of some AATTV personnel from the northern provinces. Captain Mike Wells was posted initially as an Operations Adviser, and later became the Senior Australian Adviser in Phuoc Tuy, with up to eight Warrant Officers in various places around the province.

This Australian advisory presence allowed a more frank assessment of the information stemming from within Phuoc Tuy from the Vietnamese and Americans, before it was passed on to 1ATF.

The RAAF, too, suffered from lack of information about the area. On one occasion, Flight Lieutenant Phil Cooke was flying to Saigon with Wing Commander Ray Scott, CO of 9 Squadron. They decided that the VC were probably more active along the roads, and that the best way to avoid trouble was therefore to fly across the swamps and farmland, keeping away from roads. Only later did they learn that this was exactly the wrong thing to do: the VC were strongest in the swamp and farm areas, whereas emergency landings could be made at government installations along the roads.

After Long Tan, certain items of information were recognized to have been indicators of the coming engagement, but in this the battle was no different from thousands of others in the course of military history: little or no warning was given, despite the best efforts of those concerned. No one forecast the fighting at Long Tan.

By early August 1966, the Intelligence staff at 1ATF were finding themselves in the position of 'the boy who cried Wolf'. Units were displeased at repeatedly searching areas of wet jungle and finding nothing. Some of the soldiers disbelieved the stories about the famous Vietcong, and openly referred to 'the mythical enemy battalion that is supposed to be around here'.

But others, with more experience, began to feel uneasy, though there was nothing to which they could point as solid grounds for worry. From the earliest, Jackson realized that the VC would have to engage 1ATF in a major battle somewhere, sometime, to retain control of the region.

Near the other end of the scale was Sergeant 'Paddy' Todd, an experienced Regular Army Infantry NCO, now in his third theatre of war. He had recently remarked to his Company Commander, Major Harry Smith, while having a beer:

There's something wrong with all this. It might not be us, but one of these days one of our companies is going to run into something.

Todd, a Regular, had joined the Army in 1952 and fought in Korea, Malaya and Borneo before joining 6RAR at Enoggera.

Another who had misgivings was Brian Wickens, Intelligence

Officer of 6RAR. Aided by his long experience in the British Army, Wickens struggled with the mass of information arriving before him, sensing that the enemy intended something on a large scale but unable to extract definite indicators from the sheer bulk of reports. But even Wickens underestimated the intentions of the Vietcong:

> I thought they were going to have a go at us, but it would only be harassment, mortars et cetera, like we received on 17 August. I didn't dream they'd try and tackle a Task Force HQ.

Wickens's Commanding Officer, Lieutenant-Colonel Colin Townsend, was also worried, but likewise could not seize on anything solid to show a VC/NVA offensive intention in the immediate future.

Townsend commanded 6RAR, half of Jackson's infantry. The other half, 5RAR, under Lieutenant-Colonel J.A. Warr, had been operating in the area for about a month longer than 6RAR, and had participated in the clearance of the Task Force base-camp area. Both battalions included many National Servicemen, 6RAR more than 5RAR.

Both battalions also had a leavening of officers, NCOs and men with recent experience in Vietnam. However, there was little from previous duty there to pass on to the young soldiers, apart from the obvious aspects of patrolling and similar military activities.

One man with previous Vietnam experience was Warrant Officer Jack Roughley, Company Sergeant-Major of A Company, 6RAR. In training, when Roughley spoke the soldiers paid attention, for here was a man who knew what they were going into and who had recently returned. Roughley was not in top physical condition, but had passed the medical examination, and the X-rays, by sending in a fit Sergeant to masquerade as the Company Sergeant-Major.

As stated earlier, the soldiers rapidly tired of the seemingly endless rotation of digging and working at Nui Dat, followed by exhausting patrols with little contact with the VC, followed by work at the camp, and so on. Jackson knew this but he realized that, at this stage, constant patrolling and clearing operations all around Nui Dat were his best means of keeping the enemy off balance and at arm's length. The VC had to learn that they could not assume that their presence in the environs of Nui Dat would go unnoticed, or that they could enter and leave with impunity as in days gone by. So the Australians maintained a heavy patrolling programme, despite the wet season.

Equipment was in short supply, and so were many other items necessary for a military base. The camp used by 1RAR had been stripped, but its belongings had been only a fraction of what was needed, and the tents that had served an infantry unit for a year at Bien Hoa were almost beyond any remaining useful life.

Some of the infantry NCOs were surprised and a little dismayed to be issued ex-1RAR M16s with only one magazine and no cleaning gear. How this came to happen has not been explained, the most probable reason being that these were 'extra' rifles that had been handed in at the end of 1RAR's time and did not have a full set of magazines and gear with them.

When Rod Armstrong, A/6RAR, protested about the lone 20-round magazine, he was told to take 'these little boxes of bullets' and reload if necessary.

If 1ATF was weak in infantry, it had adequate artillery in mid-August 1966. The New Zealand 161 Field Battery had been serving in Vietnam with the 1RAR Group and in the US 173rd Airborne Brigade, and it now continued at Nui Dat. Also veterans of the 173rd days were the Australian 105 Field Battery, due to return to Australia in September. Newly arrived was 103 Battery. Together these comprised 1st Field Regiment, and were equipped with 105mm howitzers. Also available were heavier 155mm M109 Self-propelled (SP) guns of the attached US artillery unit, A Battery, 2/35th Howitzer Battalion. Commanding 1st Field Regiment was Lieutenant-Colonel R.M. Cubis, RAA.

Both the New Zealand 161 and the Australian 105 Batteries were greatly experienced after their time with the US paratroopers and 1RAR. On at least two occasions 105 Battery had contributed greatly to the successful outcome of battles by providing accurate, sustained fire in support of US paratroopers who found themselves in desperate circumstances.

The Officer Commanding (OC) of 105 Battery, Major Peter Tedder, was somewhat amused at the painstaking peacetime attitudes of the newly arrived gunners, graduates of what he saw as a 'Fool's Paradise' created by the stress on safety regulations and techniques, especially the prolonged procedures for adjusting the fall of shells onto a target. But Tedder was also impressed with how quickly they adapted to the realities of Vietnam.

Major R.N. (Neville) Gair was OC of 103 Battery and considered them 'a fine group of young men' who coped well with the rain, mud and dust, backbreaking physical work, nights broken by artillery activity, only an occasional day off, and the constant possibility of attack. About a third of 103 Battery were National Servicemen, but all had the necessary positive attitude to the job and the determination to do it well.

Gair recalls one soldier as an example. In Australia he had been reckoned to be a troublemaker, so Gair had placed him in the Battery Commander's (BC) small party of radio-operators and assistants. Later, on operations in Vietnam, the soldier collapsed and was found to have suffered, some weeks earlier, a very painful perforated eardrum. But he had kept on without complaint, to the point of collapse.

Gair's Battery Captain (known as the BK) was George Bindley. Whereas the BC was normally with the headquarters of the infantry unit that was to receive the support of the guns, the BK remained with the guns and was responsible for operations there.

One thing that allowed 1st Field Regiment to adapt so quickly and so well to the conditions in Vietnam was the high level of training which had been achieved in Australia, albeit in a restrictive atmosphere of safety. In Neville Gair's words,

> battle drills are an important part of our training, the whole aim being to learn to act and react speedily whilst under pressure, in such a way as to reduce mistakes and errors to a minimum... The battle drills are practised and practised until they become second nature — a reflex.

The New Zealanders were commanded by Major H.B. 'Harry' Honner, a 1950 graduate of Royal Military College (RMC), Duntroon, who had the close relationship with Australian forces enjoyed by almost all Kiwis.

The 105mm howitzer that equipped the batteries was the Italian mountain-gun design, described by George Bindley as a

> beautiful piece of design work, capable of being broken down into man, mule and helicopter loads. It was not a field gun, and even at this early stage we were experiencing problems.
>
> There were also problems with the sights, mainly due to the tropical conditions causing mould in the lens system. We had the same experience in Malaya in 1961. We were forever requesting the technicians to fix the sights, which meant swapping sights, a routine intensely disliked by the gun sergeants and gun layers.

Control of the firepower of these four batteries was exerted from the Fire Support Coordination Centre (FSCC). The FSCC existed to advise the Commander 1ATF (Jackson, at this time) on fire-support matters; to control and direct counter-battery fire; to clear fire missions in relation to friendly troops and aircraft; to warn aircraft by radio of artillery fire; to plan and direct harassing fire; and to collect, evaluate and disseminate Artillery Intelligence.

Like the rest of 1ATF, the FSCC knew little about Phuoc Tuy and it was difficult to formulate a counter-battery fire plan; but a plan was produced by Captain Barry Campton, who went back to the basics and used World War I as a model. It was proved successful.

The three main duty-officers in the FSCC in August were three Captains: Ian Darlington, Jim Townley and Barry Campton. Townley had an appropriate send-off from Nui Dat, as on his last night there the camp was bombarded by the VC and he was able to put into effect his counter-battery fire plan.

Artillery Intelligence was provided by an 80-man detachment of 131 Divisional Locating Battery commanded by Barry Campton. With their mortar-locating radars and listening-posts, Campton's men kept a watch on the area around the base camp. He had trained them so that each man could do the jobs of others, and was pleased with the expertise of his soldiers.

The armoured personnel carriers (APCs) for the Task Force were provided by 1 APC Squadron; and 3 Troop, under Adrian Roberts, was to be deeply involved in the fighting at Long Tan. Roberts had arrived in Vietnam while 1RAR was still operating, and gained his first experiences with them and the 173rd Airborne Brigade.

Equipped with the M113 diesel-powered vehicle armed with a .50 heavy machinegun (HMG), the APC unit provided mobility and armoured protection to the infantry, or to whomever else they carried. As with the Army—RAAF problem of who commanded the vehicle — the client or the vehicle commander — the Infantry and Armour officers disagreed.

The APC crews had trained intensively in Australia, perfecting assault formations with infantry, despite the lack of radios and actual infantry passengers. After their operations with 1RAR, US and ARVN units, they were (in the words of Adrian Roberts) 'considerably more attuned to working with infantry than the infantry were with APCs, especially in combat drills'. As a result of working with the 173rd Airborne Brigade in clearing the Nui Dat area, Roberts had a mental image of the terrain and knew of a good crossing-place over the Suoi Da Bang, the river east of 1ATF, between the Australian base and Long Tan.

So, in mid-August 1966, Brigadier Jackson commanded a force that was still sorting out problems of command born of peacetime attitudes in Australia, still establishing itself in a camp located in the midst of an enemy-dominated area, and struggling with the wet season and a poor logistics system.

The nearby villages of Long Phuoc and Long Tan had been evacuated, the people being resettled in populated areas close by and the dwellings themselves being destroyed. (The land and orchards were still worked by their previous tenants or owners, who travelled to and fro.) The existence of extensive tunnel systems in the villages had led to this decision, so that an obvious base for the VC could be removed. North Vietnamese and Vietcong money and papers were found in some quantity, many Diggers acquiring samples as souvenirs.

Perhaps the situation as seen by the average Digger can be summed up in this way: Nui Dat meant constant baling out of rainwater from the flooding weapon-pits and trenches; there were not enough cleaning kits for the issued M16 Armalite rifles; and contact was so light and ammunition so scarce that only 60 rounds of rifle ammunition were carried per man.

The infantry battalions had each carried out operations in the vicinity of Nui Dat, and had fought, though fleetingly, guerrillas, local-force VC and Main Force VC. Whatever their commanders may have worried about, there was little to appear as an obvious threat to the soldiers.

17 AUGUST 1966

Mortar Attack

... and the nimble gunner
With linstock now the devilish cannon touches,
And down goes all before them...

King Henry V (II. iii.)

O N 16 AUGUST, 5RAR was scouring an area of jungle to the north of Nui Dat, where once again an enemy presence had been 'located' by 1ATF Intelligence. Recently 5RAR had conducted, with GVN police and other authorities, a successful cordon and search of the village of Binh Ba, north of Nui Dat, and had left the area of the village to search the jungles. The SAS also had recently swept the areas to the north and east of the base camp, operating in very difficult conditions in the wet weather, and had also found no trace of any large group of VC.

Recent reports arriving at Nui Dat had indicated a presence of up to 300 VC with crew-served weapons in the area, but no contact had been made, and the rains obliterated tracks and signs of passage. It was thought by some that the GVN reports actually concerned Australian patrols.

A Company 6RAR was also absent from the camp, patrolling east and north; it made three small contacts, killing two and capturing one VC, with documents that later identified two separate companies.

Many of the younger members of the Task Force were awaiting the arrival next day of the first group of Australian entertainers to perform at Nui Dat — Col Joye and the Joy Boys, plus Little Patti. Show-business facilities at 'the Dat' were skimpy, consisting of semitrailer flatbeds for the stage with seating brought by the audience, if they could find any.

28

For 103 Battery it had been a normal day: stand to, clearing patrols, stand down, breakfast, Orders Group, sick parade, exhortations to be more tidy, the laundry run, work on the barbed-wire defences, weapons inspections, anti-malarial drugs, reports on serviceability of the 105mm howitzers, preparation of the night's programme of Harassing and Interdiction fire, or H & I (George Bindley believed that 'it certainly harassed *us* — I don't know about its effectiveness on the enemy!'), update the defensive fire programme, stand to, clearing patrols, and a last word around the gun positions.

The night of 16 — 17 August was a dark night: George Bindley judged that there was little chance of action, so he went to bed. On nights when 'the Int picture was bad' or there was a lot of moonlight, he slept fully dressed, weapon to hand; but this time he stripped off.

At 02.43 on the morning of 17 August, mortar bombs and recoilless-rifle shells began to land across the base at Nui Dat. Counterfire was quickly put on the suspected enemy positions, but the bombardment caused the Task Force to be alerted to a possible attack.

Ian Darlington was on his way to take over as duty-officer in the FSCC when the mortar bombs began exploding. As he arrived in the tented office, radios were actively reporting the incoming fire. Almost at the same time as Darlington, Jim Townley arrived, and together they tried to deduce from the reports the source of the fire.

George Bindley was woken by the sound of the mortars firing: the characteristic *thunking*. His first thought was that 6RAR was firing, and he called the Battery Command Post (CP) on his field telephone for informaton.

Before the CP could answer, the first incoming rounds began to arrive 'with a roar like flying kerosene tins filled with loose stones', exploding across the Engineer unit behind Bindley and the gun position itself, a little way from the tents. His first reaction,

> apart from arriving very rapidly on the floor, was to curse 6RAR for dropping their bombs into the Task Force area, and my battery in particular. On the phone, I ordered the Regimental CP to be notified that we were being mortared. No thought it could not be friendly fire!
>
> The only — and correct — reply from Regiment was 'Send MORTREP' [mortaring report].

This did not please Bindley, who could hear more rounds being fired and was trying to dress while on the floor, wondering onto which end of his body to put his steel helmet, deciding on his head. The mortars exploded around him, close enough for him to see the red flashes.

Another salvo crashed down into the 103 Battery area, and then Bindley was out of his tent, running to meet his Battery Sergeant-Major, 'Squizzie' Taylor, who, wide-eyed, told Bindley to look back. He turned, 'to see my tent shrouded in smoke rolling down from the tree bursts'.

Swinging back to Taylor, Bindley told him to get everyone down to the gun positions, and that he would meet him again after a visit to the CP. He ended with a reminder to Taylor to put his boots on the correct feet...

By this time, fire orders were coming from the gun-control sets and retaliatory fire was going out. Bindley had time to note that all his guns were operating normally.

Reports flowing into the FSCC from 103 and 161 Batteries showed that these, and their vicinity, were receiving most of the bombardment, but it was very difficult to reduce the confusing and contradictory reports, coming from many units, to information by which the guns could retaliate.

Because of lack of previous actions, and earlier malfunctions of the ageing equipment, information from Barry Campton's radars was not given much credence in the FSCC, though later checking proved its accuracy.

After some minutes, Harry Honner, of the New Zealand guns, sent in a compass-bearing which, when plotted on FSCC maps, passed through a position previously reckoned to be a likely enemy bombardment location. All guns fired ten rounds, totalling 240 in all, onto the likely target, followed by a further 240. The VC fire ceased.

Thus, 1ATF artillery had shown that it could react speedily, accurately and effectively — even though some gun positions had come under fire in the process. And Jim Townley had the pleasure of seeing his counter-battery fire plan put into effect on his last night in Vietnam.

In a night position off to the east, 6RAR's A Company at first thought they were the intended target of the mortars. They soon realized that the bombs were going elsewhere; and then became worried, as the counter-bombardment began to fall close, that their own artillery might fall on them. Earlier, they had heard definite sounds of movement out in the night but were unable to do anything about it. It was later deduced that the VC mortar teams had passed close to them.

'Black Mac' McDonald, commanding 3 Section of 10 Platoon, D/6RAR, was leading a half-section listening-post 3000 metres outside the 1ATF perimeter, alert for any enemy approach. 'With the mortars coming in and the artillery going out, it was quite an experience.'

At his CP, Bindley found everything under control, but he 'gently reminded' Lieutenant John Griggs that the bombardment might be merely the prelude to a ground attack. Griggs acknowledged this, then equally gently reminded Bindley that defence was *his* (Bindley's) problem.

A gun detachment is fully engaged when manned in action, and other troops are normally provided to defend the positions. But 1ATF was so short of infantry that none were protecting the guns. Bindley left the CP, pondering over this aspect of soldiering as he went back to the guns.

As is usual in such situations, there were moments of humour as well as drama. While troops were standing to, officers rushed to the various command posts to see what the situation was. One gunner officer became hopelessly lost in the pitchblack dark under the rubber-trees, and after wandering about colliding with treetrunks he sat down to await the dawn. Major Harry Smith, OC D/6RAR, put his feet into the wrong boots, but did not notice until later, after running some distance and removing lots of skin.

Private Ken Tronk, also of D/6RAR, was woken by the noise, wondered what was going on, and

> wandered down to the front lines and struck the 12 Platoon Sergeant, Paddy Todd. I asked him what was happening, and he said, 'We're being mortared'. I said, 'What'll I do?' and he said, 'Go back to bed'. So I went back, put on my steel helmet, and went back to sleep.

Another soldier, doing the right thing, jumped into his weapon-pit — only to find that it was full of rainwater. Ardour quickly quenched, he climbed out again.

Brian Reilly, who was asleep in D Company, was woken by the explosions, 'and we got the word to stand to, put our gear on and went down to the forward lines until we got the word from the Company Commander'.

No apprehension was felt, as it was 'all long-range stuff'.

While A Company was away on patrol, 11 Platoon, D Company 6RAR, had moved into A's area. Engrossed in a crown-and-anchor game in A Company HQ, they paid little attention to the mortaring, which was some distance away, not sure whether it was an attack or their own artillery firing. It was not until daylight that they learnt the truth.

George Bindley arrived at his living-quarters to find a small group clustered around one of the gunners, who had been wounded in the head and later died.

Bindley estimated that about 60 mortar bombs had exploded in the 103 Battery area, most of them bursting in the rubber-trees but fortunately missing the gunpits.

The bombs had also impacted across the area occupied by the Nui Dat detachment of 1 Company, Royal Australian Army Service Corps (RAASC), inflicting minor wounds and damage — in particular to three two-and-a-half-ton trucks and a small tractor. Damage and casualties were also inflicted on the Engineers.

In a mixture of curiosity, apprehension and boredom, plus blissful ignorance, the Australians waited for what was to come. But after their own artillery fire, nothing.

The total casualties were 22 Australians and one New Zealander wounded, plus a certain amount of material damage to tents, personnel equipment, and the like. This attack, and the battle on the afternoon of 18 August, made sandbagging of all accommodation and command posts 'the rage' across Nui Dat.

Only the Australian mentioned above, Gunner Norris of 103 Battery, later died, of wounds.

Why a comparatively puny bombardment was fired on 1ATF, with no complementing action such as a ground attack of even minor size, has exercised the minds of many who were at Nui Dat that night. No document or prisoner of senior rank captured later was able to give reasons that were confirmed by other sources or other documents. Conjecture by people of all ranks includes various propositions: that the attack was an attempt by the VC to have 1ATF artillery fire its counter-bombardment plan, so that the locations where the shells fell could be noted and avoided in future attacks; that the VC planning became disrupted and the bombardment was fired one night too early, it having been intended to assist in an attack on the night of 18–19 August; that it was meant to anger the Australians into sending out a force to search for the impudent bombarding teams, and that this force was to be annihilated while a large VC formation waited to ambush anyone rushing to the rescue.

It is unlikely that the question will ever be resolved, as any information provided by the Communist regime must be suspect. But its grandiloquent claims of damage inflicted on the Australians would be belied by an examination of VC documents, if such documents were to come to light.

For George Bindley, 'the rest of the night passed quickly. It was a relief to see the dawn. The morning was bright, with clear blue skies vividly highlighting the green vegetation and still-wet laterite.'

At about 08.30, 103 Battery was visited by Brigadier Jackson, Lieutenant-Colonel Cubis and Captain Jim Townley, plus members of their staffs. Cubis disbelieved Bindley's estimation of 60 bombs falling into the 103 Battery area; Bindley stood by it but could not prove it, since most of the bombs had exploded in the treetops. Only the shredded tents showed how lucky 103 had been.

Brigadier Jackson 'was clearly delighted by our effort and said so', but Cubis told Bindley that 'the gun position was untidy and the grass needed cutting'!

It was decided at 1ATF HQ to send out a patrol to search for the bombarding teams, follow them if possible, and destroy them. No one really thought the patrol would have much success, as the VC, in their usual manner, were presumed long gone.

However, the attack was an indicator that the enemy intended some offensive action against the Australians, and 5RAR was ordered to return to Nui Dat. A/6RAR was due back in the early afternoon of 18 August, and both battalions would then be complete and at the camp, where every man would be needed if an assault was to come — for 274 and 275 Regiments, plus D445 Battalion, were still at large in the province.

B/6RAR spent the day of 17 August unsuccessfully sweeping the area to the east of Nui Dat. A Company was having several fleeting contacts with VC in the area to the north-east, but nothing indicated the presence nearby of a large force of heavily armed enemy. Barry Campton and Jim Townley analysed the craters, and fragments of the bombs and shells that had hit Nui Dat, and proved that the information from 131 Divisional Locating Battery the night before had been extremely accurate. They also positively identified the remains of one shell as a Japanese 70mm mountain-gun of World War II vintage, which raised some questions as to the weapons available to the VC.

The sense of unease about the VC/NVA allowed smooth passage for the suggestion that the patrol on 18 August be by a full company, not a platoon. Brian Wickens, Colonel Townsend and Brigadier Jackson, along with several others, believed a company was the minimum force to be dispatched.

The light level of recent contact with the enemy Main Force encouraged some people to see nothing more in the mortaring than a mere harassment. Dozens of previous patrols had crisscrossed the area, with no result. The 18 August patrol would in all probability be just another.

Accordingly, Harry Smith was told to take out D/6RAR to locate the bombardment positions, and to try to find and chastize the VC responsible.

This order, of course, annoyed the soldiers of his company. Col Joye and Little Patti were to perform in the afternoon, and D Company would miss them. The general opinion of the Diggers was that they were to endure yet more useless slogging in the wet.

Harry Smith was undisputed commander of D Company. His nickname 'Harry the Rat' was actually a shortened version of 'Harry the Ratcatcher', acquired by way of his discovery of an illegal gambling group in his unit in Malaya, and his triumphant exclamation, 'Got you, you rats!'

By far, the majority of his men were National Servicemen, delivered to 6RAR semi-trained and brought to Australian Army war standard by the officers and NCOs who would lead them in action. Lieutenant-Colonel Townsend had adopted the wise policy of making no distinction between the Regulars and the National Servicemen ('Regs' and 'Nashos') in the battalion.

Several of the Nashos recalled their pleasure and sense of being accepted when they arrived in 6RAR and were addressed by the RSM, George Chinn, who told them that there was to be no difference in treatment for any soldier in the unit, and that they were 'short-term Regulars'.

Harry Smith went further in welding his men into a family within a family, and on his own initiative ordered distinctive black-and-green camouflage bush-hats for D Company. A believer in physical fitness, he brought D Company to a high pitch, and on exercises in the field confounded the 'enemy' and umpires alike with a series of fast, hard marches that earned for D the title of 'Boots Company'. (Unit plaques to this day feature a pair of golden army boots.) A current hit-song by Nancy Sinatra, 'These Boots Are Made for Walking', was adopted as unofficial D Company song. Harry Esler described Smith in these terms:

Major Smith was a very good soldier, in that everybody respected him. I certainly did. He was a bloke you trusted with your life. Nothing seemed too hard for him. He seemed calm at all times and gave a feeling of confidence. Don't get me wrong — he could be a very hard man. The look he'd give you if you were playing up was enough to drill a hole in you.

'Pom' Rencher was Smith's batman/signaller, dragged into the job under protest while in the field on exercise. His first task was to cook dinner while Smith was on a radio conference. Rencher looked around from his disgusted muttering at fate, and was astounded to see Smith, stripped to the waist, doing his share of digging for the weapon-pit.

Rencher spent 'eight months never more than three paces from him', and came to admire Harry Smith as one of the two men he 'would unquestioningly follow anywhere'. Rencher felt 'a special pride in being a member of that company. Harry was a soldier's soldier whose professionalism rubbed off on the whole company.'

While the short, nuggety Smith and the young soldiers strode out on the training runs, the Company Sergeant-Major (CSM) was feeling his age and weight. Jack Kirby was a Malaya veteran, and naturally big in build. Unable to keep up on the runs, he nevertheless plugged along, always finishing, and earned the respect of the soldiers. At Long Tan he was to deepen and broaden their regard, with his steadiness, bravery and humour.

It was obvious to everyone that the unit was training for war, and some of the Regulars despaired of achieving the necessary standard before going into action. The Army had learnt in New Guinea, against the Japanese, how bloody a bill had to be paid when sending semi-trained troops into action, and a rigorous training programme had been set for the units preparing for Vietnam.

Geoff Kendall, a Regular officer, came from C Company to D 'with horror — involved with all these National Servicemen. However, that attitude pretty soon changed, mainly through the efforts of Harry Smith, who did his very best to inspire company spirit.' Kendall had 10 Platoon.

Commander of Smith's 11 Platoon was Gordon Sharp, who had been a cameraman on the then-popular *Mavis Bramston Show*, and his aura of glamour from show-business knowledge, connections and letters from personalities earned a certain respect and awe from the soldiers. Brian Halls remembers:

When Gordon Sharp arrived, he was a young officer who didn't know anything. We'd had a few months together by this stage and were reasonably well trained. On his first couple of trips out into the bush with us it was a real eye-opener for us as well as him — he didn't know how to pack his gear! He was totally different to the Regular Army officers. He would probably have made a better private soldier. He liked gambling, and played cards with the Diggers.

In Australia, and for a time in Vietnam, Sharp's Platoon Sergeant was Neil Rankin, who was more a father to the young soldiers than the traditional tough Army Senior NCO. When there was an unannounced inspection of the platoon living accommodation, he covered for some who had slipped out of camp without official permission: soldiers who had already been passed by the inspecting officer were told to run out, around the hut, and take up the vacant positions ahead. Rankin had the respect of the men, and there was resentment later when he was moved to Kendall's 10 Platoon, with Kendall's Sergeant, Bob Buick, replacing Rankin.

By mid-August, Kendall's platoon had only one 'kill' and there was disagreement between him and Sergeant Bob Buick on the handling of the platoon in action — resulting in the exchange of Sergeants. To Sharp's 11 Platoon, Buick was a far different type of Sergeant. Tough and no-nonsense, he was probably a good counter to the somewhat unmilitary Gordon Sharp.

This change took place in Vietnam, not long before the battle. Rankin needed some time to adjust to the switch to 10 Platoon, trying hard to get to know the men, 'but I found I was always talking to my old platoon mates. I worried about them when 11 Platoon did any patrols and welcomed them back in the wire on their return.'

'Paddy' Todd was Platoon Sergeant of 12 Platoon, which at first consisted of himself and three Regular Corporals, the Section Commanders. They had to wait until the first intake of National Servicemen completed basic training before receiving their men and officer.

> The big day arrived and we got our troops. There they were. I can remember calling the roll. We had Dettman, six foot four, an ex-tinminer, big as they come. I always remember Private Brown. I looked at him, and there was no way he was the right height for the Army. I called Jack Kirby, the CSM.
>
> 'Have a look at young Brown there, what do you think?'
>
> So we called him up, and he wasn't the height, but what happened was he had been passed by a lady doctor in his home town, on the first preliminary medical, so he'd got through. And ended up a very good soldier, joining the Regular Army, and on the battalion's second tour got an MM.

Todd's Platoon Commander was David Sabben, who had received some media publicity as a volunteer for National Service, stating that he believed in the concept. (He still does.) Graduating from the NS Officer Training Unit, which produced 'an Infantry 2nd Lieutenant', Sabben arrived at 6RAR and D Company and joined in the whirl of preparing for war.

On the morning of 18 August, as D Company prepared for the patrol, it was a band of fit young Australians with confidence in themselves and their leaders. Bound together by sweat in training and the fighting in June and July in Operations 'Enoggera' and 'Hobart', the 108 Australians foresaw nothing but the unnecessary missing of an entertainment group, and an equally unnecessary walk in the wet.

Harry Smith was briefed on the patrol at Battalion Headquarters. According to Brian Wickens:

> Harry was a Company Commander, and he let everyone know that. He would listen to Intelligence briefings, but do it his way. The briefing was, simply, that there was an enemy force out there with mortars and 70mm [mountain-guns]. Therefore it was not a small force. B Company was looking for it. I also said that because of our counter-bombardment on the mortar baseplates, they were not in a position to lay ambushes. But I suggested they might be part of a larger force, another force, coming too close to the Task Force. I wanted to find out who they were, where they were, and their strength.

The Task Force Intelligence Summary for 17 August reported the bombardment and the results of the day's patrolling — including, in paragraph 11, the estimated enemy 'Capabilities and Vulnerabilities':

> The enemy is capable of attacking up to company-sized patrols within the Task Force TAOR and of launching mortar attacks similar to that of 170240H. To move his mortars and bombs quickly, the enemy must rely on tracks and roads, which leaves him vulnerable to H and I fire.

The 'Conclusions' paragraph sketched a possible relationship between the mortar attack and the activities and contacts of 5RAR and A/6RAR on 16 August. It noted that 'An attack on the Task Force Base area is unlikely'.

The final paragraph in the INTSUM stated that the increased enemy activity in the area was probably 'to take advantage' of isolated patrols.

The unease felt by people like Townsend, Wickens and Todd was also prickling the pilots of 161 Recce (Reconnaissance) Flight, who had flown over the area and knew it to the point where locations were recognized immediately and accurately. They had sensed a change in recent days, a feeling of impending enemy action. Captain Paul Lipscombe, due to depart later that day for Australia, thought there was a feeling of expectancy in the 1ATF HQ that morning.

Moving swiftly, almost trotting, down the paths from the east came the young Vietnamese battalions. Among them were the more serious older men, the commanders and political officers, but in the platoons and companies were the typical youths of any army: the worriers, the cautious, the jokesters, the ambitious. The Northerners already had some experience, having walked down the Ho chi Minh Trail — or, as they called it, the Truong Son Trail. They had survived bombing, disease, and insect and reptile bites, and were now in the South. Some did not know where they were, nor to which formation they now belonged. What every man did know was that he was a long way from his family, and that there would be no return until the victory was won.

One force moving to the clash was expecting to go into a major battle; and the other did not expect any contact at all, despite the increase in enemy activity, and the assessment that patrols such as theirs could be attacked.

18 AUGUST 1966

Saddle Up, Move Out

... Now, soldiers, march away:—
And how thou pleasest, God, dispose the day!

King Henry V (IV. iii.)

*W*HILE THE AUSTRALIANS *searched the area within mortar range, at least seven battalions of Main Force enemy were approaching from the east. Three were moving to the north, possibly to swing round and attack Nui Dat from the north or west. Four others, including the local men of D445, were coming in towards the Long Tan rubber plantation and the small hill just north of it called, confusingly, Nui Dat. In this book, the hill will be designated Nui Dat East.*

There was probably some tension among commanders, political officers and soldiers in the battalions: they expected to be searched for, or located, by the aircraft or ground patrols of the foreigners. The tension would have increased as they closed on the Australian area, but would have been eased somewhat by the knowledge from local informants of the activities of the foreigners. These local people would have reported that one battalion had been assisting the GVN in searching Binh Ba, so that the other would almost certainly be guarding the base camp. The Australian mercenaries had therefore split their main fighting element and could quite possibly be destroyed in separate packets, a type of battle which the NLF had fought successfully in recent months against the forces of the Saigon regime. And if the band of mercenaries at Binh Ba scuttled back to the Nui Dat lair, no matter.

As they had done several times before, D Company test-fired their weapons and packed their equipment, finding room for food, cigarettes and the few luxuries a soldier settles for when every ounce travels on his back. But only the usual minimum load of ammunition was carried, despite the bombardment and the possibility that a large enemy force might be out there. No one in D Company really believed it.

B/6RAR had already spent 17 August searching without success for the mortar baseplate positions, and then an uneventful night at GR 463668. At 07.00, 48 men returned to Nui Dat for their rostered turn on leave for R & C. This might be seen in hindsight to be frivolous, but in the wet conditions it was necessary to rotate as many soldiers as possible through the sun and salt water at Vung Tau, to avoid skin diseases and attendant illnesses. Thirty-two men, from Company HQ and 5 Platoon, remained to carry on the search.

In addition, patrol after patrol had crisscrossed the area in recent weeks, and found little.

D Company itself, on its most recent patrol, had sent 11 Platoon through the rubber plantation, onto the Nui Dat East hills, and back. Peter Ainslie had been told they were looking for signs of a VC regimental radio net detected there, but nothing had been found.

The artillery Forward Observation Officer (FOO) who would accompany D Company was Captain Maury Stanley, from the New Zealand 161 Battery. Like many other New Zealand officers, Stanley had experienced the brotherhood of arms between the Anzac Armies: he had graduated from the Royal Military College (Duntroon), attended courses in Australia, served in South-East Asia with Australian officers whose careers paralleled his own, and served also in Australia.

Stanley was an experienced gunnery officer, an ex-instructor who knew his trade to the last detail and had, over the years since graduating from RMC, absorbed knowledge and understanding of infantry units such as Smith's.

On this day, D Company could not afford to have a FOO with the inexperience in heavy contact of the young US officer who had once radioed to Peter Tedder, 'Fire at will!'

Maury Stanley strongly felt the Anzac overtones of this patrol, with Aussies and New Zealanders combining on active service. In the usual fashion of maintaining personal contact between cooperating units, Stanley and his Forward Observation party had been the team supporting D/6RAR since Townsend's battalion had arrived. With him were Lance-Bombardiers William 'Willie' Walker from Gisborne and Murray Broomhall of Invercargill.

Also with D Company was a Mortar Forward Controller from 6RAR's own Mortar Platoon, who would, if required, call fire in from the 81mm mortars back in the battalion position.

At 10.35, as D/6RAR was almost ready to begin moving, B Company found VC positions at GR 473673: pits dug for 20 men, and 22 empty tubes for 75mm RCL (recoilless launcher) rounds. Tracks from the west indicated that the mortar crews had rendezvoused there and then probably gone off to the northeast and south.

Much earlier in the morning, two RAAF Iroquois had arrived at 1ATF for tasks supporting the Army. In A2-1020 were Flight Lieutenants Frank Riley and Bob Grandin, with Leading Aircraftmen (LAC) 'Blue' Collins and George Stirling; while in A2-1022 were Flight Lieutenants Cliff Dohle and Bruce Lane, with Corporal W.R. Harrington and LAC B.B. Hill. Later in the day, these aircraft and men were to fly a mission crucial to the survival of D Company.

Back home in Brisbane, people were reading that day's issue of the *Courier-Mail*, the southern Queensland daily with the largest circulation. In it were articles concerned with the alleged shortcomings of the then new and advanced F111 swing-wing aircraft; with the booing of President Sukarno of Indonesia when he told students that life under his regime was better than under the Dutch; and with statements by the Greek government and its Embassy in Australia that Greek males who wished to avoid their National Service in Australia would receive help in the form of fares back to Greece, and that Greek males were already queuing for the fares.

Readers also saw an article, by AAP special correspondent Geoffrey Murray, describing the bright future in store for the village of Hoa Long, just south of Nui Dat, which was to become the 'show-piece of Australia's civil aid programme in South Vietnam'. Hoa Long was to get a water-supply, toilets, playgrounds, schools and medicines; and its people were to receive a 'chance to work for a living'.

Brisbane's four television channels did not begin broadcasting until, respectively, 10.40, 11.00, 11.30 and (in the case of the newer Channel 0) 15.35.

In the cinemas, people were buying tickets to see Warren Beatty and Leslie Caron in *Promise Her Anything*, Peter Cushing in *Dr Who and the Daleks*, Dean Martin as Matt Helm in *The Silencers*, Elvis Presley in *Kid Galahad* or *Frankie and Johnnie*, or James Mason, Telly Savalas and Omar Sharif in *Genghis Khan*.

For those who enjoyed the big top, Bullen's Circus was performing at McCaskie Oval, on Kelvin Grove Road, tickets costing 50 cents for children and $1.00 to $2.50 for adults.

A good used car cost $1000 to $2000, and a suit from McWhirters could be purchased for $60.

Life went on in Brisbane, as it did in Sydney, Melbourne and all the other cities and towns of Australia. Vietnam was little more than a paragraph or so in the newspaper, or a 30-second clip on the TV news. Only for those with a relative or friend in the war did it assume any larger a status.

At 11.00, D Company was moving east, away from the base camp; A Company was sweeping south — back to Nui Dat, a shower, clean clothes, a steak and a beer.

At 11.05, A Company found a very old food cache, GR 474683. Patrols from B Company were searching north-east and south from the VC position found previously.

At 12.00, Corporal Jones's patrol from B Company, moving south, reached GR 471670, and found signs of two VC casualties; and at GR 468665 a site for three 75mm RCLs. They found that each had fired eight rounds, and the empty cartridge cases were nearby. Scattered clothing and equipment, and bloodstains, indicated a rapid evacuation to the east, with casualties from the counter-bombardment.

Meanwhile, in single file to begin with, D Company was led by 12 Platoon, with Sabben, a good map-reader, guiding their course. Rolling across the sloping ground, down from the stage at Nui Dat, came the sound of the Col Joye Show, the booming loudspeakers adding salt to the wounds of the men's discontent over missing the event.

It was also heard by A Company, and some of the more musically inclined young soldiers mimicked the performers, silently, using rifles as mock guitars. They pushed on to base, sure of their reward.

But the holiday spirit was kept under control, and three women met in the area were taken back as suspects and handed over at Nui Dat. Lieutenant Peter Dinham's 2 Platoon, discomfited by the slowness of the captives, came along behind the rest of A and were last to arrive.

Dinham's men were more than impatient at their captives' slowness because they had to carry the bananas the women had been collecting in the groves when detained. The heavy bunches of fruit, added to the considerable weight each man carried, made the last stretch of the return journey seem to pass more slowly. And this was the hottest part of the day.

At 13.00, D and B Companies met. The mortar and RCL positions were shown, VC tracks and other marks were examined, and Smith decided to follow the trail to the east.

No one felt overly concerned, and a few were complacent.

Brian Reilly, 12 Platoon, had been with 1RAR, and had then transferred to D/6RAR to complete his tour of duty. He spoke to a few friends in B, looked at the enemy positions, and in the quietness found it easy to accept what the B Company people said — that 'there's nothing out here'. D had already swept back through this very area on its previous patrol a few days earlier, and found nothing.

For Reilly, 'it was fairly mundane patrolling' until they met B Company. 'We had a look around at the mortar baseplates, and that was it.'

'Black Mac' McDonald, in 10 Platoon, had no idea of any enemy force in the area, or of its size.

Word from B sped through D, adding to the sense of being on another useless patrol. And A Company was also out, to the north, with no enemy to report.

To the east, four battalions of Vietcong and North Vietnamèse (for simplicity, henceforth referred to as VC) were approaching the eastern edge of the Long Tan rubber plantation. Knowing, from the absence of air and artillery action, that they had been undetected, the commanders were reasonably confident that they would remain so, for they knew that Nui Dat was lightly defended. With the usual afternoon rains due in a few hours, their approach to the final positions would also be covered. Their confidence spread to those around them, boosted by the lack of enemy activity.

At Nui Dat, the Col Joye Show, with Little Patti, was entertaining the soldiers, the first entertainment group to come to the 'sharp end', the combat area. Brigadier Jackson had resisted the misgivings of the more cautious, who thought it not safe enough for civilians to be at Nui Dat, especially after a bombardment; since the show was to be in daytime, and evacuation could easily be arranged, he had allowed it to go ahead.

Brian Wickens was arranging a helicopter reconnaissance over the area to the east of 1ATF's camp, to look for trails or signs of passage and to compare what could be found with what was already marked on his map.

Alan Hutchinson, a FOO with D/5RAR, was experiencing the expectancy, the beginnings of impatience and the relief of a man coming to the end of a year of accompanying infantry companies in the field. It was time to unsaddle, begin to relax and think of a life back in Australia.

In the towns and villages all around, and in the cities, the pace of life was beginning to liven after the noontime siesta. Officials were going back to their offices, shop-owners bestirred themselves for an afternoon's trading, farming communities carried on with the endless routine of their lives, rubber-tappers began moving along the cool dark rows of valuable trees, bargirls went to hairdressers, cyclos and taxis began their slow cruising for fares. Those Westerners for whom no day was long enough breathed a sigh of relief that the locals were now up and about and the country could get moving again.

First Contact

He that outlives this day, and comes safe home,
Will stand a tip-toe when this day is nam'd...

King Henry V (IV. iii.)

B COMPANY BEGAN its return to Nui Dat, and at 15.00
Smith moved D Company along the track he had selected,
generally east, into the Long Tan rubber plantation. After about
300 metres this track divided into two, both running east-south-
east, some 300 metres apart and roughly parallel.

*A small group of VC set off from one of the main positions. Who
they were and what they intended to do is not known, but they were
probably moving to the western edge of the rubber plantation to
observe the area, watch for Australian patrols, or fulfil some similar
purpose. They may have been going as far as the Suoi Da Bang, to
reconnoitre possible crossing-places, but this would most likely have
been done or planned with the help of local guerrillas. They apparently believed that there were no enemy soldiers close by.*

Smith considered the new tracks and the change in direction,
and altered D Company's disposition to cope with the situation:
two platoons forward, followed by his HQ, and the third platoon
following in the centre-rear.

Kendall's 10 Platoon was on the left, Sharp's 11 on the high
ground on the right, followed by Sabben's 12 Platoon. The
company frontage was about 400 metres, and the same in depth.
With visibility about 150 to 200 metres, the platoons and Company
HQ were in visual contact. This dispersion, tactically normal for
the Australians given the terrain and growth, was much greater

45

than that usually adopted by the ARVN or US units. Later, the VC were to have difficulty in coping with so widespread a force.

Suddenly, from the right (south), about six VC literally walked, nonchalant, between the leading section and 11 Platoon HQ soldiers. Buick immediately fired, wounding one; and the others turned and fled. It was 15.40 hours, GR 478673.

'Bluey' Moore's 5 Section was swiftly after the VC, the young fit Diggers covering ground easily. One VC was killed.

Flying back to the south-east, with the speed the hunted always seem to have, the enemy were soon some distance away, followed by a volley of fire. As keen as any other platoon, Sharp's men turned after them. It was by 'kills' of enemy soldiers that performance was judged, and so far in the tour they had had few opportunities.

Adrenalin began pumping through the 108 Australians: safety-catches were thumbed off, firmer grips were taken on weapons, and eyes now keener swept the rubber-trees stretching off into the distance.

But the VC had gone, and most of the Australians thought that this had been just another small, fleeting contact.

Back at Company HQ, Maury Stanley moved to Harry Smith and checked the location, prior to any firing of artillery. Each had been following the course on his map, and it was common sense to agree on their position.

On the radio, Gordon Sharp called that the enemy were not in black pyjamas (the dress of village guerrillas) but in khaki uniforms.

Further back, with 12 Platoon, David Sabben realized that the enemy were 'a special group'. However, in the excitement of the chase no one else, Sharp included, seems to have understood the significance of the observation. Village guerrillas could be likened to farm dogs, in that they might attack a stranger who seemed afraid; but green or khaki uniforms denoted enemy Main Force soldiers, who rarely travelled alone and could be relied upon to fight, even if it was a fighting withdrawal. Tigers, not farm dogs.

At 15.42, artillery from the NZ 161 Battery was fired onto GR 482668, a position about 500 metres south of the small firefight, in case the running enemy were heading that way.

A/6RAR was entering the camp as the guns fired, but no one paid much attention. Salvos were often fired onto likely enemy locations, and by now the Diggers were used to it. Not so the Col Joye entertainment group, who provided an unrehearsed laugh for the audience when the loud noise made them jump with fright, like all new arrivals. Adrian Roberts, of the APCs,

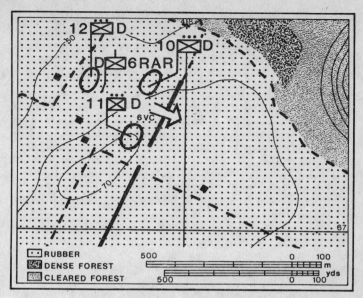

Initial contact in the rubber plantation

was showering. Peter Tedder, 105 Battery, was at 1st Field Regiment HQ, talking to Captain Ian Darlington in the FSCC. Darlington had left the Col Joye Show to assume control of the FSCC at 16.00 hours.

Alan Hutchinson, one of Tedder's FOOs, had returned from the bush with D/5RAR and was trying to find a place in which to sleep and live at 105 Battery, since he had completed his last operation and was returning to Australia in a few days. This was easier said than done, however, 'as no one wanted to know me: FOOs were regarded as the grubby itinerants who stomped through the weeds out there with the grunts'.

George Bindley was enjoying a hot shower from the standard Army canvas bucket, which was suspended from a tent ridge-pole, near the gun position. He heard the first firing by the New Zealand guns and thought it unusual, as the day had been so quiet. Bindley continued to 'relish' the hot water, and enjoy 'the view across the gun position to the hills in the south and west, where a tropical storm was developing'.

Rob Rich, an Australian Army pilot flying a Sioux observation helicopter, commonly called a 'bubble' because of its appearance, was waiting for the order to fly. At the control room of the

Army's 161 Recce Flight, beside the airfield at Nui Dat, Private Ernie Sparahan was passing another day. No one there knew of anything developing, and the radios were not even tuned to the D/6RAR frequency. The first indication 161 had of the contact was a call from Task Force HQ on the telephone landline.

Among the resting and waiting VC, there would have been surprise and consternation. Success depended on attacking an enemy that had little or no foreknowledge of the assault. The young soldiers began putting on their equipment, placing their hands on their guns, looking towards their leaders for information, orders, some sign of what would happen. Each commander was looking towards the sound of the firing, of the artillery bursting; perhaps motioning to a platoon leader to come to him, before sending him out to see what was happening. Automatically they would have recalled the tactical slogan, 'The Three Firsts':

> *First to occupy critical terrain;*
> *First to open fire;*
> *First to assault.*

These gave the VC the initiative, and kept their foe at a disadvantage.

Also alerted by the sound of firing, the 32 men of B Company halted at GR 458665, awaiting information over their radios.

Sweeping forward, Smith's HQ reached the initial scene of firing. Later, Harry Smith would realize the significance of the well-cared-for uniform and equipment borne by a healthy young male — it signified a Main Force soldier — but at the time, he was too involved in keeping track of his platoons to stop and reflect.

Firing was continuing from 11 Platoon up ahead as Sharp manoeuvred his men after the retreating enemy. A rubber-tappers' hut was in front of them, and it was thought the enemy had hidden there. Sharp radioed that he was putting in a platoon attack on it; and Geoff Kendall, now off to the north, today distinctly recalls thinking, 'Sharp, you lucky so-and-so!' It was every Platoon Commander's dream: a platoon attack, bowling over an enemy section or squad — and picking up an MC on the way through.

So far, for all concerned on the Australian side, it was merely another platoon action.

The platoon swept through the area of the hut, finding nothing: any enemy there had fled. With his three sections abreast — 6 Section on the left, 4 Section in the centre and 5 Section on the right — Sharp pushed on further and further through the young rubber-trees, approaching a clearing in the plantation and the green wall of bush beyond. He was carrying the AK47 picked up from the dead VC at the start of the action.

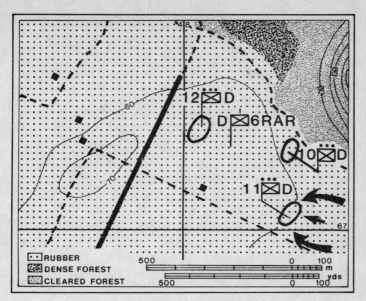

11 Platoon comes under fire

Behind the inscrutable green mask, enemy platoons were readying for action. The fleeing survivors of the short fight must have come running in, panting the news. Peering through the shrubbery, the VC would have seen Sharp's men, green figures advancing towards them among the rows of slim unmarked rubber-trees. Quickly orders were given and relayed to the lower echelons, hands checked weapons, men wriggled into firing position, platoons scurried off to the flanks in preparation for the rush around the sides of this group of about twenty or so foreigners.

In extended line, 11 Platoon reached a barbed-wire fence running through the trees, when, in Peter Ainslie's words, 'a million little lights seemed to come out of the rubber, from knee height to above our heads, and a helluva noise'.

It was 16.08 and 6 Section, on the left, was hit by 'fairly heavy fire'; the fighting began to change its character. Sharp radioed that he was under fire from what was estimated to be a platoon of enemy, and Kendall and Sabben, listening, also received this information.

Bob Buick counted at least two light machineguns firing on 11, saw about four soldiers hit, and thought, '*This is it. Let's get into them, and hope they don't bug out the way they've always done.*'

49

He was to find that the VC had no intention of 'bugging out' this time.

Smith began to close up Sabben's men with the HQ, and to move forward to 11 Platoon. Peter Ainslie 'wondered how any of us could have survived. Two fellows were killed immediately. The platoon fell back and attempted to get into all-round defence. Gordon Sharp was still carrying that AK47.'

After the initial burst, the VC fire stopped and Sharp ordered his 5 Section to move out and sweep across the front of 11 Platoon to clear the ground there. The men had moved out to about a 45-degree angle in relation to the others, when the enemy fire burst out again, on a larger front. In the words of 'Paddy' Todd, back behind Smith's HQ:

> We had hardly moved 12 Platoon when the greatest firepower you've ever heard went, and that was 11 Platoon walking into the enemy... Mortars started falling, and we couldn't dig in...

Never had 11 Platoon seen such a hail of fire as crashed out of the greenery in front of them, a veritable storm of tracer three or four metres high, flailing the trees. Brian Halls, in 11 Platoon, recalls these moments:

> We all went to cover. It was a natural reaction bred into us before going to Vietnam. Section Commanders took control. I remember being left out forward by myself, and Johnny Haslewood from Brisbane was next to me. There was a VC coming up on my right ... [Johnny] yelled out, 'Can you see him?'
>
> I said, 'No!'
>
> 'Well, keep your bloody head down', and he fired across the top of my head and got this bloke, then said, 'You're right now, you can pull back'. And we did, into a straight line.

The remorseless mass of bullets streamed through the platoon position, shattering tree-branches, shooting leaves off, sending latex spurting.

Barry Meller felt something slap his face, put his hand to the spot and was surprised to see blood on it: 'Shit, I've been shot!'

Bob Buick looked across and called, 'Well, keep shooting!'

Like all the others, Geoff Kendall, with his 10 Platoon to the north behind Sharp, heard the rolling crash of the volley of gunfire, and the growing strain in Sharp's voice on the radio.

> The firing was increasing and getting very heavy. Sharpy came up on the radio and said, 'I think it's too big for us. They're in at least platoon strength.'

I told my fellows to drop their packs and shake out into a loose assault formation. Knowing Smithy, my immediate thought was, if there was a platoon there we'd be doing a quick company attack, and I was certainly in a perfect position to hit from the left, so I assumed I would get the job of being assault platoon while Sharpy supplied fire support.

VC were pouring automatic fire into the area of the foreigners out there in the rubber-trees, while platoons ran to begin their outflanking moves and attacks.
'First to open fire; First to assault...'

But even as Kendall's 10 Platoon shrugged out of their heavy packs, it became obvious that Sharp was in trouble, and Kendall heard him say, 'I think it's bigger than I thought it was. *They're* going to attack *us.*'

The drumroll of VC fire poured on and on.

Called for by Maury Stanley, artillery fire from the New Zealand guns began to fall beyond 11 Platoon, among the massing VC. Stanley was out of sight of the platoon, and had to be careful that the shells did not fall among the Australians. Even if they were not exploding as close as they did later in the battle, these salvoes landed amid the VC unit organizing to attack the small force that had suddenly appeared almost on top of them.

Back at Nui Dat, few realized what was developing out in the Long Tan rubber-trees. Alan Hutchinson, the nomad FOO whom no one wanted to house in 105 Battery position, gave up and, 'a bit miffed', returned to D/5RAR. Adrian Roberts, of the APCs, had been to the Col Joye Show and was having a shower. When the artillery began firing regimental missions (i.e. all 24 guns at once), he realized that something was wrong. Then, a soldier arrived at the showers to tell Roberts that he was wanted by Major Hagerty, and that he should take his map.

At the FSCC, Peter Tedder, with eleven months' experience in Vietnam, was talking to Ian Darlington. As the messages came in, Tedder realized that the VC were staying to fight, and that it would be a battle not a fleeting contact. He said this to Darlington, who looked at him, not yet comprehending, and Tedder left for his battery position, probably the first man outside D Company to grasp what was happening.

David Harris, an Armoured Corps officer at 1ATF HQ, unofficially telephoned Major Hagerty, commanding the APCs, and warned him of a possible need for his vehicles.

Buick, prone among the soldiers of 11 Platoon, estimated that the fire being thrown at them must be coming from an enemy company. RPG rockets were blowing rubber-trees apart, and at first he thought these were explosive bullets. The volume and accuracy of the fire, plus the rapid sequence of casualties, was frightening.

Behind all this, Harry Smith was bringing his HQ and 12 Platoon forward, attempting to join 11 Platoon and moving out of the area where about 20 mortar bombs had just exploded. Maury Stanley briefly conferred with the MFC, agreed on a compass-bearing taken on the probable source of the VC mortars, and transmitted the information to Nui Dat.

At the FSCC, Ian Darlington saw the bearing and ran across the map through an area he had previously noted as a likely mortar position, a thick clump of trees at the road-junction at Long Tan itself. Glen Eure's battery of US 155mm cannon fired the counter-bombardment — and the mortaring stopped. It was not known whether it stopped because the VC could not see their target, or because the big 155mm shells had arrived at their destinations (and this was never checked after the battle); but at the time it appeared as though the shells had had the desired effect.

In the 6RAR area at Nui Dat, Chaplain Les Thompson was visiting C Company when the firing alerted him and the Battalion Medical Officer, Vic Bampton. They hurried back to Battalion HQ and listened over the radio to the battle as it developed, quickly realizing that Harry Smith was in trouble.

In fact, 11 Platoon was in very deep trouble indeed; but training and discipline held them together against the shock effect of the VC reaction. Brian Halls describes the Australians' response:

> For the full duration while we were out there by ourselves, it was very well controlled. Everybody knew what the bloke next to him was doing, and how he was reacting. It was like a very tight family. We all worked very well together. That control came from Sharp, down through the Section Commanders, and after he was killed the control was still there in Bob Buick, who took over the platoon.

A series of group attacks was made by the VC, rushing out of the foliage. Sharp radioed that enemy were to his left, front and right. It was now obvious that their force was much more than a platoon, probably at least a company. The information flew back to Smith, and then to Nui Dat, where it was gradually becoming known that D/6RAR was engaged in heavy contact.

Ron Eglinton, a machinegunner, found himself somewhat forward of the line of 11 Platoon, and in a good position to bring accurate automatic fire onto the waves of enemy charging out of the bush. Although wounded, he held his position, mowing down the enemy as they came forward time and again.

The first explosions of the artillery shells among them showed the VC commanders that surprise was now lost. But the enemy was only a minor unit, and could easily be overpowered and annihilated with a quick attack using numbers of men and asserting firepower superiority. A Battalion Commander quickly snapped out orders, and subordinates nodded, rose from the group and ran back to their men.

Control of his weaponry was repeatedly demonstrated by Corporal 'Bluey' Moore, leading 5 Section, who calmly directed fire into the approaching VC, halting the attacks before the position was overrun. Artillery also crashed down into the VC in the rubber-trees and bush, flinging bodies and shrubs in all directions.

After the first few minutes of shock, of adjusting to the idea that the VC were 'having a go', Bob Buick found that he was too busy 'doing what had to be done' to worry. Movement around the 70-metre-square area was severely hampered by the hail of fire, but control was kept by shouting.

Peter Ainslie could see the VC coming out 'in extended line: it seemed they would attempt to attack very strongly one part of the platoon; that would wither a bit; then they would attack another part very strongly'.

Buoyed up by the success of their undetected march so close to the foreigners' camp, and excited by the roar of firing and the knowledge that they held the initiative, had firepower superiority and outnumbered the band of enemy over there in the rubber-trees, young VC ran forward, past their comrades firing from the bushes; spread out along the edge of the shrubbery; moved out into the open, running over the bundles of rags they recognized as more comrades, dead or wounded, their weapons scattered about in the dirt; realized that their own wave was melting away; dived to ground or turned back for the scrub, perhaps dragging a wounded fellow.

At this moment, 12 Platoon was still with Smith, all moving forward to get to 11; 10 was preparing to move down to help 11; Maury Stanley was advising the FSCC of the situation; and Smith was radioing 6RAR with the best information he had — that 11 Platoon was being engaged by a probable enemy company.

The men of A Company, just back from patrol, were showering, putting on clean dry clothes, looking forward to the expected beer and steak. The artillery fire was nothing to worry about. But in the audience of the Col Joye Show, some soldiers and officers were beginning to sense that the gunfire meant that something was wrong...

George Bindley, 103 Battery, had returned to his tent after his shower, was dressing and heard all the batteries firing in earnest; clearly there was a regimental fire mission in progress. He went to the CP, found out what had happened, listened briefly to the radio net, and then returned to the gun positions.

There were no problems at the guns, and even the men who had been to the concert were back — where they were needed. Then,

> a series of fire missions followed with quite unprecedented calls for ten rounds fire for effect, plus repeats. It quickly became clear that if fire was to be sustained at this rate, ammunition was going to be a big problem.
>
> I warned the Sergeant-Major and Section Commanders, but I need not have bothered. For the entire duration of the battle I needed only to monitor ammunition handling, not interfere with it in any way. The Sergeant-Majors involved did a magnificent job.
>
> The physical effort involved in moving 105mm ammunition should not be underestimated. A box containing two 105mm rounds weighs just under 100 pounds [45kg], and unpacking poses special problems. It is crated and packed to withstand rough handling and does not fall apart when needed.

The boxes were braced by steel rods and these were secured by butterfly nuts, which could become corroded or bent; so that time and force might be required to open the boxes. When removed from the box, the ammunition had to be laid out for inspection by the senior ammunition member of the gun crew.

The projectile weighed 15kg, and was fired by muslin bags of propellant. These bags could be removed from the cartridge to provide the necessary range.

After fusing, the shell was loaded, an action requiring stamina and skill. Bad timing could result in injuries: lost fingers (cut off by the breech block), broken legs, or worse. A good gunner developed a rhythm with the recoil, virtually becoming a part of the gun himself. An error of judgement could be fatal.

Now, at all gun positions, the training and experience of the officers, NCOs and gunners was embodied in the smooth sequence of preparing, loading, firing, checking and adjusting, to keep the shells falling in response to Maury Stanley's calls.

Out to the east, where the shells were landing, the infantry fighting and manoeuvring went on.

Gordon Sharp, in his first major battle, like countless sub-alterns in armies round the world, was reacting to his training; trying to see, hear and digest everything, to command and look after his men, to inflict damage on the enemy, to keep his superiors informed. He was continually moving around the small area held by the Australians, raising himself to see what was happening out there, ignoring Buick's calls to stay low.

In the shrubbery, a VC scanned the target area, saw movement: a foreigner ducking and reappearing... Quick, fire!... The distant man went down ... did not reappear. Keep firing in that direction... More comrades went past and off to the side, moving to attack...

Sharp was hit in the throat and killed at once, still holding the captured AK47. Bob Buick took command of the beleaguered platoon. 'I kept on telling the Diggers that the company was coming, and so were the APCs with the rest of the battalion, and only to hang on a little while longer.'

Kendall's men, originally some 200 metres behind and roughly to the north of Sharp, were advancing towards the firing, alert for contact. It began to rain. 'And when I say rain', Kendall emphasizes, 'it rained like it rains in Vietnam in the afternoon. It absolutely started to pour monsoonal rain.'

Pushing on, going for the estimated centre of firing, Kendall's 10 Platoon ignored the rain, peering ahead for the enemy from under dripping hat-brims.

In the words of Kev Branch: 'The next thing, we went down and up a bit of a dip, and onto level ground, and came across all these VC lying with their backs to us! There was a bit of a hump on the ground, and there were thirty to fifty VC, I think.'

Suddenly, Kendall saw, to their immediate front, an assault-wave moving almost due south, going in on 11 Platoon.

I estimated it was probably at least a platoon frontage, and we could see thirty to forty people. They were assaulting with pretty much the same tactics we would use, walking forward, well spaced. They hadn't seen us because they'd gone slightly past us.

Branch heard Lieutenant Kendall saying, 'This is it. Keep going, keep going' —

and I'm thinking to myself, *Christ, he's mad! We'll be able to shake hands with 'em soon!* We kept going, and with all the commotion going on they didn't know we were there. Next thing we got the order to fire.

Kendall:

> I just sang out to my fellows something like, 'Fire!' I dropped down on my knee and started firing and we knocked over all their right-hand element. I don't think they knew where the fire was coming from.

Harry Esler was 'surprised to find I was calm, no fear, because I could see a target'. Kev Branch was

> blasting away from the hip with my SLR, but after about ten rounds or so, I said to myself, 'This is no good, I'm wasting them'. I then knelt down and took aim. I certainly knocked over a few. They were really surprised. I think we cleaned up about twenty in a few minutes.

Kendall:

> The guys over to the left appeared to me to do a left turn, apparently under orders, and to break into a trot, away, out of our sight, to the east, in good order, without ever returning fire at us at that stage.

The survivors of the VC unit moved back, the senior man reporting the clash: that a superior and aggressive force of foreigners had appeared behind them, and was probably moving south to the aid of those already in battle. Their commander sent a runner back with the information. More enemy? How many? How far away? Peering through the rain and the deepening afternoon gloom in the trees, he tried to see what was happening. He sent a few men to observe and report. The enemy artillery was suddenly doubled or tripled in force, and he started his men digging shallow trenches for protection. What was to be done now? What was the plan?

Smith's HQ had been able to see, in the distance, Kendall's men sweeping south, but had then lost them from view. A burst of firing broke out from that direction. It had been obvious that a single battery of guns would not be sufficient to provide support, and the entire regiment, 24 guns, was called onto succeeding targets. At 16.19, 1st Field Regiment, controlled by Maury Stanley, fired on GR 487674, and the first great hammer-blow of the afternoon smashed down into the VC positions.

Skittering around above the trees, trying to see what was happening below, hampered by the artillery, the rain, the failing light and the layered mat of green foliage below, Brian Wickens was frustrated because the radio frequency of D Company was not known — it was changed at the start of the fighting.

Meanwhile, 11 Platoon fought on, with VC surging past on all sides, falling to the controlled fire of the young Diggers, blasted away by the artillery dropping among them, getting up and going on, crawling or staggering away, leaving weapons and equipment scattered among the branches and leaves, all under the streaming rain and splashing mud.

Maury Stanley called corrections to another regimental fire mission at 16.22, moving the deluge of high-explosive back and forth over an area of 200 metres. Unable to see in the rain and murk exactly where the rounds were falling up ahead around 11 Platoon, working entirely by communication with Buick over the radio, from a folded map held in his hand, constantly wiping off the splashing mud and running rainwater, this New Zealand officer was calling on every ounce of his experience and training. His M16 rifle lay unattended in the water, despite the repeated reminders of his radio-operator to keep it in his hand.

For Rob Rich, waiting at the helicopter pad, 'the contact was just a routine call to us. The NZ officer came rushing down with his maps and we got airborne straight away. As normal, I asked him where they were. He pointed to the hill [Nui Dat East], and said, "Over there".'

So away I went. He was still organizing his radios and maps. I was orbiting this hill and became aware of a tremendous amount of enemy ground fire. In a helicopter, this is quite noisy. These tracer bullets were coming up past the helicopter, and I tapped him on the shoulder, and said, 'Are you sure this is the right place?'

He then looked out and saw all this stuff coming up, and said, 'No, No, that's *them*, that's *them*. We're over there somewhere.' So we flew away from that hill.

At 16.30, A Company 6RAR was warned to go back out to D/6RAR. B/6RAR — that is, the 32 men comprising it in the field that afternoon — was told to move back to the battle. It might be of interest, to whoever likes to ponder the 'ifs' of history, what the outcome of the day would have been if these 32 men, and not the 108 in dispersed platoons of D/6RAR, had encountered the VC force.

A Company, under Captain Charles Mollison, began to saddle up again, their dirty clothes conveniently to hand.

In the rubber plantation, amid the rain, the mud and the din of firing, Geoff Kendall still had to shove through to 11 Platoon.

I got my blokes back up and we continued. We'd only just barely started to move when we walked into a hail of fire from three sides, certainly from the front and left and from what appeared to be a HMG with plenty of tracer rounds from the higher ground of the Nui Dat [East] feature some 400 metres away to our left.

Quickly reacting to information concerning a second unit of foreigners moving south, the VC Battalion Commander sent platoons to take them under fire and keep them separated from the first group, so as to achieve a battle of destruction in pockets, with each enemy group a separate weak element.

In the first burst of fire, which was an absolute hail [Kendall continues], I had four or five guys wounded, and unfortunately, one of the first was my radio-operator, Brian Hornung, who took a round through the top of his chest and through the radio. He seemed to be OK, it was a clean enough wound, but the radio wasn't OK. My radio communications were lost at that time.

Kendall's 10 Platoon was forced to ground and to a halt by the mass of fire threshing the area. About 100 metres ahead was the embattled 11 Platoon, still fighting on alone, amid walls of artillery brought down by Maury Stanley, with VC dead and wounded almost all around them. The rain was pouring down on all, blinding impartially, splashing mud, forming pools and rivulets.

Crawling carefully around, well out from the foreigners, slithering through the wet red mud and sodden leaves, at least one VC sniper made his way to the rear of 11 Platoon and then just as carefully crept closer. Ignoring the shrapnel and automatic fire, he climbed a tree, bracing himself in the lower branches. Peering through, he could make out the forms of the green-clad enemy, now black-wet with rain. Still they fired, resisting, their backs to him. He took aim at one of them.

Harry Smith now had all the makings of a serious situation before him: 11 Platoon heavily engaged and unable to move, ahead in the rain and rubber-trees; and 10 Platoon, going to their aid, last seen before a massive roll of firing, suddenly out of radio contact. Then, the wounded from 10 began to filter back through the trees. And overhead thundered the salvoes of artillery, slamming down like giant doors closing, up there where the enemy were persisting in their assaults.

Kendall's men were now prone, fighting off the attacks, and Smith began to put artillery down, rather blindly and hopefully, to assist them.

But the VC showed no signs of slackening the pressure.

At the artillery positions of 1st Field Regiment, men were

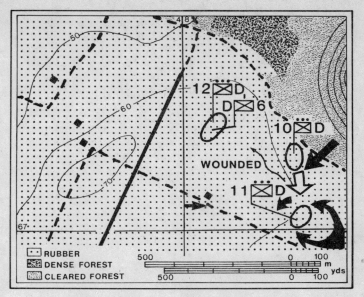

The attempt by 10 Platoon to reach 11 Platoon

busily preparing the heavy shells for firing. Normally, about 100 rounds per gun were on hand, with 300 more per gun in the battery dump. The seven-man crews were fully occupied serving their guns; soon, the discarded packing and boxes began to pose a problem. Other men had to be brought in to keep the boxes moving to the position, and to carry away the debris building up. And the rain kept coming down.

At 15 minutes' notice, 1APC Squadron was ordered to be ready to lift a company of 6RAR to the battle. All 24 of 1st Field Regiment's guns were thundering almost without pause. The Col Joye Show had broken up — partly because of the overwhelming noise from the guns and partly because of the rain. Little Patti was riding through the area on an APC, much to the delight of the soldiers; but to her consternation, she was abruptly left at the helicopter pad.

Ian Savage, commanding the vehicle, was told to get it back to the unit as soon as possible. It was normally used by Adrian Roberts, Savage's Troop Commander.

It was decided to fly the entertainers back to Vung Tau at once, but before Col Joye could climb aboard the Iroquois he was 'kidnapped' by a Sergeant, who drove him away to drink with the soldiers. A good scout, Col went more or less willingly.

Little Patti, looking back from the helicopter as it threshed its way south, saw the continuous flash of gun-muzzles, which she took for enemy explosions in the camp. No one explained these things to her, and she spent a worried night recalling the new, confusing and (as she understood it) dangerous situation at Nui Dat.

Artillery Crescendo

O God of battles! steel my soldiers' hearts;
Possess them not with fear; take from them now
The sense of reckoning, if the opposed numbers
Pluck their hearts from them!...

King Henry V (IV. i.)

B Y NOW IT WAS becoming obvious to all at Nui Dat that
something serious was going on. The constant and heavy
artillery fire was like nothing that had been heard before. In the
province capital, Baria, the repeated booming on the rain-soaked
afternoon caused some alarm among the GVN and ARVN —
because if the newly arrived Australians were in trouble, it
would surely flow on to *them*. Captain Mike Wells, the Australian
adviser, tried to find out what was happening, but the Vietnamese
knew nothing of use. He flicked the frequency of his radio
to that of the Task Force, and he listened to the battle as it
was reported on that net, piecing together items of information
and using his knowledge of the Australian Army to read between
the lines. He was careful not to show any alarm: it was not so
long ago that the ARVN had been decisively beaten by the VC
all over the country, and the memory of the debacle at Binh Gia
was still fresh.

At 16.40, Task Force HQ put 1 APC Squadron on 15 minutes'
notice to lift a rifle company from 6RAR to the scene of battle.
Adrian Roberts called his men to readiness. The M113s were a
little old and tired, some of them having operated with 1RAR
during its tour, and were in need of a good overhaul. Some had
no protective armour-shield on the .50 HMG mounted at the
commander's hatch; and some had no intercom system, though
this was attended to by fixing a string to the left and right

61

epaulets of the driver, so that the vehicle commander could give him steering directions. The APCs' pivot-steering (the method used in water crossings) was worn out, and this presented great problems when swimming the flooded Suoi Da Bang.

Brigadier Jackson was waiting for the commencement of the usual afternoon briefing, but was called away by Dick Hannigan to the Command Post as the contact grew more fierce. It became obvious that there was a time-lag in the receipt of information from D/6RAR: Harry Smith had first to acquire it from his platoons, and then to compose and send a message to 6RAR, who then passed it, along with any other that they had, to 1ATF. If necessary, of course, Smith and 1ATF could communicate directly, but this would mean bypassing and thus making useless the parent battalion, which had a definite role to play.

It was at the nearby FSCC that information was coming in directly and accessibly, and Jackson moved there to gain a better understanding of the immediate situation. Group Captain Peter Raw was close by his side, estimating what RAAF support might be called for on this day.

At Nui Dat were two RAAF Hueys, commanded by Flight Lieutenants Dohle and Riley, which had been used for the transport of the Col Joye entertainment group.

In the Operations Room of 9 Squadron at Vung Tau, Flight Lieutenant Phil Cooke was duty-pilot. At first, the only thing known was that an Army unit was in contact with the enemy in the Long Tan rubber plantation. Then, information arrived that a large enemy force was engaging that unit.

The VC Battalion Commander, his Political Officer looking on, was receiving reports from the members of his Reconnaissance Platoon: runners moving up through the rain, with mud and water dripping from them, eyes shining with excitement or dull with fatigue as they reported. Stumbling past, heading east, were the wounded, their bandages soaked, the water-diluted blood lost against the black-wet clothes and dripping to disappear in the mush underfoot.

Members of the VC 5 Division Medical Unit were busy with stretchers and medical haversacks, hurrying the casualties to the central collecting-point. The usual priorities prevailed: the wounded, the weapons, then the dead.

Messages from his higher HQ arrived: he was to continue the attack, crush these two small units of Australians, and remain ready to go on to the camp.

To the west of the two platoons engaged by the VC, Harry Smith, with his HQ and David Sabben's 12 Platoon, was still pushing eastwards through the rows of trees, the rain, and the tremendous clamour.

In Smith's HQ was 'Yank' Akell, second radio-operator. 'The noise was frightening, just like sitting in the middle of a company rifle-range, with the crack of shots falling all around you. I was wet, cold and frightened.'

At 16.46, Maury Stanley brought down another rain of shells on GR 487669; and then 'walked' the destruction back and forth, and to the right, over a 200-metre area.

Harry Smith, in contact with the survivors of 11 Platoon, was told that they were surrounded, unable to move, and almost out of ammunition. Smith decided to move forward with 12 Platoon, in an attempt to reach 11 or get close enough to allow 11 to move back to him. With 12 Platoon leading, they began pushing south-east. Although 10 Platoon was still out of communications contact, wounded from it were arriving.

Brian Halls, 11 Platoon, remembers 'Bluey' Moore, the Section Commander, 'telling people with automatic weapons to fire only single rounds, not to fire them on "Automatic", to conserve rounds. By now we all realized we hadn't come up against another listening-post, but something heavy!' And Bob Buick recalls:

> We lost communications with the company because the an-tenna was shot off the radio. Vic Grice, the radio-operator, replaced it, but during the ten minutes of no communications, 10 Platoon had moved to the north-west to assist us. Not knowing this, and having seen what I thought was enemy to my left rear, I requested artillery fire into that area.

Having no direct contact with Buick, Maury Stanley did the best he could, controlling the artillery fire by a combination of listening and plain experience.

Geoff Kendall was fighting his own little war in the rain, amid the rubber-trees and noise.

> I'd stopped moving forward at this stage and put the guys on the ground, to establish what had or had not happened. We were still under *very* very heavy fire from all sides, coming through a foot or eight inches above the ground, so you had to stay low or take the chance of being bowled over.
>
> One of the fellows wounded was the 2ic [second-in-command] of my forward section, so I got the Platoon Sergeant [Rankin] to get the wounded, if they could move — walk or crawl — back under the care of this wounded 2ic. I told him to crawl back, straight behind us, the way we'd come in, until he

broke clear of the immediate area of fire, and get the blokes back to CHQ, and tell them that my radio had gone, I was still virtually intact, and I was moving on to see if I could get close to 11 Platoon.

At Smith's HQ there was another radio, normally used for Administration matters but not much needed on this day. The radio-operator, Akell, decided to run forward with it:

The 10 Platoon radio-operator had been brought back into the centre. Behind us, Corporal Phil Dobson had found a small hollow where he set up an aid-post. I decided to go forward with my radio so that at least 10 Platoon would have a set they could put onto the company frequency.

Armed with an Owen gun of World War II vintage, Akell set off across the bullet-swept ground between Smith's location and Kendall's men, out there somewhere in the rain and trees. Enjoying a high reputation in action against the Japanese, the Owen was less popular in Vietnam because of the light power of its 9mm ammunition, and some preferred to carry a heavier, longer rifle. But Akell still had an Owen.

At Nui Dat, Brigadier Jackson and Lieutenant-Colonel Townsend discussed the action by telephone; and it was decided, after some strong talking by Townsend, that A/6RAR was to be taken to the battle by a troop of APCs, with Townsend also going to take command at the scene. Adrian Roberts was ordered to go to 6RAR as soon as possible with his APCs.

At 6RAR, standing at the long buffet table set up for the A Company after-patrol steaks and beer, Rod Armstrong, one of Lieutenant Peter Dinham's Section Commanders, was talking to two replacements for the platoon who had arrived just that day. Suddenly, Warrant Officer Jack Roughley, the Company Sergeant-Major, appeared, and shouted that the APCs were coming and everyone was to be ready to move, with basic webbing, in five minutes.

The happy crowd dissolved in a flash, men running to their tents to dress and collect their gear and weapons. As they came running back out again, the Sergeants were standing by the ammunition bunker, handing out as much ammunition as anyone wanted.

Peter Dinham changed out of his fresh dry greens into the wet dirty ones he had so recently taken off. Peter Bennett, a machine-gunner, actually managed 'one mouthful of a steak sandwich', and had to go.

But at this stage, at least as far as Rod Armstrong was concerned, it was merely a matter of riding out to give assistance to D Company and then returning to Nui Dat.

Sergeant Frank Alcorta, Peter Dinham's Platoon Sergeant, also had no information about what was going on. He had migrated to Australia from Spain in 1959, joined the Army later, and seen service against the Communists in Malaya as well as against the Indonesian invaders during Sukarno's 'Confrontation' campaign. Alcorta had only recently returned to Australia, with his wife and young children, but had volunteered to go to Vietnam with 6RAR. He passed out ammunition and grenades to the Diggers, who could take as much as they wanted.

A Company, a little excited at the prospect of action but regretting the steaks and beer, prepared to go back into the field.

Ken Tronk of D Company had been left out of this patrol because of heel trouble, and was at the Col Joye Show. He returned to the company area when a call came for all members of D/6RAR to do so, went to the Command Post, and listened to the messages coming over the radio.

> I think for the first time since I went to Vietnam, I cried my eyes out. I prayed for mates I had, as I didn't know who had been killed and who wounded. But prayed. I've never prayed so much in my life.

Alan Hutchinson, the unwanted FOO from 105 Battery, had returned to D/5RAR, and was about to begin eating when word came that D/6RAR was in heavy contact. He and others left the Mess, and went to listen to the radios.

Another artilleryman who found it hard to be of use was Barry Campton, commanding the radars and listening-posts to collect information about enemy mortars.

> What the problem was [he recalls] is that there were so many rounds in the air that you couldn't pick up what was incoming and what was outgoing. It just completely flooded the radar. There was no positive information, mainly because of the heat of the battle.

Meanwhile, Bob Buick and 11 Platoon were still hanging on, desperately waiting and hoping for rescue. Brian Halls heard

> a lot of yelling from their [the VC] side of things. I suppose this was to get their adrenalin pumping so they would have the courage to stand up and walk in. They were not running, just walking in, groups of ten to fifteen, no more than that. There was only one sort of a wave at a time. I couldn't say

65

how many in all . . . one would finish and another would come in, all from the one area on our side. A similar thing was happening on the other side, but they had heavier weapons, they seemed to have .50 [machineguns], in fact they moved one of them across in front of us. Ian Munro, the machine-gunner in 4 Section, tells [of how] he took care of him with good accuracy with his machinegun. Later on, they did find the .50, right out in front of our position, with the bodies. So it is quite true. [In fact, no .50 MGs were captured. It was a wheeled 7.62mm gun.]

To their north, Geoff Kendall ordered his platoon to move forward using fire and movement, a basic tactic.

It wasn't really successful because we couldn't identify targets to shoot at. It was pouring with rain, and fire was coming at us from people in, I believe, dug-in positions. At least some of them had quickly dug shell-scrapes. We got about 40 to 50 metres forward, took another couple of casualties, and I thought there wasn't a great deal of point in going further, as I'd just lose my platoon to people I couldn't even see.

Corporal 'Black Mac' McDonald, one of Kendall's Section Commanders: 'My section and Corporal Buddy Lea's section were to move forward with fire and movement, and we moved as far as possible until the fire got too heavy.'

The Heavy Weapons Company of the VC battalion swiftly prepared their mortars for action, firing a short bombardment of the area where the foreigners had engaged a platoon. The number of bombs they could use was controlled, as each had to be carried by a man or woman, and might be needed for the attack later in the evening.

So Kendall 'held there, on the ground, firing at opportunity targets, and at that stage received twelve to fifteen mortar rounds, right in the platoon area. Luckily, it didn't do us that much damage.'

Neil Rankin could hear firing from 11 Platoon, and see artillery and mortar fire falling all around.

I was calling to no one in particular to lift the [artillery] fire, when I saw a blue flash at my feet, felt the air suck me up into the rubber-trees, and the marker-panel bag being torn from my shoulder, and I landed with a thud but unhurt. I believe it was either an artillery or a mortar shell.

Kendall was looking back to where the Platoon Sergeant and stretcher-bearer were, 10 to 15 metres behind him, and in fact saw a round explode which looked to me right on top of them. I thought, *Gee, there goes poor old Neil Rankin, gone west!* But really, it exploded between our groups, and no one was hurt. I don't believe we had anybody hurt from that first load of mortars that dropped on us.

'Black Mac' McDonald was also pinned under the fire: 'We had orders to withdraw, but couldn't straight away, as one of my riflemen was wounded and had to be found before we moved out at all.'

About 100 metres away, in the gloom, rain and drifting smoke from artillery, 11 Platoon grimly held on. Brian Halls thought that the VC

realized they were making a mistake, and then started using snipers. In fact, a sniper put a bullet through the rubber-tree I was hiding behind. It was [because] I was on the wrong side of the tree that I'm here today. The trunk was about one foot across and the bullet was [from] above head-height. I passed this on to Barry Magnussen and he, in fact, killed that sniper, who was about five rubber-trees out from us, up in the branches. He had killed the person on my other side, with a bullet in the head. Presumably he got him initially and was coming across the section for the rest of us.

Bob Buick was continually taking stock of the platoon's situation.

The rain was very heavy, and visibility about 100 to 150 metres, when I decided to call artillery onto my own position, knowing that with ten of us left out of 28, and no ammunition, we could not survive more than another ten or fifteen minutes.

Captain Maury Stanley reminded me of the rules of artillery fire when I requested the fire mission, but I told him of our situation. The fire came, and landed about 50 to 100 metres to our front, and right in amongst the heaviest concentration [of enemy]. That's the 5 per cent luck.

Halls watched a wave coming in, and it 'disappeared in a howl of artillery fire! At the right time, *very* close, too close! The ideal thing, just what we wanted.'

Ian Munro was out of ammunition, reduced to cheering the gunners as their shells crumped in among the VC. Peter Ainslie saw 'people blown away almost in front of your face. It was very, very close and we were very, very grateful.'

Harry Smith had requested fighters with napalm and bombs to attack the ground from GR 486669 to 487674, and these began to take off. He also asked for an ammunition resupply. It was obvious to all concerned that resupply would have to be by air: it would be impossible by land.

Made restless by the activity and the lack of information, Flight Lieutenant Frank Riley had gone from the helicopter pad to the 1ATF HQ complex to find out what was happening. He soon realized that D Company was in trouble, and that the only way ammunition could be delivered to them in time was by helicopter. And helicopters were what he was trained to fly.

Bob Grandin had accompanied Riley to the complex, knowing that Riley 'was always looking for action, and maybe to slow him down a little bit'.

Together with the others there, the pilots could hear the radio messages flowing between Smith and Nui Dat, and were particularly struck by the constant requests from Smith for ever-closer artillery support. Despite the concern by Brigadier Jackson that it was falling too near, Smith insisted.

Ignoring the 'general support' rule, and the ban on taking aircraft into insecure locations, Riley offered to fly the ammunition to Smith. Bruce Lane was prepared to fly alone, if necessary. Bob Grandin 'was sure we would be killed', but would fly with Riley.

Discussion followed. A current Department of Air order (Grandin recalls), dealing with the general support role of the helicopters, clearly stated that the squadron's role was not to be offensive, and that aircraft were not to be risked; the only exception was to be flying for the SAS. Bob Grandin did not think the mission was 'possible or sensible', because

> with that number of people and the type of day it was, we were going to have great difficulty going out there unescorted, as there was not time to arrange any gunship cover. If the position was as described, and they were surrounded, then how in the heck were we going to provide them with ammunition in that predicament?

> However, Frank was adamant that we would go, and he insisted that he was the detachment commander and therefore had the responsibility for the aeroplanes, and therefore could launch them and would be held responsible for anything.

Group Captain Raw rapidly assessed the situation and the offer, and accepted the latter without clearing it with Wing Commander Scott, the Squadron CO. Riley was present, had heard the radio conversations, and was aware of the risks involved. Referring the question to 9 Squadron at Vung Tau would have meant loss of precious time while Scott was brought up to date and to a complete understanding of the situation as seen at Nui Dat. Also, Scott may 'not have been in a position to authorize it'.

Riley and the others began to prepare for the flight.

The VC commanders were busy discussing their next moves. The foreigners had been unexpectedly hard to eliminate, and their small-arms fire, plus the unstoppable artillery, had caused many casualties. No one was sure exactly how big the enemy force was, but it maintained a deadly fire. It might still be possible to wipe out this unit, if its centre could be located and its numbers ascertained. After that, either attack any rescue force, or lure a large group from the camp further out into the jungle, where both regiments could fall upon it; or push on to the camp itself, for a night attack, withdrawing before dawn into the safety of the eastern jungles. But first, the unit that was fighting here must be eliminated.

Some runners had come in with reports of yet another band of foreigners behind the two groups that were known. It was decided to send a company in that direction, to sweep through and attack . . .

Meanwhile, Akell, with the spare radio from Harry Smith's HQ, was making his way through the dangerous ground between the scattered sub-units of D Company. Meeting two VC, he killed them with the Owen gun, and pressed on through the rain and murk. As Kendall remembers it:

> Smithy sent a radio with a fellow called Yank Akell, whom I subsequently recommended for a decoration, because I thought his performance in bringing the radio forward was quite magnificent. In retrospect, it may be that he wasn't aware of what he was getting into!
>
> My recollection is that he came running through the rubber from behind us, singing out 'Mister Kendall! Mister Kendall! Where are you?' at a time when it was almost bloody fatal to stand up. He was probably a little lucky not to get knocked over. I believe that he had a brush with the enemy on the way forward. Anyway, he got the radio to us, which was a big relief, and I got onto Smithy and told him what was going on, and where I was.

Akell moved over to the side of Neil Rankin, staying with him until the move back from the position, and with 10 Platoon as their radio-operator until the end of the battle.

Out in front, heavily pressed by the VC, 11 Platoon had been asked to throw a smoke-grenade so that the arriving jets could identify the platoon's location and could bomb away from it. Brian Halls threw a grenade, but 'made the error of throwing it in front of us, blinding us, and we couldn't see the enemy. With the rain, the smoke didn't rise, but hung there. So we had a smoke haze in front of us, with the enemy coming through and us trying to pick them up.'

Above the fighting, Brian Wickens had to move out of the area so that the jets could come in, and sat watching from the bubble cockpit of the Sioux. Flying slowly and lower, he could see the smoke from Hall's grenade, but the jets had difficulty and radioed that they could not make accurate passes. Unable to go down low and slow, hampered by the weather, the three F4 Phantoms dropped their bombs on the easily seen Nui Dat East. This was the sole air-support mission by fighter-bombers during the actual fighting that afternoon.

David Sabben, back with Smith, took his 7 and 8 Sections to try to push through to 11 Platoon, leaving his 9 Section with the HQ group. Bullets were snapping through the trees around and above them, flying past from the fighting up ahead. And still it rained.

'Paddy' Todd, Sabben's Sergeant, had soldiered in the tropics, in Malaya and Borneo; 'but to the day I die, I'll never forget that rain. I've never known rain like it. The plantation was just mud.'

In addition to the air-strikes, which had been of no immediate value to him, Smith was waiting for the ammunition resupply. How to get it to him was exercising the minds at 1ATF. Around the small dip in the ground where Phil Dobson was treating the wounded, D Company was represented by its HQ group, one-third of Sabben's platoon and the wounded of 10 Platoon, with the survivors approaching through the darkening rows of rubber-trees. No one had returned from 11 Platoon since the battle had begun in earnest.

The dip in the ground was over the crest of a small rise, on the side away from the VC. The soldiers were thus somewhat sheltered from VC fire from further down the gentle slope, and many of the enemy's rounds passed overhead. The VC did not seem to realize that D Company was on a slight reverse slope.

Maury Stanley and his fellow New Zealanders, Walker and Broomhall, were prone in the mud, communicating with the FSCC at Nui Dat. For much of the time, all of Stanley's senses were concentrated on the map in his hands (steadily dripping with water and mud splashes), on the radios, and on the sound of shells crumping into unseen targets ahead.

Everything from the platoons was being radioed back to 'Pom' Rencher, Smith's radio-operator. Rencher then passed the information verbally to Smith or Stanley. Pressure started to build 'when things were getting really warm and grid-references were flying thick and fast to adjust arty [artillery]. Communications deteriorated, and I had to keep repeating "Say again, over" because I couldn't hear the grids properly. I started to get really worked up and began shouting into the handset.'

> I remember starting to get panicky, until a quiet voice came over the net and said, 'Calm down, Pom'. The near hysteria burst like a pricked balloon and I carried on with the war. I have searched memory and heart, and can say it was caused by frustration and fear of letting the platoons down, rather than fear for myself.

Rencher looked around and saw Harry Smith, like 'a rock, always cool and collected; but the calmest man in CHQ was Maury Stanley, calmly working out fire orders as if he was on exercise back home'.

The slender lifeline from D Company to 1ATF — and to the powerful artillery there — was the radio link. Major Harry Honner was in continuous if 'sometimes tenuous' communication with Stanley, and his greatest worry during the entire battle was that this link would be broken, either by malfunction or by damage to the set or its operator.

One of the factors among those often classified as 'luck' was that 1ATF was equipped with modern US PRC-25 VHF radios. In Honner's opinion, 'without these and the far more reliable communications than those provided by the replaced HF radios, there might well have been a different outcome to this whole battle'.

Everything for the Australians now depended on that fragile radio bridge, as the VC began to swarm around them to determine their numbers, their location and how best to annihilate them.

Geoff Kendall was unable to make progress from his position, but was talking on Akell's radio to Harry Smith, about 200 metres behind.

> He said to withdraw to his location, so under cover of the artillery fire we pulled back, by fire and movement, out of the immediate area, and then up at a low shamble (as you might describe the action) back to our own position.
>
> Smithy told me to put my guys down around CHQ in all-round defence. He'd kept a section of 12 Platoon back with him, so I put my guys down again facing back the way 12 Platoon had gone, which was the way towards 11 Platoon. I put two sections up and one behind me, and then tried to work out what happened next.

Harry Esler, one of Kendall's men, had been caught up the front and, 'like a silly bugger', was one of the last to get back.

I'd been having a bit of fun, and looked behind and the boys had gone. Peter Doyle was the guy that told me, 'For Christ's sake get down! Get back!'
I nearly got left up there. I remember running back. That was the strangest feeling, because unlike marching towards them, you had a funny feeling a bullet was going to hit you in the back. You were tense, and it was worse than approaching them. Meantime, it was pouring down rain. Pissing down, and we couldn't see much.

Kendall's men moved back from the VC, away from Buick's dwindling band, to link strength with Harry Smith's group.

More messages arrived at the Battalion and Regiment HQs. Poring over their maps, as beset by the rain as their Australian and New Zealand counterparts, the VC commanders tried to understand what was happening. The first unit of foreigners was still in its position, but moving slowly where it was, to avoid total encirclement. The second group, moving from the north to assist, appeared to have withdrawn west, with some wounded but leaving no dead behind. And there seemed to be yet another gang in there to the west somewhere. If only they were not so dispersed, it would be possible to pinpoint them and put a quick end to this fight, which had gone on far too long already. But attacks cannot be launched until the enemy position is known and the enemy can be fixed there by firepower.

Frank Riley and the other pilots, Grandin, Lane and Dohle, were thinking of the flight into D Company. On everyone's mind were the abominable weather and the conditions in the battle area. Heavy rain and cloud, plus thunderstorms in the mass of it, made *any* flying dangerous, let alone flight into a location occupied by at least hundreds of well-armed enemy. The artillery was plunging into the immediate vicinity of D Company, who were so short of ammunition that it would be perilous to cease the fire support to let in the Hueys carrying the resupply.

Also, it was one thing for the pilots to be told of the location of the ground unit, but quite another for them to find it, quickly and accurately, in the cloud, rain and gloom, over a featureless mass of rubber-trees that had been pounded by high-explosive.

Army Aviation may have been quite willing to attempt the mission; but the Sioux helicopter was unsuited to the task, since it could not carry enough ammunition to make it worth while if the Hueys were available.

The weather was so bad, and the afternoon so advanced, that in Vung Tau it had been decided to stand down from readiness to fly. An Army unit was known to be in a firefight, but there were already two Hueys at Nui Dat, the ones that had taken the Col Joye party.

The crews had retired to the Mess and, as Ray Scott recalls, 'were about to have our first beer' when word came that every available helicopter would be needed to support the Army. Five more were made ready as Scott tried to find out what was happening.

To Ray Scott's north, under the rain and the steadily disintegrating rubber-trees, the scouting, the probes and the attacks went on.

Kev Branch, 10 Platoon, now back in the D Company position, was aware of 'the *sound* of bullets, the *sound* of rain, coming off my nose, off my lips, off my eyelashes. I was saturated. The skin of my hands was as if they'd been in a bathtub for an hour.'

Harry Esler moved back and lay down beside Doug Mitchell and his mate Jack Jewry. 'Jack was a few feet away from me on my left.'

Lieutenant Adrian Roberts had been to HQ 1 APC Squadron, where he was told to take his 3 Troop to 6RAR and report to Battalion HQ. He set off with two sections of three APCs, and four additional APCs from his HQ. Normal strength was 13, but his numbers were down.

> My APCs had been used by 1 Troop, up in Bien Hoa: crew communication was by very old radios. One of the sections, commanded by Sergeant O'Reilly, came from 2 Troop, and had no gunshields, and no intercommunication at all — this had to be done by shouting or by cords tied onto the back of the driver's tank-suit.

Roberts drove to HQ 6RAR. There he was told that 'D Company is in bad trouble', and his briefing was quite simple: 'Take A Company out to D Company, and break up the attack.'

In the CP he noticed Lieutenant-Colonel Townsend and an Artillery Major (Honner) working on their maps, the intention being that they would go by helicopter. The location of D Company had been marked on Roberts's map, in the form of a circle 'about the size of a grid-square'.

That was the extent of his briefing, and of the orders for his mission. He did expect more detailed orders and information, but passed on what he had to his subordinates. All further orders would be transmitted to him by radio as the APC sortie progressed.

So Roberts 'moved off and picked up A Company. They'd been out on patrol, and were in the middle of a shower, trying to eat and gear themselves up to go out again.'

Roberts watched what he called 'organized chaos' as soldiers ran by, eating as they went, dressing, flinging webbing over their shoulders, carrying cans of ammunition. In a remarkably short time, they were ready.

Ian Savage, Roberts's 2ic, realized that the situation was serious, and exchanged promises with his driver that if one of them did not get back, the other would tell his wife what had happened — 'corny things like that', as he puts it.

But for many of the young soldiers of A Company, there was no dread; just excitement at the prospect of action. Peter Bennett, with almost all of his steak sandwich left behind, was looking forward to the possibility of action. As machinegunner in Ross Smith's section, Bennett was one of the few who stood in the opened top hatch of the M113, his M60 machinegun ready to add its fire to the .50. Tall and blond, a self-confessed 'character', Peter was 'always ready for a fight in those days'.

Lieutenant Peter Dinham, thinking ahead to the engagement, realized that there were few points at which the river (the Suoi Da Bang) could be crossed, and worked out in his head the probable route to D Company, whose exact location was not known anyway. There was so much activity in A Company, Dinham recalls, that there was no time to be worried by the thought of action: 'the tiredness seemed to disappear', though they had just come from a patrol.

Rod Armstrong asked the two new arrivals if they wanted to come on the mission, and with the zeal of the unblooded they accepted the offer, although they had not been officially allocated to a section or given a duty (such as rifleman, or number-two on the machinegun).

In basic webbing, with packs not needed, A Company was ready. They began to climb aboard their assigned vehicles.

Peter Dinham, his radio-operator and his Platoon Sergeant (Frank Alcorta) were sitting on the hatch edge. Dinham looked down and saw all the faces inside 'just looking at me. So I had to be fairly cool and calm. At that time I realized I had their responsibility on my hands.'

Across at 1ATF HQ, tension was so deep in the FSCC that Peter Raw noticed that those present — listening to the radios, projecting themselves out from the tent and into Harry Smith's location — seemed to be drained of colour by the intensity of the feeling in the group.

In the artillery positions a problem began to emerge, caused by the continuous firing and the heavy rain. When a shell is fired, the resulting fumes are toxic, especially if not dispersed. The storm was unaccompanied by wind, and the rain fell vertically, preventing dispersion of the fumes.

Soon the sheer physical exertion of manning the guns was compounded by difficulty in breathing, and George Bindley became aware that a lethal haze was developing around the positions.

While the battle went on, information from the regimental radio net was relayed to the gun positions of 103 Battery by Lieutenant John Griggs, in the CP, heartening the gun crews with reports of the direct effects of their efforts in support of the embattled infantry.

A wave of volunteers from units adjacent to the guns, not involved in the battle, came into the gun positions to help.

The gun crews kept on in the rain and mud, when 'any misadventure could have caused disaster: poor laying, fogged sights, an incorrect charge of propellant, an incorrect fire order'. George Bindley further explains:

> With indirect artillery fire, a tremendous responsibility rests with the individual, particularly those in the gun detachment. Each round fired is potentially as lethal to our own troops as to the enemy. Even under the most favourable conditions, an inattentive or inexperienced layer can shoot on a moving bubble [i.e. before the gun is properly steadied], or a Section Commander can be distracted long enough to allow an incorrect charge of propellant to be fired.

Off to the east, 5000 metres away, all elements of D Company were under fire. The HQ could not move because of the number of casualties collecting in the dip; 11 Platoon was still isolated, unable to be reached; 12 was engaged in heavy contact in the area between Harry Smith's HQ and Bob Buick's isolated position. The VC were maintaining a constant fire with small arms, all types of machineguns and small mortars, sending in attacking waves despite the artillery falling among them.

No one knew what lay between the 1ATF camp and the Long Tan rubber plantation. Intelligence had tentatively located a second regiment of VC to the north of Nui Dat, possibly moving to hook round and approach Nui Dat from the west.

One Intelligence theory is that an enemy's intentions can be linked to his capabilities. In that case, 1ATF might be attacked in the next few hours. Brigadier Jackson reported this to General

Jonathan Seaman, Commanding General of II Field Force Vietnam (IIFFV); and it was agreed that if the VC did in fact make such an attack, IIFFV would move to surround and cut off the enemy.

But D Company was still fighting for its life and no one knew whether it could be saved.

Armoured Breakthrough

We few, we happy few, we band of brothers;
For he to-day that sheds his blood with me
Shall be my brother; be he ne'er so vile,
This day shall gentle his condition...

King Henry V (IV. iii.)

STILL THE UNENDING RAIN poured down, as much a hindrance to the VC as to the Australians, though it is unlikely that any man in D Company took any comfort from this, even if he did think of it. Russ Perandis, CHQ, took his M60 over to support members of 12 Platoon, with 'the rain bouncing off the machinegun, hitting me in the face and eyes, making it hard to see. I had to keep my ammunition belt in a puddle of water, to stop mud from getting onto it.'

In the VC units, the numbers of wounded and dead were growing with every minute as men were hit by small-arms fire and artillery shrapnel. The confidence on the faces of the young soldiers who had earlier joked and played was gradually being replaced by a more serious demeanour. The unending roar of rifle and machinegun, RPG rocket and artillery had flattened their earlier buoyancy. Somewhat later than their leaders, the men in the companies and platoons realized that this was to be a bloodier battle than they had imagined.

Companies from a battalion not committed to the assaults were called to help evacuate the injured. Many of the casualties were quiet, the stoic Asian wounded; but for others the shock and pain were too much, and they groaned, cried out, called for their mothers or friends far away in the North, back along the Truong Son Trail — months of travel from this terrible, dark, wet, noisy rubber plantation in the South.

The unending blizzard of fire snipping through the trees overhead made the Diggers so conscious of keeping close to the ground that, as Brian Reilly later joked, 'We didn't stand upright for days!'

Time and again the accuracy of the artillery impressed the infantrymen, so that it was averred that Maury Stanley 'must have measured the distance in front of us! You would see VC arms and legs flying up into the air. Another thing [I remember] was a VC up a tree. It got hit, and half of this fellow hung up there by a leg, the other half fell out.'

At A Company, 6RAR, Adrian Roberts was waiting, and 'at about a quarter to six we got them all on. I never got any clear orders. We moved off, still not really sure how bad it was out there.' Roberts had been mentally checking the advantages and disadvantages of various routes from Nui Dat to Long Tan, and, in the light of his experience in the operation that had cleared the Nui Dat area, selected a place where bullock-carts could descend the banks, near a dam that would prevent the APCs being swept downstream. Further north from this spot, entry to and exit from the river was difficult if not impossible.

Roberts was leading his M113s to a gap in the Task Force perimeter barbed-wire fence where the APCs could get out. 'Unbeknownst to us, they'd closed the gap. We then had to go and find someone from the nearby Engineers who knew where the gap was. And they were having their evening meal. I had to stop.'

While the APCs halted, waiting again, engines rumbling, like an impatient herd of elephants, some of the infantry watched the frenzied activity in the nearby artillery positions. The ammunition stored for ready use near the guns had been fired long ago, and now every available man was busy removing the shells from their wooden travelling-cases and passing them along a human chain to the hungry muzzles.

Cooks, clerks, drivers, anyone and everyone available was slaving to feed the guns, to keep that avalanche of high-explosive falling out there where Maury Stanley was directing it onto the waves of attackers.

It was then that some of A Company began to understand how desperate D Company's situation was — that a fierce fight was imminent, and that there was a real possibility of death or mutilation in the Long Tan rubber plantation.

'*At last*', thought Rod Armstrong, '*we're really going to go out there and do something.*'

Ross Smith took in the scene at the guns, and thought that this could well be his last day on earth.

Finally an Engineer came running, and showed them where the barbed-wire barricade could be pulled aside. The engines of the APCs roared, puffing exhaust, and the squat vehicles rolled forward, jerking and swerving on their tracks, carefully weaving through the temporary gap in the defences, before increasing speed in the direction of the river, the Suoi Da Bang.

After passing through the barbed wire, Roberts received a radio message: that 'the CO of the infantry battalion now wished to go out with us to D Company. So I sent back Lieutenant Savage and one other carrier.' Ian Savage roared back to 6RAR to embark Lieutenant-Colonel Townsend and his HQ group in vehicles 30B and 33A.

Normally, the artillery battery CO travelled with the infantry battalion CO, but on this day it was decided that Harry Honner would remain at the 6RAR HQ at Nui Dat rather than risking the possibility of a break in communications between himself and Stanley. So Townsend took with him a smaller HQ party in Savage's M113s.

While the arrangements for the relief force were being made, the Chaplain and Doctor had discussed between them where they should be, and agreed that their place was with the people going out to D Company. Since Les Thompson was the older of the two, it was decided he should approach Townsend about it.

I raced across and walked beside him as he was briskly going toward the APCs. As you can imagine, he was on fire, ready to go, and I suggested to him that it might be a good idea if he took us with him to the Long Tan area.

He didn't take the bait of our enthusiasm at all, and quickly retorted that because of the heavy rains and the darkness, he was positive that the wounded would be brought back through the battalion lines, up to the Task Force HQ, and we would be needed there when the wounded came back.

What tremendous pressures are put on guys like this, in the heat of a battle, being asked all sorts of questions, by all sorts of people.

I went back and told the Doctor and we stood our ground there, chewed our fingernails there.

Roberts knew the banks of the Suoi Da Bang. He had operated there before, as long ago as May, in the clearing action to prepare the area for the arrival of the Task Force. In the region of the river there was swamp, as well as terraced paddy-bunds and a bullock-cart trail. Heavy rain poured down as the APCs growled along to the crossing-place.

Later, Roberts wondered if the curtain of rain had shielded

the vehicles from view, from possible VC observers on the high ground on the eastern side of the river. It was another of the afternoon's unanswered questions.

Wanting to avoid the terracing formed by the paddy-fields, Roberts moved south towards Phuoc Long and selected a spot where the river could be quickly crossed by APCs. He went there, receiving a message from his HQ to halt and wait for Townsend. But on his radio, on another channel, Roberts heard that D/6RAR was in trouble; so he ignored the order and pressed on, urged forward by Charles Mollison, also listening to the infantry radio net.

At GR 463649, the Suoi Da Bang was flooded and running swiftly — too strongly for an APC to cope adequately with the current. Roberts left one APC, commanded by 'Tiny' O'Shea (twice wounded in previous actions), to guard the crossing-place, and took the others across, choosing a dam area so as to prevent the APCs being swept downstream. Even so, the APCs, lacking pivot-steering for the water journey, were swept around, sometimes describing full circles before they reached the far side.

As the APCs charged forward out of the river, Peter Bennett was filled with a sense of adventure. 'I realized that D was in real trouble, and the adrenalin began pumping.'

Sergeant Frank Alcorta, sitting on the back of his APC, had 'absolutely no information of D Company's whereabouts or the casualties they were sustaining. I suspected something serious because of the hurry, but not how serious it was, or the nature of the battle itself.'

On the far side of the river, when in the middle of the paddy-fields, Roberts was again told to halt; and again he ignored the order. Choosing a track running in the right direction, he placed his seven remaining APCs on the sides and drove on, with 23 Section (commanded by Sergeant O'Reilly) and himself on the left and 32 Section (commanded by Sergeant Richards) on the right.

In the passenger compartment behind him, Mollison was becoming impatient, demanding more speed.

Now to the left of them, the artillery thundered on and on, the shells screaming away across the dark, grey sky. It was common for the VC to ambush likely approach routes for rescue forces, and at any moment the vehicles might come under a hail of anti-tank and machinegun fire. But they had to go on; on into the deep, green rubber plantation.

Frank Alcorta, perched up in the rain and soaked to the skin, looked down into the crowded body of the M113 and noticed that the Diggers were quiet.

Usually there was a lot of bantering and jokes between the Diggers who rode on the APCs, but not this time. They were silent, as if they suspected a test of some kind, perhaps even on their lives, may be imminent.

The VC commanders sat on the sides of the hastily dug pits, their small HQ groups close by. All around under the dripping trees were the VC wounded, some of the dead, and some who were yet to go into the attack. More messages arrived by runner:

It is believed there are four separated bands of the stubborn foreigners, who are perhaps trying to move together, perhaps trying to go on up to the original ones still at bay in the same area. These foreigners do not abandon the battlefield; they fight whenever NLF units are met; none have surrendered. They are causing considerable upset. The way they move, the area they cover, the fire from them, shows that there must be more than a small part of a battalion. Perhaps it is a whole battalion which is caught here. That would be worth destroying... The commanders encouraged the men of the Reconnaissance Platoons, and sent them off again.

Meanwhile, David Sabben, with two sections, moved south from the HQ position of Harry Smith to the rubber-tappers' hut mentioned by Sharp at the start of the battle, intending to turn east from there and go on to 11 Platoon. As they came to the hut, Brian Reilly noticed observation holes made in the walls. These holes had not been there when D/6 had swept through on its previous patrol a few days before.

Sabben 'didn't know exactly where 11 was. When we got to the vicinity of the [hut], we bumped the guys circling 11. I formed a two-section position to evaluate. Are we going to be attacked or is this just another probe? We were maybe 200 metres from 11, but couldn't locate them in the rain.'

Enemy groups flooding in between 10 and 11 Platoons began to fire on 12. Sabben 'could see the rounds going straight through the rubber-trees. We were getting attacks from the south and north, and nothing in between, so I worked out that was where 11 was. We couldn't hear firing from there, 11 was way out of ammunition.'

The VC platoons pressing on to the west past the isolated group of foreigners encountered yet more of them, aggressively firing and moving east to that isolated first band; and this information was sent back. How many of these foreigners were nearby? Where were they all coming from? Why had their proximity not been known?

Sabben 'picked up my guys and we started walking but were under so much fire we started taking casualties, so we went back

81

down again. It was obvious that if I kept on, the casualties would not have been worth it. The only alternative was to get 11 to come to us.'

Kev Graham was one of Sabben's machinegunners. Moving along through the rubber-trees and mud, he too was concerned and surprised by the sheer mass of tracer streaming from ground-level to four or more metres above, and was nervous until their own first shots were fired. Then calm flooded through him.

Graham fired 150 rounds, the M60 stopped, he got up on his knees to clear it, and was hit. He fell over, got up again, and was taken back by Bob Topp. Sabben asked him, 'Can you crawl back to the company?'

'Crawl?' said Graham. 'I can fuckin' run!'

Around Sabben and his small force the VC manoeuvred, while behind him, to the north, Harry Smith was organizing the establishment of the position to which the platoons would withdraw.

Further back to the west, at Nui Dat, Ian Savage and his two APCs collected Townsend and his party at the HQ of 6RAR, then returned to the river, moving rapidly to catch up with Roberts, since 'he had about a 15-minute start on us. The rain was starting to come down fairly heavily.'

Savage's driver arrived at the Suoi Da Bang at full speed, did not stop to lower the board at the front which keeps water from flowing up into the open hatch, but 'just leant over, pushed it forward, and we hit the river. My driver did a marvellous job, crossed it no problem, made it flat strap.'

Roberts, like armoured-vehicle commanders since the beginning, had the problem of trying to see out of his vehicle.

I had a board across the hatch, and sat up on that. A silly thing to do, but that's how I was, head and shoulders up. I had to be up like that, I had to be able to see what was going on. My Troop Sergeant was behind me, with the Infantry Company Commander. It wasn't written down then, but in those days we were in command while we had the infantry aboard.

Mollison believed the opposite: that the infantry commanded.

Inside the body of their APC, the men of Ross Smith's section held ready belts of ammunition for the M60s operated by Bennett and Bond, who were preparing to fire from the hatch. Peter Bennett, ready to shoot, adrenalin pumping, was still unconcerned: 'in blissful ignorance', as he puts it.

As the APCs ground on towards D Company, the RAAF crews prepared to deliver the ammunition requested by Harry

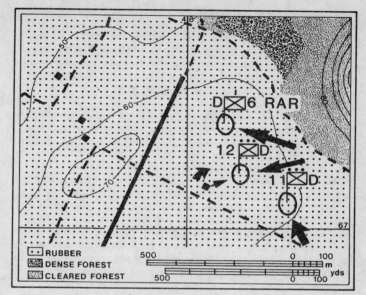

The attempt by 12 Platoon to reach 11 Platoon

Smith. The very bad flying conditions, the unknown enemy situation out in the Long Tan rubber and the unending artillery salvoes made the prospect of the resupply flight into D Company's location very dangerous.

Flight Lieutenant Frank Riley wanted to go at all costs, even without orders, to support fellow Australians in difficulty; as did Bruce Lane, who was prepared to go alone. All the crews had misgivings about the chances of success, but they manned their Hueys and flew over to the 6RAR helicopter pad to load the ammunition.

Warrant Officer 1 George Chinn, RSM 6RAR, rounded up volunteers to carry the heavy boxes to the 6RAR helicopter pad. Then there was a short period of indecision, about whether the ammunition should be delivered loose, or ready-loaded into magazines, or just in boxes. It was decided to drop it in boxes, and to wrap the boxes in blankets to cushion the drop.

Chinn supervised the loading of the boxes, and climbed aboard with Major Owen O'Brien to do the actual dropping. An experienced soldier, with previous service in Vietnam, Chinn had been awarded the DCM during a tour of duty with AATTV. Keenly aware of the problems faced by D Company, he was determined to do everything in his power to get the ammunition to them by helicopter.

While this was going on, Bob Grandin was busy sorting out maps and codes, in preparation for the mission. The pilots had decided to use a technique developed with the SAS. Cliff Dohle and Bruce Lane would take most of the cargo, and would follow one minute behind Riley and Grandin, who would locate the correct spot for them.

As soon as Riley and Grandin had some ammunition aboard, they lifted off, into the rain. 'We were going to have to try and find the rubber plantation, which we all knew', Grandin recalls. 'It was lightest to the south of Long Tan, so we cut across to pick up the road and follow it up into the plantation.'

The D Company area was relatively small, and it was absolutely necessary to stop the artillery while the Hueys flew in.

Cliff Dohle, in command of the second Huey, was quite experienced, having initially been trained as a wireless-operator/air gunner, and then remustered to pilot training. He had flown jets, including the Canberra bomber, in Australia, Malaysia and Thailand, and found the helicopter 'very heavy and sluggish to lift off'. He had intended to follow Riley and Grandin, but soon after take-off they lost visual contact in the storm.

The intensity of the rain reduced the efficiency of the rotors, and the engine was in danger of 'flaming out'. The heavily laden Huey was able to fly only at treetop height, at reduced speed. Dohle remembers it as 'uncomfortable'.

Ahead, Bob Grandin was straining to see through the wetness streaming around them.

The rain was heavy, visibility was very, very poor, we could not quite pick out our position. When we slowed down and did this we realized we'd gone past the position, to just past Long Tan [village], so we turned around and came back at about 20 to 30 knots, above the trees, as we had to get up for visibility. We were in rain, we identified the rubber plantation, and moved slightly to the south, as we were over the position given as the enemy's.

Thrumming on behind Riley and Grandin, just above the treetops, straining to see through the 'atrocious' weather ('it was absolutely pissing down'), Bruce Lane was startled to glimpse 'something' leap out of the shrubbery below and in front: a dark moving mass, a big bird, animal or human — unknown, but enough to frighten him as they swept on over it.

D Company, still fighting off attacks coming through the rows of rubber-trees, had been told by radio that the helicopters were coming with ammunition, and preparations were made to receive and distribute it. The artillery had stopped, to allow the helicopters to fly in and return. The VC began to surge forward.

Sergeant Neil Rankin, from Geoff Kendall's 10 Platoon, was back in the D Company HQ position. 'It was while we were waiting for the helicopter with the ammo that Jack and I noticed a constant flow of enemy moving to the road, carrying their dead and wounded. In a matter of about fifteen minutes, about 100 metres away, I estimated at least 400 passed us.'

Harry 'Horse' Esler was not allowing the situation to get him down.

> I lay next to Doug Mitchell, and said to him, 'OK, you're supposed to be a crash-hot shot' — this is true, I'm not exaggerating — 'I'll bet you a can of beer you can't hit that bloke in the stomach.' He'd have a shot, then say to me, 'A can of beer if you can hit him in the head'...

The two friends lay there, firing steadily.

Waiting for the promised helicopters, Neil Rankin heard the firing from another assault on his platoon area, and could tell by the return fire that ammunition was low and that 'each man was counting his shots'.

Riley and Grandin made radio contact with D Company, and called for a smoke-grenade. Peering out, Bob Grandin saw a wisp of colour, and radioed 'I see orange'.

The reply was urgent: 'No! No! Wrong! Wrong!' The smoke from D Company's grenade should have been seen as yellow.

Riley immediately broke off his approach, both he and Grandin assuming that the VC were listening and had thrown their own smoke-grenade to decoy the helicopters.

A second smoke-grenade was thrown. Grandin identified it as red, and received assurance that this was in order. Later, it was decided that the yellow smoke thrown earlier had been diffused and dispersed by the weather, and perhaps coloured by smoke from shellbursts among the trees, and that this must have led to the misidentification; for both clouds of smoke had come from the same place.

Grandin called Cliff Dohle and Bruce Lane, guiding them to the company location.

> We saw their aeroplane quite quickly. They'd put on their red light on the top, to give us an easy identification. We directed them in, straight in, to the position, gave them a little left and right steering at treetop level, and as they approached it we told them to break and they rolled onto their side over the

position, all of the ammunition being able to fall down into the company while they were turning and already on their way back.

Cliff Dohle saw the smoke below, and felt the helicopter lightening as the heavy boxes slid out, straight into the trees immediately below them. It seemed to take forever, but the heavy rain gave him a slight feeling of security, visibility being 'practically zero'. At last, Dohle heard a crewman call out that the drop was complete. He has no further recollection of the mission.

Below them the attack had petered out, Rankin thinking that it was possibly the approach of the helicopter which had caused this. Then 'a smoke-grenade was thrown and down came the ammo wrapped in blankets, which were given to the medic'.

Those few metres above, yet so remote from D Company, the pilots heard the happy voice on their radio: 'You bloody beaut, that was smack on!'

Riley and Grandin 'then dived from the height that we were sitting on up above, and did a steep turn, which allowed us to push all the ammunition out of our aeroplane, and headed off back to the Task Force'.

Bruce Lane, flying with Cliff Dohle, had fully expected to lose at least one of the aircraft on the mission. But as they wheeled for base, he realized that no enemy had been seen; and later found that no one had seen the VC, or knew of any fire being directed at them. 'We dropped it and got out, and that was it.'

During the entire flight, Bob Grandin had seen 'no sign of people on the ground, we didn't hear any firing in our direction, but it would have been camouflaged fairly extensively by the rain'. He felt 'it was amazing that we were just staggering around above the trees, quite visible, at such a slow speed — it's a wonder somebody didn't wake up to what we were up to, and fire at us'.

The ammunition crashed down into the centre of the position, only metres away from Kirby and Rankin, but was still securely packed. It was needed at once. Rankin recalls that he and Kirby

had trouble trying to break open the boxes to get at the ammo, it seemed to take ages. And firing could be heard to our front again... Belts of machinegun ammo and rifle ammo were carried back to our position and *thrown* to each group ... magazines were refilled, return fire resumed, and the enemy withdrew for the third time.

The moment the helicopters radioed that they were back in the 1ATF area, the guns began firing again. The crews went over to the HQ to find out how it had gone, and were told of the accuracy of the drop. Bob Grandin was relieved to be back. He remembers that

Frank was quite high, he really felt it was the right thing to do and nothing was going to happen on these sorts of things. We then sat around trying to keep tabs on how things were going.

While the helicopters had been making their drop, Dave Sabben had still been trying to locate 11 Platoon. At the same time, unseen below the helicopters, Roberts's force of M113s had been pushing on to D Company.

Peter Bennett, in the APCs with A/6RAR, noted that they were quickly traversing the bush area, and approaching the dark mass of rubber-trees. He began to hear the sound of fighting over the roar of the M113 engine, knew he would soon be in battle, and deliberately 'began to psych myself up, thinking of my friends in D Company, wanting to go and help them'.

Roaring along behind the other APCs was Ian Savage, carrying Lieutenant-Colonel Townsend. 'I had my radio tuned to Adrian, and one back to Squadron HQ, while Colonel Townsend was on the air to D Company, issuing instructions through me to Adrian.'

Meanwhile, below the electrical storm, the gunners at Nui Dat were carrying on under difficult working conditions. In the New Zealand position, Gunner Deacon, manning the switchboard, was thrown several metres when lightning struck; he was dazed, but later recovered and returned to duty. Staff Sergeant Day had been standing on a steel-mesh plate, and the shock of the lightning knocked him over. The others continued to serve the guns.

Back in the mud of the company location Geoff Kendall, in his 10 Platoon position, watched as

another group moved across the front of my right forward section — that is, to the south — a bit too far out to engage with small arms. They were being engaged with some success by fire directed by Maury Stanley.

About this time we saw them forming up for the first of the major assaults. They formed up maybe 300 metres away, across what was probably a company frontage. We saw them move off, again much as we'd do it: well spaced, at a fast walk. We saw their reserve line pull in behind them, with the same frontage. The assault-wave was still about 150 metres out from us, and the reserve line 100 metres behind them, and our own artillery came in and completely wiped this reserve line out; they were just like a pack of cards falling down. This was a big factor in assisting us in stopping the assault.

The constant blaring of bugles was heard from the trees as the VC units manoeuvred for their assaults. In the waterfall of sound enveloping the scene, shouted orders would easily be lost, whereas the sharper tones of the bugles pierced the noise of explosions and firing. There seemed to be no tune or melody, just blasts to signal 'Wait!', 'Ready!' and 'Go!'.

Brian Reilly heard someone say, with dry Aussie wit, 'All we've gotta do is hit the fuckin' bugler!'

To Reilly, it seemed that the waves of enemy rose up and surged forward on each bugle blast, putting out a 'horrendous fire'. Neil Rankin watched the assault-wave come in:

> We were in position about five minutes when a force of about 200 enemy appeared to our front, and I could see them picking up cable from the ground. I later found they laid cable on the move. They hit us with heavy machinegun and small-arms fire from a wide front, and we opened fire on them at a distance of 60 to 80 metres, cutting into them. After about ten minutes, they broke contact. Then mortars started falling into our position, and we were trying to dig in with our bare hands, as our entrenching tools were with our big packs, out somewhere the enemy now held. I could see them moving forward collecting their dead and wounded, along with weapons.

Realizing that the unarmed VC were equipping themselves with the weapons of the fallen, Rankin yelled to the men, 'Shoot them before they pick up the bloody things!' Later he was to feel remorse at having shot unarmed men; but at the time it was literally a life-and-death decision.

For communication from Regiment HQ to the battalions, 275 Regiment was equipped with Chinese field-telephones, and the crews moved forward, laying wire as the HQs advanced. Radios were not liked because of the difficulties in supplying batteries, and the problems imposed by range, weather, terrain and enemy interception.

Not all the enemy lying out there around D Company were dead or wounded, as the Australians soon became aware. 'Unfortunately, the ones that weren't killed by our fire went to ground among the bodies', Geoff Kendall notes, 'and it was from these guys that we were taking our worst casualties. They just lay there, waiting for the next assault-wave to come in, and between-times they'd crawl forward and snipe at [any of] our fellows they could see.'

Russ Perandis was at one point 'exchanging shots with an enemy machinegunner using a .30 gun on wheels, which we later captured. When it opened fire, I was behind a small rubber-tree. I could see the red-and-green tracer coming. I didn't know a person could move around so quickly on his stomach.'

In the heat of the action, reacting to their training — and to the leadership of Harry Smith, Jack Kirby and the other officers and NCOs — the Diggers had no time to worry about themselves but were concentrating, like Brian Reilly, on 'knocking them out ... picking our targets where we could see them'.

Another large group of VC appeared in front of Kendall's 10 Platoon, about 200 metres away, and the platoon fired. Kendall could see some of them go down. 'Our firing wasn't terribly effective so I told the blokes to hold their fire. They moved right across our front and across to our northern side, into the area where our echelon packs were. It certainly appears they did get into the packs, because some of them were opened and Neil Rankin had his camera stolen.'

Jack Kirby turned up near Reilly's position and called to the nearby Diggers: 'Do you know who that is? No? Well, shoot 'im!'

'Black Mac' McDonald could 'see the enemy closing in around us, their firepower was devastating. We could see them going through our packs (which we'd dropped for our first assault), pulling all the gear out of them, and they gave us quite a few targets. It wasn't long before there was a pile of bodies where the packs were.'

The Medical Unit of 5 VC Division was with the attacking force, busy across the battle scene, its unarmed members running into the fiercest fire to drag away wounded. They themselves became targets.

Harry 'Horse' Esler remembers noticing one member of the enemy in particular:

There was a big fellow running around in a white dustcoat. He seemed taller than the rest, giving orders, shouting orders... Anyway, I had a few shots at him. I don't know if he had on a bullet-proof vest or if I'm a lousy shot, but I couldn't get him. Corporal Green, in 11 Platoon, said later that he got the bastard, but he was never found among the dead. I remember him as a big, tall bloke, and whether he was a medical officer or one of the big nobs, I don't know.

Salvoes of artillery were crumping down, closer and closer to the Australians, as Stanley 'walked it in' under control. The chunks of shrapnel could be heard flying by, sometimes so close that Kev Branch thought, *'Well, if the VC don't kill you, you'll be killed by your own stuff!'*

The Australians were now fighting in three separate positions, roughly in a line running south-east: from Harry Smith's HQ; to Sabben's two sections, brought to a halt but hoping somehow to get Bob Buick's group back to Sabben's position; and finally, furthest east, to the survivors of 11 Platoon — still as cut off as they had been when the battle had erupted. Time was running out for 11 Platoon and Bob Buick knew it.

Visibility was now about 75 metres, it was getting towards last light, and I considered it time to go. The artillery had taken the heat off us, but we were still being engaged by all types of weapons, though not so heavily.

About ten or twelve of the platoon were still alive, with one or two wounded. I had no idea where the company was, or what was going on outside our small area of real estate.

I decided to withdraw to the west, and if necessary hide for the night and move back to 1ATF next day if I could not find the company. The only way to do it was by a clean break [while trying] to help back the wounded. My prime task was to save as many of us as I could.

The word was passed that when the order came, everyone was to run back 100 to 150 metres to our rear, and regroup.

As the order was given, the survivors rose to go. Grice was shot dead in that instant, and several others were wounded.

Barry Meller stood up and a round thumped into his leg, sending him down again. He began to crawl away, held back in the slippery conditions by his wounded leg. Barry Magnussen came over and pulled Meller onto his back, trying to piggyback the wounded man through the mud and water, the shattered trees and the deepening dark. Behind them, the VC began to advance on the spot now held only by the dead of 11 Platoon.

Brian Halls 'remembered my training for getting out and staying low: put your rifle by your side and roll over and over'...

I was rolling quite well, and rolled into Dougy Fabian, from Brisbane, and he was going the opposite way! So we sort of had a little discussion on who was going the right way. Luckily I won, because he was going the wrong way. So we stuck together. Johnny Haslewood was with us, and once we got that initial break we got up and ran. Then we'd hear a burst of fire — didn't matter where it was coming from — and we'd hit the ground and *slide*! About ten yards. It was raining, with very red mud. So we were gaining ground every time we went down.

Behind, to the west of 11 Platoon's position, was Sabben's small force, under fire from north and south, unable to move further east. Down there, they knew, was 11 Platoon. In the uproar of the battle it was impossible to communicate by sound, so Sabben 'got one of my Section Commanders to throw smoke. We chucked yellow smoke, which 11 saw, and they withdrew to us. When 11 got to us they were carrying wounded, and my medic, Davies, from Lismore, was tending the wounded and got shot.'

Bob Buick collected about eight men. Looking through the rain, he saw a yellow smoke-swirl some 100 metres away, thought it was D Company, and led back the small party, yelling and screaming so as to identify themselves.

Buick felt a surge of relief, for 'at least we were with friends, and a sense of security returned. But not for long: 12 was under heavy fire from the south, and Sabben was ordered to withdraw [and return to the D Company HQ position].'

Back in amid the slush and fallen trees, Barry Magnussen was having little success carrying the wounded Meller — who realized this, and told him to leave and come back later.

As Magnussen disappeared into the rubber-trees, Meller had no way of knowing that he would see no friendly faces until the next day. One other wounded man, Richmond, was nearby, but everyone else who passed that way during the night was Vietnamese.

Magnussen met Peter Ainslie, and together they went back to D Company.

Bob Buick spotted, among Sabben's men, fellow Sergeant 'Paddy' Todd, and had a cigarette. 'Paddy told me he was hit, but I couldn't find any wound on him and told him he was too bloody old for this bloody game. He then moved away and I went to Sabben.' Earlier, Todd had felt as if someone had hit him across the feet with a bat; but when he had looked down, there had been no sign of a wound.

Sabben had been away from D Company for some time, and could do little more out where he was. 'At this stage we'd collected what we could of 11 and knew we'd got to go back. We could see groups doing fire and movement on us from two sides, which we were fighting off, and the VC were following up 11 Platoon.'

Sabben then ordered Corporal Laurie Drinkwater to take his 7 Section, together with the survivors of 11 Platoon, and begin moving back towards the D Company position. As rearguard, Sabben would remain with Bob Buick and 'Chico' Miller's 8 Section.

As 12 began to go back, Laurie Drinkwater noticed that 'Paddy' Todd was facing back towards the enemy, and asked whether Todd was all right. 'Yeah, keep going, keep going.'

Drinkwater's group moved away, going north-west in a direct line to the D Company position. Todd got up to go, believing himself to be the last man, and found that he could not walk. He fell over every time he took a step, and began to feel foolish; but then he looked at his legs again and found that he did have wounds, in both of them.

Unknown to Todd, still nearby were Sabben, Buick and Miller's 8 Section. No one in Drinkwater's group looked back, as they knew that the others were coming along behind them.

Believing that the rest of the platoon had moved away, Todd thought he was alone, in a part of the world swarming with enemy. He knew the platoon had moved south, then east, and decided to cut across to the D Company position; so he began crawling, first west and then north.

But not far away, 12 Platoon was about to encounter another mass of the enemy.

The Drinkwater group was engaged by enemy to the north-east, and the perimeter was reformed to hold off this probing attack. No one noticed that Todd was missing. As the attack died away, the move back to Harry Smith's location was resumed, with Drinkwater's men leading, followed by Miller's, and finally Sabben and Buick.

But once again the move was interrupted by the enemy. Dave Sabben remembers the moment:

No sooner had we got up than someone said 'Hey, look at that', and we all sat down again. On the far side of the hut was line on line of enemy in the rubber-trees. They were forming up, one to each tree, and a few minutes later they came up, about three ranks, about fifty in each. They couldn't have known we were there, they were just standing there waiting for the whistle to blow.

So I told the guys to put the machineguns down the avenues and just wait — and sure enough, we opened up and we blasted them. They immediately went down, and sort of crawled back, allowing us to get back to headquarters.

And of course, unknown to us, Paddy Todd was in front of them, crawling north. Had he looked around he probably would have got up, ankles and all, and run!

Sabben then got his platoon up 'and did a tactical move back to headquarters. We didn't do a fire and movement, we didn't have to fire on the way back. I imagine that as soon as we were out of the area, the enemy did a lovely set-piece attack on our empty rounds. The last three guys out were Bob Buick, myself and one other, and we were each carrying three weapons.'

Behind them was only wreckage and one M60 — which Sabben put out of action by shooting into it with his M16. But still out there was 'Paddy' Todd.

How Todd came to be alone without at once being missed by the rest of the platoon can be explained by the fact that the heavy rain was creating a 'ground mist', about 30 centimetres high, among the many fallen branches of rubber-trees littering the ground. Mist and branches combined to screen his crawling movement away from the soldiers, whose attention was taken by the attack from the north-east when Todd began crawling west, and was then diverted to the VC assembling in lines near the rubber-tappers' hut.

Brian Halls was coming back from the 11 Platoon position, with a few other survivors.

Myself, Johnny, Dougy, Ian Munro, all sort of huddled in this one area... We could hear firing off to the flanks, and see movement behind us, but were unsure of who it was.

Then the helicopter came in. We saw the yellow smoke, and heard the helicopter. It didn't come in over the top of us, but from the Dat. We then made a group decision that it must be CHQ, or at least our people. So the helicopter was the beacon, and we realized they were friendly people behind us, but up to that time we were unsure.

When we made the dash from our tree to there, we were the last of our platoon to come in. In fact, talking to the fellows later on, they'd seen our movement out there and were unsure of it. Thank goodness they didn't start shooting at us, or we would have ended up taking potshots at each other. There was excellent control in the company area.

Peter Ainslie and Barry Magnussen came into the position, where they 'were immediately greeted by CSM Kirby, who grabbed us and gave us some ammunition, and we were sent to a break in the defences'.

Sabben and the survivors with him came back through Kendall's platoon position, which was facing the way both 11 and 12 had gone earlier that afternoon. Kendall asked Buick, 'Where's Mr Sharp?' Buick replied, 'Oh, he's been dead for a long time, sir'.

Kendall recalls that 'It sort of drove home the fact that we were in some sort of difficulty'.

Buick moved past into the centre of the company, where he met Jack Kirby passing out ammunition and 'giving support and encouragement. He asked me if I had seen Paddy, and I told him he should be back here.'

'Paddy' Todd, shot in the ankles, was dragging himself grimly back through the rain and mud.

About half-way back, to my right, there was a bit of a hedge, not big, where the VC would run along. As I was having a spell I could see these two coming. To this day, I don't think they saw me — couldn't have. I carried an SLR. At 20 metres I fired, killed one, hit the other, but don't think I killed him, as I saw him crawling around. I carried on.

Bob Buick moved on through the D Company position to where the remainder of 11 Platoon had been allocated a section of the perimeter — on the west, or facing towards Nui Dat. It was quiet there, though 10 and 12 Platoons were being heavily attacked from the south and north-east. Rain still came down heavily, and the night deepened its gloom under the trees.

The helicopters had come once, but darkness would make it impossible to repeat the mission and find D Company again. APCs with A Company were on the way, but no one knew where they were, when they would arrive, or even whether it would make any difference. D Company's world was their small area of rubber-trees; their horizons were lined with dead, wounded or very much alive VC.

The horizons back at Nui Dat were considerably wider, and the fighting in the Long Tan rubber plantation was only one of the pressures on the commander and staff. The VC seemed to be in a fighting mood today, persisting in attacks on D Company despite the steady and accurate artillery. What else did they intend? When? From which direction? How many of them were there?

At least one battalion of enemy had appeared 5000 metres away, and was showing great determination. Would a solitary battalion approach so very close to the Nui Dat base? Where there was *one*... After all, two regiments were available to the VC...

How was 1ATF to find out before it was too late? It was raining so hard that aerial reconnaissance would be greatly hampered, if not useless, and night was coming on rapidly. Ground patrols could not move fast enough to be of use for any great distance outside the perimeter.

The soldiers in Smith's D Company were concerned with more immediate matters. Harry Esler's cigarettes, in his thigh pocket, were ruined. He wanted a smoke, looked around and saw 'Buddy' Lea lighting up; so he casually rose, ran across and

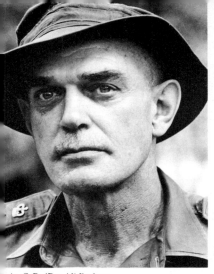

rig. O.D. (David) Jackson

Col. Colin Townsend

Maj. Harry Smith,
WO2 Jack Kirby,
Sgt Bob Buick

GpCapt. Peter Raw and
AirCdre Jack Dowling

Nui Dat in August 1966

Capt. Maury Stanley

Maj. Harry Honner

Capt. Mike Wells

Col. Dat

North Vietnamese troops, with Soviet-bloc weapons, at a political rally

NVA soldiers coming south

A Vietcong 57mm RCL team

NVA soldiers with Soviet LMG (left) and rocket-launcher

Main Force VC, using captured US weapons

A Vietcong supply column

WO2 Jack Roughley

Cpl 'Buddy' Lea

Sgt Neil Rankin

Cpl Rod Armstrong

WO2 Jack Kirby and Maj. Harry Smith, firing a Chinese HMG

FltLt Bob Grandin

FltLt Frank Riley

Cpl Bill Harrington

RSM George Chinn,
who flew on the
resupply mission

FltLt Cliff Dohle

FltLt Bruce Lane

LAC 'Blue' Collins

LAC George Stirling

Lts Adrian Roberts, David Sabben, Geoff Kendall

Cpl Rex Warren, in the exposed machinegun position aboard an M113

Lt Ian Savage

Adrian Roberts's M113 APC

Lt Peter Dinham

Sgt Frank Alcorta

re Peter Bennett

Cpl Ross Smith

Inside an APC

A 105mm howitzer,
161 Battery RNZA

...mnel in 3 Troop. Front row: Tpr Tomkin (holding 'D for Dog'), Tpr Newman, LCpl Mitchison, ...owes, Sgt Richards, 2Lt Savage, Lt Roberts, Lt Howard, Sgt O'Reilly, Cpl Gross, Tpr McNamara. ...re left: Tpr Prior, Tpr MacCormack, Tpr Clifton, Tpr O'Rourke. Centre right: Cpl Carter, ...McMillan, Sgt Chester. Rear: Tpr Scammel, Cpl Robinson, Cpl Smith, LCpl Graf, Tpr Turner, ...Behan, Tpr Wilson, Tpr Maloney. Absent: Sgt Bannister, Cpl Burrel, Cpl Clements (died of ...ds 27/8/66), LCpl O'Shea.

Pte 'Pom' Rencher

Pte Harry Esler and Pte Peter Doyle

Pte 'Sting' Hornett

Two typical young Australians,
Pte Mark Minell and Pte Neil Baker

Pte Paul Large, killed in the last stages of the fighting

Pte Kev Branch

Cpl 'Black Mac' McDonald and Cpl Laurie
Drinkwater on the morning after the battle, in the
clearing from which the wounded were flown out

Chaplain Les Thompson

Lt David Sabben scans the battle area, 19 August 1966. The ground is littered with branches
and twigs shot off the trees during the fighting. In the background is a wheeled 7.62mm
machinegun used by the VC.

Ptes Hodder, Burstall and Dettman in the battle area
the day after, with a pile of Australian weapons

Cpl Phil Dobson, the medic

Capt. Brian Wickens (left), with an ARVN
interpreter, questioning one of the wounded
VC captured after the battle

Pte 'Custard' Meller, with face and leg wounds,
after spending the night alone on the battlefield

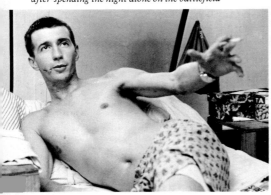

LAC B.B. Hill attending to a captured
wounded VC in an RAAF helicopter

Sgt 'Paddy' Todd, wounded in the battle,
recovering in hospital

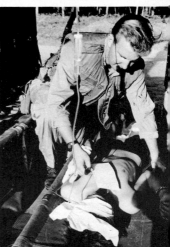

Presentation of gifts by the South Vietnamese government after the battle. Facing the camera is Capt. Charles Mollison.

Australians of D Company after receiving dolls and gifts. Front: Pte Noel Grimes, Pte Allan May, Pte 'Yank' Akell, Pte Neil Bextrum, LCpl Bill Roche. Rear: 2Lt Geoff Kendall, Sgt Bob Buick, Pte Geoff Peters, Cpl 'Bluey' Moore, LCpl Barry Magnussen, Pte Ian Campbell. (Ranks as at time of presentation.)

Banner congratulating the Australians on the Long Tan victory

Commendation certificate awarded to Tran van Tranh, of C2/D445, for his actions during the battle

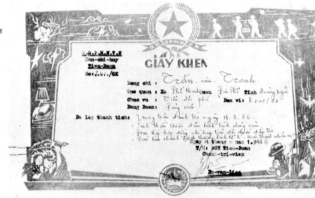

Memorial cross erected at the battle site in 1970

'bludged a cigarette off him, lit it up, ran back and lay down. It was the sort of stupid thing you do.'

Jack Kirby noticed a wounded machinegunner, Webb, and ran up to the exposed position, picked up the tall soldier, and carried him back to the aid-post. The M60 could not be retrieved and had to be put out of action by rifle fire. Webb had joined the company only a few days earlier, as a reinforcement.

Crawling on, determined, through the chaos on the field, 'Paddy' Todd edged closer to the Australian position.

I could see our kids lining me up — I couldn't blame them. All they could see was a heap of mud crawling along. I was yelling all the Australian adjectives: 'You silly bastards!' and 'Paddy Todd!' Out of the blue, Buddy Lea heard me and came tearing out and grabbed me.

We were going back to where the medic had set up a little aid-post, 50 metres or so behind the perimeter, and on our way there was a reasonably big tree. We had a spell there, and I looked up and could see these two characters coming, in black. I said, 'Hey, Buddy, have a look there'.

Buddy said, 'That'll be A Company, they're on their way'.

I said, 'Well, they must have changed uniforms, mate, because they're all in black'.

Buddy went behind a tree. One VC was in front of the other with an AK47. Buddy stepped out and let go, but this fellow was too quick and got Buddy in the left shoulder. I had to laugh. I had a giggle — it was unbelievable. I said, 'You silly old bastard'. The kids had seen him kill these two fat tigers... We both ended up in the aid-station, and from there on it was a matter of waiting to see what happened.

The Diggers in Kendall's 10 Platoon had been watching the man crawling towards them, through all the dead and living bodies. Someone in Kendall's right-hand section shouted, 'He's one of ours!' Then Kendall called out, 'Take your hat off!' and they saw him do so. 'We knew it was one of ours. A couple of guys raced out and dragged him in.'

Neil Rankin recounts a different version of Todd's arrival:

More movement could be seen to our front, and it was one man crawling on hands and knees towards us. He came closer and I could see it was Paddy Todd, Sergeant of 12 Platoon. I wondered how in hell he'd got in front of us. Corporal Billy Roche and myself went out and tried to pick him up, but he was in too much pain. We escorted him back, I asked him was he OK, and he said 'Yes'. Then I asked him would he be able to hold the gap between two of my groups, gave him a spare rifle I'd picked up, and left him facing the enemy. I last saw him crawling towards the aid-post some five minutes later.

With the wounded from three platoons collecting in the dip in the ground, Corporal Phil Dobson, medical orderly, had his hands full and won the admiration of all the men. In Harry Esler's opinion, he 'should have been given the Victoria Cross for what he did. You'd see him run up the front, out of sight, bring back a wounded fellow, patch him up, and away he'd go again. He was a champion, that bloke.'

Brian Reilly noted and was impressed by the actions of men exposing themselves to VC fire to grab and pull away wounded friends, taking them to the aid-post, and returning. Eventually there would be 23 wounded in Dobson's care, some of whom would have died but for his skill.

The Regimental Commander nodded, and then tapped his map. At last the position of the enemy had been defined. The small groups fighting on the eastern, northern and southern sides had now all withdrawn into the centre. His North Vietnamese battalions had been fully occupied engaging the foreigners on their east and south. Now to send the local unit, D445, around to the west, to make a battalion attack from there and end this fighting, which had gone on far too long and cost too many casualties. The enemy battalion would be obliterated. The runner with the message moved off.

The fighting conditions amid the rain, mud, water, leaves and debris were beyond what anyone present had experienced, and the weapons began to fail under such abnormal stress. 'By now, the machineguns were jamming', Neil Rankin explains. 'My rifle had to have each round put up the spout by using my finger, as the mud had started to seize the working parts and would not allow the breechblock slide to go forward enough.'

The continued calmness of their leaders, outward though it may have been, could not fail to be noticed by the soldiers, who were kept confident by it. Harry Esler heard 'Major Smith, or someone, behind us, getting on the radio, saying "Don't worry, we can handle it", and I'm thinking, *Christ, we must be doing all right*'.

A short distance from Esler, in the CHQ position, 'Pom' Rencher was beside a rubber-tree, calmly and busily operating his radio, passing messages to Smith and Stanley. Next to him was one of the New Zealanders. All through the battle, rounds had been cracking overhead and tracer flying past. For some reason the two looked at each other, then faced front again — 'to

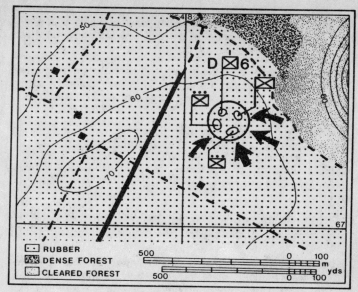

The final D Company position, under attack

see a huge tracer floating towards us at head-height, seemingly moving in slowmotion'.

The world stopped as I waited to see who it would hit. No fear, just a fascinated expectancy. After an eternity it passed exactly half-way between us! I *knew* then that I was going to come through the battle in one piece and nothing was ever going to be the same again.

Out on the thin perimeter of D Company, Laurie Drinkwater was watching the area to his front when Jack Kirby came by and called: 'Drinky, you can shoot anyone you don't know!'

Away to the south-west, coming on through the rain and scrub, Roberts's small unit of APCs was steadily covering the ground into the dimness of the rubber-trees — still alert for an ambush, but knowing that they had to keep moving forward. Hanging on in the back hatch of the lurching and rocking APC, rolling on through the evening, pressing on under the artillery fire, Peter Bennett, machinegunner, had only a blurred impression of the shellbursts, for 'everything was happening very quickly'.

Further to the south-west, going as fast as he could to catch Roberts, knowing that if anything happened to Roberts he would have to take over command of the APCs, Ian Savage was given an order from Townsend for Roberts:

Adrian was to do everything he could with the troop to get to D Company, as Major Smith had said to the Colonel that the enemy were forming up for a bad assault, and he was expecting to be overrun.

In the dimness, walking in towards where they knew the foreigners must be, with the crash and slam of the artillery never-ending . . . walking in among the unseen bullets and shrapnel, through the falling branches, twigs and leaves, peering from under their rain-sodden hats, with water running over their faces . . . the VC attacked again.

For the young Australians, prone by their trees, semi-hidden in the water, the falling rain and the mud, the VC lines presented good targets. To Harry Esler,

it was just like a kangaroo shoot. They were coming in waves. They were blowing bugles off to the left, in front, and across to the right. I remember thinking, *By Christ, I wish I had a set of bagpipes here. I'd put the fear of Christ up these blokes!* The bugles did get on your nerves, and have an effect on you, when you heard them blowing.

Brian Reilly heard Jack Kirby call out, pointing to a group of enemy, 'Do you know who that is? No? Well shoot the bastard!'

Momentarily diverted from his concentration on the artillery net, Maury Stanley heard a young infantryman close by talking to himself as he engaged the oncoming waves: 'Steady . . . aim . . . fire!' — and this seemingly trivial episode reassured the New Zealander about the condition of the small force around him.

But in 9 Squadron's Operations Room at Vung Tau, Phil Cooke was 'depressed'. The only information coming through to him spoke of Australian dead, wounded or missing, and of a platoon cut off somewhere; it made no mention of VC losses. The impression was that the Australians were taking a hiding.

In the D Company position, Barry Magnussen was suffering from a painful back, injured somehow during the day. At one stage in the afternoon, he had been lying in the mud, with Brian Halls 'rubbing his back trying to get a bit of circulation back into it'.

For many of the Diggers, once they were in the position from which they knew they could not move away (and *would* not, if it meant leaving the wounded), things became more simple. 'Once I got settled down, that was it. You just fired. It was like having a picnic, shooting at them. You couldn't miss.' Kev Branch, for one, understood that 'by doing our job, we overcame our fear, and our stamina became greater'.

As the attacks began to roll in on the small position, with the fire unabated and no help in sight, Laurie Drinkwater turned to David Sabben.

'Do we look like getting out of this?'

'I don't think so', was Sabben's reply.

With the ammunition starting to run low again, Jack Kirby came over and took the unused magazines from the New Zealand artillery party, leaving them one magazine each.

In the embattled D Company position, Kirby continued to move around underneath the flights of bullets, steadying the soldiers. A long-standing joke in the company was Kirby's insistence that Harry Esler was in fact a Private Ralph, who had last been heard of on a patrol in Malaya.

'You remind me of that bludger', Kirby would say to Esler; and on his journeys around the perimeter that afternoon, Kirby would remark: 'How are you, Private Ralph?' and 'You're not going to get back if you don't watch out'. Undismayed, Esler would reply: '*I* will. You make sure *you* do.'

Alone, out in the shambles of rain, mud, trees, bodies and scattered equipment, crawled Barry Meller . . . on and on he went, not knowing in which direction he was moving at any given time.

When 'Buddy' Lea was wounded and the Section 2ic killed, 'Black Mac' McDonald was told to take command of Lea's 2 Section, leaving his own 2ic with 3 Section.

Now, in the gathering gloom, the darkness deepened by the rain and the spreading rubber-trees, VC were able to slither closer to the Australians. 'Yank' Akell, with his Owen gun, was sharing a tree with Geoff Kendall. He dug the officer in the ribs, saying, 'Hey, have a look at this!' Kendall looked —

and Akell just shot a Vietcong who was about five metres from us, between us and the forward section. This guy had crawled in behind the forward sections. Yank noticed him and let him have half a magazine in the top of the head. That was what they were doing between the major assaults.

D Company held their positions, lying in the mud, picking their targets, wondering what would happen when night came. The VC showed no signs of slackening.

Throughout the battle, the Vietnamese made every effort to carry away their wounded, coming very close to the Australians to do so. 'For some unknown reason they would just keep running up and taking their wounded away', Kev Branch reflects. 'You knew you had to kill them, and you did, because they'd come back and kill you, anyway.'

Harry Esler would 'knock one bloke over, and about four of them would pick him up and drag him back. Well, you couldn't miss them. And they were close, you could hear them talking.'

Another assault-wave formed out there in the rows of trees, their reserve behind them, and began to advance. Again Stanley called in artillery, which arrived exactly on the reserve line, but the assault-wave came on, this time getting closer to the Australians. Geoff Kendall's men

> could actually see people standing up and joining the assault as it came forward. That was apparently one of their tactics. They got to within about 30 or 40 metres of my forward section before the attack petered out. The same thing happened again. We had immediate close firefights with these guys who were crawling around 30 metres out.

Neil Rankin looked over and saw a Digger to his left, on one knee, firing his machinegun at the enemy those 30 metres away. Rankin yelled at him to get down, but the Digger was killed.

Jack Kirby looked out of the perimeter and saw, perhaps 50 metres away, a VC heavy-machinegun team setting up the weapon. In a few moments they would be able to rake the position. He lunged forward, killed the crew, and returned.

As the darkness deepened and closed in on the men of D Company, Esler heard Harry Smith send another message: 'If you don't come within half an hour, don't worry about coming for us.'

Later, analysing the wave attacks, 6RAR Intelligence Officer Brian Wickens was told by the survivors that 'they would hear a loud babbling in the rubber, then a yell, and the VC would come for them. The babbling was [the enemy] psyching themselves up before the attack, and that's when a bugle sounded, a short blurt.'

The companies would be led to the position from which they would go into the charge; they would spread out into lines, and lie down or crouch; and the Political Officer would give a short speech about the war, the reasons for it, why it was necessary to attack these foreigners, in the name of independence and liberty. Volunteers in the unit would perhaps shout their resolve to destroy a machinegun, or to penetrate into the heart of the enemy position; all would be caught up in shouting the chosen warcry — the regiment motto, or simply the old cry of the Vietminh, Tien len! *('Advance!'); and the leading wave would rise and go forward to the enemy.*

The VC would come along [Wickens continues], come under intensive fire, and then drop. A very short time afterwards, the same thing would happen, and another line of 200 or 300 would come through. They would be taking casualties like the first lot, but when they reached the point where everyone else had dropped, all those capable of standing would get up and fill the gaps. So you got this rolling effect, which you couldn't stop while they still had the manpower — an automatic re-supply of people as they went along.

Their attention focused on the fighting to their right (the east), D445 Battalion, with a few wounded already sustained in the earlier shelling, moved into the position in which they would arrange themselves for the attack. From here they would spread out in their companies, move north a little, then turn east for the attack. The Regimental Commander had given to them the honour of the final, decisive assault. With luck, the enemy commander could be taken alive, along with some of his men.

D445 Battalion would be in the forefront of the future battles in the area, sweeping the foreigners and the puppet troops of the Saigon regime into the sea.

Through the streaming rain in the darkening plantation, D445 gathered for the last stages of preparation, peering through the lines of trees towards the foreigners, crouching a little under the tremendous slamming noise of the shells, maintaining a neat series of arrowhead formations.

The sound of their engines swallowed by the noise of the artillery and the rain, the M113s rolled through the trees, approaching the unsuspecting VC of D445.

Riding atop his APC, which was too crowded for everyone to fit inside, Rod Armstrong was watching 'the orange glow as a shell would hit a tree; there'd be a ball of fire... It was about that time [that I decided] I didn't care how crowded it was inside the carrier, I was getting inside! I couldn't see anything anyway, I had spots in front of my eyes.'

Then Roberts 'ran into the first company. The right-hand-side carrier commander, Corporal Gross, said over the radio, "They're the enemy" — because when I first saw them I thought they were D Company, they were moving in such a disciplined formation. And such a lot of them, a hundred-odd blokes.'

Not wanting to shoot at fellow Australians, Roberts had his vehicles hold their fire. Marching along apparently unconcerned, clad in wet green clothes, floppy hats on their heads, carrying their weapons in the rain of the dimming afternoon, the group of men among the trees simply did not look like the attacking VC about whom so much had been heard that day. In addition, Roberts had been given only a general position for D Company: just an area marked on his map. They could have moved.

Then a VC fired, and the spell was broken.

Rod Armstrong told his machinegunner, Leo Kucks, to fire; but Leo replied that they might be Australians. Armstrong turned to the APC commander, who was watching the distant men through his field-glasses: he saw him drop the glasses, grab his .50 and begin firing.

Armstrong swiftly brought up his M16, got a running figure in his sights and fired — forgetting that the line of sight is some 5 centimetres above the barrel. His barrel was not above the gunshield of the .50, and his 5.56mm round drilled a neat hole through it. Later the hole was exhibited as a close call suffered by the APC commander during the battle. Armstrong was able to laugh this off, and disillusion the credulous.

Some of A Company, Dinham's platoon over on the right, started their own little war. Here were some of those elusive VC at last!

Looking down from the APC hatch, Peter Bennett suddenly noticed that there were many people scurrying about just below him, in the mud and trees. Rain-blackened clothes . . . Were they Australians? D Company? Then he saw a man propped against a tree, white bandage on his head — and sandals on his feet. VC! 'I shot him and the contact began.'

Like the others, Peter Dinham did not know of the presence of D445, 'until we were right in amongst them, and these people suddenly stood up, in the thick scrub and rubber immediately in front. We had come out of the rain, surprising them as much as us. There we were on top of them.'

Frank Alcorta was conscious of the 'eerie silence' around them, when 'suddenly the whole undergrowth exploded with enemy soldiers. They were screaming, covered with camouflage, and with the typical pith helmet of the Vietcong. They swarmed all around our flanks, firing indiscriminately.' Adrian Roberts takes up the account:

Then we started to fight. The right-hand infantry got out of the tracks and went forward. I yelled at the infantry commander [Mollison], and we got 'em back in again. We were edging forward, not howling along, and there was a lot of firing and what-have-you. The enemy retreated in good order.

Roberts noted that the enemy had cane-loops tied to their calves, and saw how some would rush to a VC who had been hit, grasp the loops and pull him away, while others provided fire support for them. He was impressed with their battle discipline.

(He later realized that, being a commander, he had no business swinging a machinegun around, shooting people, but should have actually been thinking more of his command responsibilities. He recommended that a unit commander in his position should not be behind a machinegun at all.)

Armstrong fired his magazine and ducked down to reload, while 'Greg Cooper took over, firing out the side of the carrier'.

Peter Dinham's Platoon Sergeant, Frank Alcorta, on top of the APC, was caught by the heavy machinegun fire directed at the vehicle. As Dinham recalls it, Alcorta exclaimed 'Fuck this, I'm getting off!' and rolled back off the rear of the M113. All around him was the startled but reacting enemy, and Alcorta was the only Australian on the ground.

Peter Bennett, too, remembers how Frank Alcorta 'jumped down off the APC and in traditional John Wayne style dispatched quite a number of the enemy'.

Alcorta fired a whole magazine at the nearby VC, who he thought had 'no discipline at all', and he saw several of them fall. Then, the tracer round showing he had only one round left flashed out, hitting a VC in the face, 'and the whole thing disappeared in a mess of blood and flesh'.

Dinham and the others standing in the hatch had ducked out of the VC fire. Dinham now rose and yelled to the vehicle commander to stop and lower the ramp, 'so I could de-bus the platoon, because I couldn't leave my Sergeant out there'.

Alcorta was alone, magazine nearly empty, VC all around him. Then, Dinham recalls, things happened quickly:

I had the platoon out, forming an extended line, and while we were doing it there were dozens of the enemy, some dressed in pith helmets, some in floppy hats, a lot with a form of netting hanging over the back as a type of camouflage — they started standing up in front of us and streaming from left to right (that is, west to east), running back towards their parent formations.

Private Brett, machinegunner, appeared at Alcorta's side firing his M60, and Alcorta believed that 'doubtless he saved my life, because he gave me a chance to bring a fresh magazine from the pouch'. (In February 1967, Frank Alcorta was able partially to repay Brett, piggybacking him away when Brett was badly wounded in the leg by machinegun fire; the leg was later amputated.)

Standing under a rubber-tree, firing his M16, Dinham was

> not appreciating the danger, when all of a sudden I felt something wet splatter on my face, and when I looked up there were a couple of bullet-holes in the rubber-tree immediately above me, so I immediately adopted the prone position!
>
> We literally had a turkey shoot at that time, and later conservatively estimated that we killed at least 40 of them. Subsequently, when we swept through the area about two days later, we picked up only eight bodies.

There was no hand-to-hand fighting, but much close-range shooting as the VC moved across the platoon front. Occasionally one of them 'would turn, go to ground and fire at us, but the general noise that was around drowned their shooting — you couldn't hear it unless you got a couple of close ones'.

Frank Alcorta was surprised to see that the VC 'panicked and broke ranks, fleeing to the east, throwing weapons, equipment, everything'.

> I just couldn't believe my eyes, because they certainly had the numbers. Had they pressed an attack, I don't see how we could have stopped them. We were a depleted infantry company, only our platoon was engaging them, and there were only eleven APCs [in fact, seven]. The enemy certainly had RPGs, which they abandoned, and with which they could have taken the APCs almost at will. There were hundreds, literally hundreds of them around us. Yet they broke and ran.
>
> We were grateful anyway, and exhilarated, as we were out of immediate danger.

Only one man in Dinham's platoon was hurt — a slight graze across the eyebrow — and another had a round strike and pass through his basic pouch. The virtual ineffectiveness of the VC return fire was the result of the surprise and shock inflicted on an unprepared enemy.

Dinham looked up to see the APC commander making hand-signals to him, to the effect that the infantry were to get back on board. They climbed aboard the vehicle and it drove off.

Events had moved so quickly that only the men with Dinham had dismounted, engaged the VC and remounted. Rod Armstrong's vehicle-load remained aboard, firing from the hatch.

Roberts marshalled his force of seven vehicles and moved off again, towards the artillery and fighting, through the trees ahead. Then, at front and to their left, they encountered a second group of about a hundred VC, moving east. Roberts thought that these VC 'had obviously heard us coming — they were withdrawing as we hit them. [They fired at the] carrier just across the road from me ... there was a tremendous explosion and a rubber-tree went down.'

Confident of their ability even in this situation, the picked and trained members of D445 Reconnaissance Platoon prepared to engage the enemy machines. Their 57mm RCL was able to destroy an M113. It took dedicated men to operate an RCL so close to the enemy.

They were attacking Corporal Carter's APC, 39M, fitted out as an ambulance but without the huge Red Cross markings. Roberts, still perched on his plank,

> thought they'd had it. I couldn't get them on the radio, but could see them, just across the road. There was an RCL team with it on their shoulders, and the fellow firing it was down, and the one loading it was kneeling at the back just like in a military textbook. They fired a second round, and it hit the branches of the tree they'd just shot down.

Roberts watched as 'the Corporal, his machinegun jammed, leaped up with his Owen submachinegun, killed the crew and a few people around. He was standing on top of the vehicle, and the driver was throwing up magazines.'

Engraved on Roberts's memory was the picture of Carter leaning forward, braced, firing the Owen, looking just like an illustration in a training manual.

Not knowing how many RCLs were there, but suspecting that they operated in pairs, Roberts drew to a halt, searching for the second anti-tank gun.

> On the other side of the road, the left, O'Reilly's section had been well and truly raked. O'Reilly [in the centre-left APC] had been knocked unconscious by a bullet-graze; I could not get him on the radio. Further out, Corporal Clements [in the far-left APC] had been shot through the stomach. He dropped down inside and a couple of infantry tried to climb over him and get at the gun, to get on with the war.

Clements's driver kept the big machine advancing, driving right over the machinegun that had hit Clements and two others. Roberts continues his account:

The Company Commander inside [Mollison] was urging me to get on, but he was down inside, and here am I sitting up on the board, taking in the whole scene. He wanted me to get someone over to take command of the APC, and tried to shove McCormack, my operator, who didn't have very good eyesight. But I just said 'No', and said to my Troop Sergeant, Lowes, to get out and whip over and take command of Clements's carrier — which he did, and ran across about 200 metres of bullet-swept ground, past three carriers. The fellows on board thought he was an enemy and nearly clobbered him.

He reported Clements very badly wounded, and other casualties; so I said, 'Right, take the carrier back'.

Mollison protested at this removal of a fighting vehicle and its men, and demanded that the order be cancelled. But Roberts thought Mollison had not understood that there were wounded in the APC; and the M113 swung away, rolling back west.

Unbeknown to Roberts, one of Mollison's Platoon HQs was on the APC, and these men were carried away from the action. The decision did nothing for Infantry—Armour relations. Roberts later admitted that the M113 should have remained.

Several people have criticized him for sending back the single APC carrying the wounded Clements together with a Platoon HQ and some men. Yet none of these dismounted to climb aboard another M113: all allowed themselves to be borne away. Also, no one criticized the loss to the APC force of the three vehicles necessary to guard the crossing-place and to bring up Lieutenant-Colonel Townsend. The elements of A Company lost to Captain Mollison by this demand (i.e. the three APCs) far exceeded those represented by the *one* M113 carrying wounded. A Company, seriously depleted, would have been in great difficulty if it had had to dismount and fight its way on foot before Ian Savage arrived.

The .50 on one of the left-hand APCs stopped at one point, because of a bullet jammed in its barrel. All around were VC. The driver and commander somehow decided, in an apparent leap back through the ages of Man to the body language of their forebears, that if they did not look at the VC, the VC would not look at them. Accordingly, the driver stood up in his seat and unscrewed the heavy barrel; a new one was fitted. This done, they looked up at the enemy — who had, amazingly, ignored them — and got on with the action.

The VC had brought the APCs' thrust to a halt; but they did not have the capability, or the commander on the spot, to react at once and hold them there. It was their last chance for any sort of victory on this day.

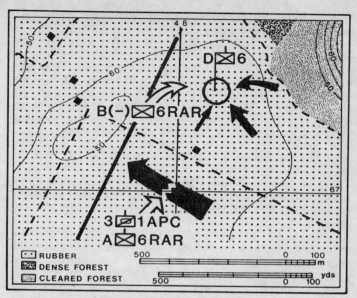

Arrival of the APCs and A/6RAR

Again, the right-hand section, not grasping the full extent of what had happened on the left, had roared on, alone, rolling straight into and through the artillery barrage, through the VC, right up to D Company. Then, realizing that Roberts and the others were still away back behind them, they wheeled east past the cheering infantry and then sped on back through the barrage to Roberts. It can only be imagined what impression of the situation — and of the number of APCs in the action — the VC reports of this foray must have given to their commanders.

Ross Smith, Section Commander, standing next to Bennett in the open APC hatch, saw trees disintegrate in front of the lumbering vehicles, 'the ground being pulled to the sky by some evil force, with no reason, and I realized we were in the midst of the artillery. Everyone got inside, the driver went blind over trees, and outside we could hear the RPGs and small arms firing.' Outside was dark, wet, a mass of multicoloured tracer bullets. To Peter Dinham,

the noise was tremendous: the Task Force guns, enemy mortar fire, constant small-arms fire, and the roar of the tracks. The only way I could communicate with the vehicle commander — we didn't have intercom — was by standing up, putting my mouth to his ear and yelling. You could almost feel the concussion pressing in around you.

Frank Alcorta was struck by the overpowering smell of explosive, which blotted out the normal 'wet' odour of the jungle and rubber plantation. Alcorta began to reload his empty magazines while Corporal Vickers, a Korea veteran, 'fired almost unceasingly from the open hatch' at the huge numbers of enemy among the trees. The noise continued without pause, and normal voice-communication was almost impossible.

D Company was doggedly holding on, aware that the VC were pressing closer, massing out there in the dark. And still the artillery crumped down all about them.

Jack Kirby came around, doling out the meagre ammunition available, and asking Harry Esler, 'You all right, Private Ralph? Doing a good job?' He dropped twelve rounds of ammunition by Esler's side.

In the pressure of the attacks, some soldiers did not have time to do what they had been taught to do in training: remove the empty magazine, put it in a basic pouch, take out another, clip it in... Magazines were dropped into the mud, and left there when the man had to move. And it was Kirby, Peter Ainslie recalls, who would 'miraculously find a magazine from somewhere and load it'.

In D Company HQ, peering through the trees, Harry Smith saw a mass of dark figures forming to one side, and called, 'Righto, Private Esler and you others had better turn around and look behind you'.

'What, sir?' asked Esler.

'Can't you see them?' But Esler could not see what it was that Smith was indicating.

'They're forming up to hit us from behind.'

Then they saw the VC flitting from tree to tree, moving into a patch of thick scrub behind the Australians. The bugles sounded again.

'Christ', said Esler.

Every shot had to count. Esler heard Smith say, into the radio, 'If you don't come for us in half an hour, don't bother to come at all'.

They began to hear a dull roar, 'like a couple of bulldozers'. At first no one knew what it was; 'and then all of a sudden it struck me! It was the nicest sound I'd heard in my life!'

For hours, D Company's attention had been concentrated on their own small world. Now they at last realized that help was on the way. David Sabben heard 'heavy firing behind us,

.50s — we knew they were coming, they had been coming for an hour'.

When the thudding of the machineguns was heard, the cheering started. The Diggers watched the huge M113s jerking and swerving as they rolled through the mass of VC, crushing some beneath them — so that next day, all that could be seen of these men would be feet or an arm poking out of the mud.

A VC stood up to throw a grenade at an APC. The commander tried to get the .50 depressed far enough to hit him, but could not. Esler and Mitchell saw this, aimed, and fired. 'I think I got him first', claimed Esler as the VC was flung backwards and the grenade went off next to him.

Buick and the remnant of 11 Platoon 'jumped up, yelled and waved to identify our position, just like in the movies. I felt like one of those Yankees saved from the Indians.'

The APCs of Roberts's right-hand section which were carrying Dinham and his men had pushed on to D Company, not knowing that the others were temporarily held up. Charging on alone, they had swept up to Smith's position, seen that they had become separated, and roared past the cheering Diggers; but to the dismay of the passengers, they had rolled back into the artillery barrage again.

Dinham watched the rubber-trees disintegrating around him, realized that the shells were airburst, and thought to himself that airburst shells were dangerous. But he was more conscious of the constant pressures of airwaves from the explosions, and regarded the scene with a degree of abstraction.

Roberts had looked around, and seen that the right-hand section of his force had gone 'roaring up, zooming up the road'. They saw D Company, 'did a loop around them, and came whipping back to me. They had to drive through the artillery, pretty horrendous. It was here that Lieutenant-Colonel Townsend, with the other three APCs, came up and asked me to assault eastwards.'

Barrelling along behind the main group of APCs, Ian Savage caught up with Roberts's force at the edge of the artillery zone and drove on into 'the browny-grey bursts, which were not so loud due to the engine noise and earphones'.

The surprised D445 gathered themselves some distance away and new orders were given. The armoured vehicles must be prevented from advancing; they must be stopped. None of the VC units was trained or experienced in close combat against armour on the move. Their preferred method was to set an ambush, on their own ground, to be fought when they had the initiative. But spirit and battle discipline can overcome such disadvantages. Word was passed to the HQ that a force of armour was approaching from the south-west.

The radio chatter among Roberts's crews was heard by Alan Hutchinson and the gathering at D/5RAR, listening to the battle into which they could be flung following A/6. They listened to the APC crews fighting their way through the mass of VC around them:

'Look out, there's someone by the tree there... Wait for the lightning flash... See him?'

'They're pointing something at us... OK, let's go for 'em!'

'Check fire! Check fire!' — this from Roberts, who was very much aware of the power of the big .50 machineguns on his vehicles. The APCs and A Company were pushing through among the artillery explosions, shoving along northwards.

Fighting was still going on around D Company, as VC units that knew nothing of the relief force carried out their orders to attack.

Time and again, amid the water, rain, mud, falling leaves and branches, the soldiers had to react, under fire, to the training they had received in faraway, peaceful Australia: strip their weapons, clean them, reassemble them, and go on firing. One machinegunner, forgetful of where he was, knelt alongside the machinegun, as he had done in less dangerous times, and calmly put it back into working order, oblivious of the bullets flying by.

'Horse' Esler heard one of the nearby Diggers 'yelling and screaming', so he called out to him. 'I think my leg is gone!' came the reply. Esler crawled the 20-odd metres between them. 'Well, why don't you have a bloody look?' he told the Digger. 'It's still there, as far as *I* can see.' Esler examined the wound.

What happened was that a bit of mortar shrapnel had cut through his boot, the ridge around the sole-edge, the laces and the top, and even put a hole in his sock — that's how lucky he was. He must have thought his leg was gone. But I got up him, and said, 'I crawled all the bloody way up here for you, and you didn't even have a look!'

D Company's need to stay close to the ground, combined with the long exposure to the rain, made it awkward to urinate, and some of the men did so without bothering to open their trouser flies — they were so wet and muddy that it made no difference, except (as one of them pointed out) that it was 'warming your legs up'.

Before the fighting, in the heat of the day, 'Pom' Rencher had drunk a lot of water and it now began to make itself felt.

I resisted it as long as I could, but finally had to give in to the pressure. Civilization (or Pavlov) took over, and with large numbers of VC firing even larger numbers of bullets at me, I actually started to stand up and have a private leak behind a tree!

Sanity returned and I eventually added my contribution to the thousands of gallons of rainwater that I was already lying in.

In the midst of the attacks, with no help in sight, one or two of the soldiers began to show signs of strain. Jack Kirby would then place his large hand on the soldier's shoulder, saying, 'Get a grip on yourself, son. You're paid to kill these people, and here's your chance to earn your money. Get over there.'

To many of the Diggers that long afternoon, he personified the traditional image of a Sergeant-Major. One of the men later likened him to the imperturbable British Regimental NCO who told the redcoats to 'do up your buttons, and never mind the spears'.

At Nui Dat, the only information available to the units was coming over the radios. Those who were not in HQs or CPs were informed by word of mouth, which lost nothing in the telling. The non-stop artillery fire accentuated the scraps of battle news being passed around.

Men in combat postings in Vietnam, when coming to the end of their twelve-month tour of duty, tended to grow superstitious, and also to ponder the well-known legendary deaths or mutilations of those who had offended Lady Luck by going on that one last operation. Alan Hutchinson was experiencing the sinking anticipation of being called upon to go with D/5RAR, the nominated reaction company to follow A/6RAR if necessary. 'I'd called Peter Tedder and said, hopefully, "You don't want me to stay with these guys, do you?" But he told me to stay, as I knew them and had operated with them.'

Outside, the rain streamed down, the guns roared relentlessly... To George Bindley, 103 Battery,

the gun position seemed to slip into another dimension like some great engine of the Industrial Revolution, roaring and flaring in great billowing clouds of smoke and steam. The fierce downpour gave an eerie shine to the guns, reflecting the muzzle-flashes against the gathering smog, which cloaked the movement of men toiling with ammunition, their shadows showing only in the glare, while the roar of the guns, with 'fire for effect' in force, created a bedlam. It was our El Alamein, but a little damper.

The APCs under Roberts, aware that their presence was known, were moving more cautiously onward, but still closing the distance between themselves and Harry Smith's position. In the words of Ian Savage:

> We were moving two up at that stage, with Adrian in the centre — that's six vehicles forward. I was behind with two vehicles. It's a scary thing to be second-in-command, as you have plenty of time to think, and you may have to take over at any minute. I'd rather be commanding: you're doing too many things to be worrying.

Deeply conscious that he was shoving forward into the unknown, but that the infantry he had come to save were out there somewhere among the groups of enemy, certainly well within range of the heavy .50 ammunition, Roberts did not want to add to Smith's troubles. 'A big problem I had was that I wasn't sure where D was, so I kept shouting to my people, "Check fire! Check fire!" because I didn't want any overshoots.'

Roberts watched the dark mass of VC that they had passed 'scampering away to the right'. But they were not fleeing, and poured a heavy fire back towards the formation of slab-sided M113s, continuing this as the vehicles rolled on north-eastward.

With his earphones on, and the engine and artillery noise all around, Roberts could not hear the VC firing; but he could see 'the tracer and stuff coming up at you'.

Ian Savage looked out at the mass of enemy firing and moving about, but was unable to pivot his machinegun to shoot at them. 'It was most frustrating seeing these fellows firing at you and trying to dodge the tracer. It seemed to be coming towards us in slow curves, but it was like ducking tennis balls.'

The APCs arrived in the vicinity of the rubber-tappers' hut around which both Sharp and Sabben had manoeuvred, and Roberts changed direction, to north, to go on up to Smith.

Savage maintained his position as 'Adrian swung us around, in the same formation, intending to ride through to D Company, and push the enemy back. We were moving at about walking pace.' All around in the dusk were enemy, and the infantry were leaning over the sides of the hatches blazing away at fleeting targets.

Frank Alcorta saw wounded VC 'who did not have the strength to get out of the way' being run over by the M113. The driver was concentrating on his place in formation and was unable to see the VC under the bushes, close to the big APC. Visibility has always been a problem with armoured vehicles.

Ian Savage was caught up in the spirit of the advance. 'You

see these little buggers running around, and you want to kill them. It was quite an exciting ride in, to the east.'

Savage opened fire with his .50, shooting between Roberts's vehicle and the one next to it, but 'Adrian got pretty dirty towards me, as I was firing pretty close to his vehicle, so I eased off on my firing and concentrated on backing him'.

One RPG exploded near the tracks of Dinham's APC, rocking it and throwing people around, but no damage was done. The hail of fire from their section of APCs and infantry on the right of the Australian force 'routed them, and we later found it was D445'.

Crowded into the APC, Rod Armstrong looked at the two new men who had arrived that afternoon and come out into the battle, and saw that 'they'd gone white — probably wondering what they were doing here, and if this went on every day!' Roberts points out:

> The fire that came back at us as we went in there was absolutely enormous: small-arms and machinegun fire, from the front. I think that we survived because we kept coming on and they were firing high. I put my tin hat on, as an instinctive reaction, going through the artillery.

Savage noticed that whereas he normally sat up, exposed, behind the machinegun, he was now standing on the seat, about half inside the vehicle; though he saw that Roberts, up ahead, was still exposed. He believes that their advantage came from the failing light and the torrential rain — which drowned the sound of the engines, not allowing the VC time to decide on how to use their 57mm RCLs. In these conditions, much of the enemy's fire went high.

Having pushed the VC back, Roberts 'broke off the thing at the Colonel's request and fell back onto D Company'.

Several of the soldiers saw Mollison charging in, pistol in hand, firing away from the top deck of the M113. Maury Stanley, having controlled a great weight of artillery for several hours amid a continuous storm of small-arms fire, looked at Mollison's 9mm pistol and thought it ridiculous by comparison. Only then did he realize that Mollison was part of the relief force.

They stopped, came back to D Company and drove into the HQ, where Dinham saw Maury Stanley 'calmly calling down the fire from a crouched position behind a tree' — and almost at once, after four or five shots, 'all was very quiet'.

Rod Armstrong, in Dinham's platoon, saw Harry Smith 'standing there waving his arms around, giving directions to everybody' in the D Company position. Nearby was Jack Kirby, sitting on an ammunition box. An APC crunched over Russ Perandis's M60; so he picked up an SLR, ready to continue the fight.

Dinham looked around and saw two Australian soldiers carrying back their dead friends, shot in the last flurry of bullets as they stood up to cheer the arriving APCs. He thought it remarkable, and a credit to their training and presence of mind, that they were also carrying the dead men's weapons.

On his own initiative Dinham moved his small force out, into part of D Company's eastern perimeter. The remainder of A Company was still to the west, not yet at the actual position. When they did arrive, Mollison kept calling Dinham on the radio, telling him to come in and secure a part of the perimeter, and Dinham kept replying that he was already there.

For Peter Bennett, the advance on foot over the last stretch of ground to D Company was a matter of holding his fire, so as not to risk shooting any friendly troops up ahead.

About this time the rain slackened at last — but then began to pour down again as heavily as before. Dinham was trying to dig a small shell-scrape in the ground, but the water kept running in and 'eventually it was a matter of pushing the mud aside to make a bit of a hollow you could get into'.

Frank Alcorta waited for the next attack. 'But suddenly, they were gone. Only the moans of the wounded, and the jungle silence, remained.'

At first Roberts formed his APCs into a line facing east, with the A Company soldiers filling the gaps between them and everyone waiting for the VC to surge back; but they did not. Then the APCs formed a hollow square around D Company, and the force waited for the expected next attack, intending to go to Sharp's 11 Platoon. 'There was a lot of sniper firing, but no assault.'

Kev Branch, 10 Platoon, 'passed Doug, my fellow scout and mate, lying there with a hole in his head, and I thought sadly, *Well, well!* and just burst into tears'.

In the darkness and water, the promised help had arrived. But out there still were the determined VC.

The Night

Now entertain conjecture of a time
When creeping murmur and the poring dark
Fills the wide vessel of the universe.

King Henry V (II. vi.)

WHILE THE VC were being distracted and forced back by the charge of the APCs, the under-strength B Company also arrived in the area, after light contact with the enemy to the west of the position, and halted at GR 482673 to cover that direction.

With the VC at least temporarily driven off, and reorganizing, the Australians had won breathing space to do likewise. Lieutenant-Colonel Townsend assumed command of the force, and they prepared for the further attacks expected. It was now night, and the possibility of more reinforcements arriving from 1ATF was very slim.

However, the position was now more strongly held, with a reasonable supply of ammunition brought in by the APCs. Whether the VC would be capable of night attacks was not known, but they had certainly attacked with determination all afternoon.

The artillery continued to fire on probable enemy locations, halting while four air-strikes were placed on the area, 2000 to 3000 metres to the east.

The expenditure of artillery during the afternoon had been high and a resupply was necessary. US Army Aviation Chinook helicopters were made available to lift the heavy cargo in, while 5RAR patrolled the outer reaches of the landing-zone, with HQ Company 1ATF providing the workparty to assist the gunners. All this was to be done in the dark and rain.

A night resupply by the big helicopters was not normal practice, and indicates the severity of the situation.

No one on the Allied side could state confidently that the trucks of 1 Company RAASC would be able safely to make the road journey from Vung Tau to Nui Dat. But 'there was no question' in Operations Officer David Ferguson's mind 'about supplying 1ATF. All [at 1ALSG] were willing, an instant professional reaction.'

Confident of their ability to make the trip but aware of the obvious possibility that the VC were in ambush positions along the road, the RAASC trucks, with ammunition already loaded aboard, drove instead to the airbase, where the cargo was transferred to the Chinooks.

During the height of the storm, lightning had begun to strike in the gun positions, and some of the artillery radio-operators had suffered burns when it struck the aerials. The gun-barrels were so hot that they took on a dull-red glow, and the rain sizzled on them.

At 1ATF HQ, Jackson was faced with the possibility of further attacks on the force at Long Tan, which would require artillery support but for whom he could do little more until daylight, after what the night might bring.

In fact, 1ATF itself could well be the target of attacks by ground forces, and in the darkness and the weather conditions the VC would be able, if they so decided, to close on the defences before being detected. Determined assaults could penetrate the perimeter and inflict severe damage on the Task Force. Some material could be replaced at once from the huge US supply system, but the remainder had to come by ship from Australia.

It seemed obvious that the VC would try to occupy and destroy the gun positions, and then possibly the Engineer units; and after that, while the night lasted, would create havoc in the remainder of the Nui Dat camp. As dawn approached they could disperse in almost any direction, and disappear into the jungles, swamps and mountains close by.

And now, at night, Jackson had only five companies of infantry to protect the base — seven if he used the Support Companies of 5RAR and 6RAR. While individual units in the camp could be expected to defend themselves, he would need infantry on the perimeter to seal off breaches, and for counterattacks.

No one at Nui Dat could state with any probability of being correct what the VC intentions now were.

They had appeared undetected only 5000 metres from 1ATF's base; at least one battalion, and probably more, had doggedly hung on around D/6RAR from mid-afternoon until night, despite heavy artillery fire. No enemy identification had been received at 1ATF, but they were definitely Main Force and clearly looking for a fight: 1ATF was the most obvious target.

If they did attack 1ATF, and lost many men, they would still achieve a propaganda victory by the very daring of the assault. It would take the Australians, with their limited resources, some time to recover, and the VC would make the most of the time gained.

And there was still another regiment out there somewhere. In the past weeks, no source of intelligence had been able accurately and repeatedly to locate the enemy for Jackson; nor had any of his sources been able to confirm information provided by any other. The Task Force was still new in the area. On the night of 18—19 August the VC had the initiative in Phuoc Tuy Province.

They knew where the Australians were and, roughly, their numbers; they could assume correctly that 1ATF would be on the defensive. But 1ATF knew only that heavy fighting had taken place close to their eastern perimeter, and that two regiments were nearby.

Crouching around the dim light in the CP, the VC commanders finalized plans for their withdrawal. The attack was no longer possible, and priority had to be given to evacuation of the hundreds of casualties. Many would require at least two people to carry them, and apart from a few small groups for protection the entire force would have to be used for this. All the wounded who had been brought back before dark were already on the way east, and the fourth of the battalions, which had not been used in the battle, would move from the eastern slopes of Nui Dat East to scour the battlefield for as many other wounded as possible.

The heavy rain had at least kept the fighter-bombers away, but there was no way of knowing what the weather tomorrow would be. If they were found in fine weather, a storm of high-explosive and napalm would envelop them.

The heavy casualties were regrettable but the foreigners must have been badly damaged as well. The duration and intensity of the fighting must have annihilated part of their force. Also unfortunate was the complete lack of enemy prisoners.

But now, in the darkness, the battlefield must be searched for wounded comrades, and all those remaining on the scene must be on their way east well before dawn.

In Brisbane it was also night, and in the homes of the 6RAR soldiers no one knew of the intense fighting of the afternoon, or what the absent sons and husbands had been enduring. Television programme guides werc being consulted: What next: *Gunsmoke*, *The Roaring 20's*, *I Spy* or *Peyton Place*?

At Nui Dat, the RAAF helicopters were assembled. Wing Commander Ray Scott now had seven helicopters at Kangaroo Pad, waiting for what was to happen.

> We sat at the base and were not about to leave our aeroplanes, because I'd been told that we had a very critical situation on our hands. We were standing by our aeroplanes, and it was quite some time before we had anyone come down from the Army Ops Room to tell us what it was all about.

The guns were firing steadily, and almost beneath the muzzles, in the dark, were the helicopter crews. 'All we knew was that there was a bit of a battle going on and things weren't too good.'

With the others, Bob Grandin 'sat around the aeroplanes. They were all cocked, ready to go, in case anybody did attack us. We were asked to sit there, which we did, hour after hour.

'I remember being nervous all the time, the sort of nervous energy that keeps you on edge ... but we remained ready to do whatever we had to do.'

In the pitchblack night and rain amid the Long Tan rubber, Lieutenant-Colonel Townsend conferred with the Company Commanders. They agreed that heavy casualties had been inflicted on the VC. Townsend decided that it was not possible to secure the battleground, or to locate the sixteen missing soldiers, in the present conditions; and that the force should move back to a cleared area where helicopters could evacuate the wounded and dead. Some of the Diggers had been hit hours before and needed medical attention.

Jackson and Townsend spoke on the radio, and Jackson agreed to Townsend's proposals. Preparations for the move back began in the rubber plantation.

During the night, Smith refused an order to go back to Nui Dat and then on to Vung Tau, insisting that D Company be used to go in to get the bodies of its dead, find the missing, and assert a psychological dominance over the area — along the lines of climbing back onto a horse immediately after a fall.

At 21.00, 1ATF was informed that 18 men would be the total load for the helicopters: four dead, six walking wounded and eight stretcher cases.

Overhead the artillery still roared, breaking now and again for air-strikes to go in. Probable VC withdrawal routes were bombed and shelled throughout the hours of darkness.

Lying there in the dark and the mud, after the excitement of the ride in and the fighting on the way to D Company, some of the A Company soldiers were deeply concerned about the missing Diggers. Apart from being friends they were fellow Australians, and everyone had heard stories of the way the VC treated their prisoners. (Of course, the VC had heard similar tales about the foreigners.)

It was very hard to remain inactive when some of the moans and movements out there could be coming from wounded and lost members of 11 Platoon.

The CSM of A Company, Jack Roughley, had fought in Korea, and had already served in Vietnam with AATTV. He crawled forward, alone, out into the night, and searched the area to the north of the position. Moans had been heard, and it was possible that they were from an Australian. While Roughley was out there the noise stopped, and he was unable to locate any Australians. He returned to the Australian perimeter.

Further around the position, Ross Smith decided that he could not leave his fellow Aussies out there: he too left the position, searching for missing men of D Company. He went to the south-east through Peter Dinham's 2 Platoon, first arranging with him for 2 Platoon to be informed of his expedition.

Peter Bennett accompanied Ross Smith on the crawling penetration of the unknown, as 'one of my very good friends was still lying out there. I wasn't sure whether he was dead or wounded. I wanted to locate him or any other Australian before the Vietcong did so.' Ross Smith remembers:

When the lightning flashed in the distance, we saw these people, the enemy, in front of us. Peter Bennett grabbed my leg — my leg was shaking enough to fall off, and his hand was shaking — and said, 'Did you see that?' and I said, 'Shit, I saw that too. They're in front of us.'
'They're coming in from both sides, too.'

Smith checked the compass and held out his arm: 'Follow that direction. When I start shooting, keep going, don't stop.' They crouched, ready to fire, but did not have to. They got away unharmed.

When Peter Bennett 'got out there, and realized we were in no-man's-land, I started to shake'.

It was unbelievable. It was dark, there were people groaning and moaning everywhere... I didn't really know who we were trying to make contact with. We just continued to crawl along the ground to that noise, to that groan ... obviously hoping that we'd locate one of our own. The thing that I noticed was that as we got closer, the groans would move away ... we seemed to be losing whatever contact we made. It was very dark — you couldn't see a few feet in front of you — and raining.

Peter Dinham sat next to his own radio-operator, listening to Smith's whispered reports.

They returned to A Company, in the dark, 'introduced ourselves', and went back to the 3 Platoon area. Later, they decided to go out again, and took the radio-operator, Ernie Dare, ignoring the orders of their Lieutenant to remain.

Again, every time they crawled towards a sound of groaning, it would move away. The three edged across the dark battlefield, calling Australianisms; but they found none of their own people.

Smith could not remain quietly in the position, as 'we knew they were missing, and we had to do something for them. If they were dead, injured or otherwise, we still had to go out and find 'em. We kept going and going, but didn't see anybody. We returned, crawling, to the A Company location, and told them we couldn't find anyone.'

In 9 Squadron's Operations Room at Vung Tau, Phil Cooke's earlier feeling of depression had gradually lightened as word filtered back that the soldiers had put up a good fight — the gloom being swept away by a message from Nui Dat to the effect that enemy casualties were not known, but were estimated to be equal to 'Don Bradman's highest score'.

At Vung Tau, 1 Company RAASC also felt deeply for the position of the infantry, away up in the darkness and rain, when the sobering news of the casualties came through, and in particular the number of missing.

At midnight, 1st Field Regiment notified 1ATF of the ammunition expenditure for the day: 2639 rounds of 105mm, and 155 rounds of 155mm.

It is believed by some who were at the gun positions that this figure is on the conservative side. Australia and New Zealand were the only two Allied nations that paid their way for US materials used. Because, each month, a certain amount of food, fuel, ammunition and equipment was paid for, whether used or not, commodities such as ammunition tended to accumulate unofficially. The common-sense view was that since it was being paid for, why not take it! It 'could always come in handy some day'.

Also at midnight, Brigadier Jackson issued orders to the effect that the remainder of 6RAR would move to the battlefield in APCs as soon as possible after first light, and that D/5RAR was to join them by helicopter. Lieutenant-Colonel Townsend would command the force on the spot and nominate the arrival-points for the incoming companies.

Quietly creeping across the muddy wasteground, softly calling in Vietnamese, small teams of VC searched for their wounded. As these were found, they were carried back to the dimly lit assembly areas, and guided off on the evacuation route. All around in the wet blackness were the soft squelchings of the carriers, the stifled moans of the wounded, quiet orders and conversations. No one shouted or called out.

Tran van Tranh, C2/D445, tirelessly covered the area, sending back injured comrades. He did his best to ensure that no living were left behind.

Gradually, carefully, the plantation was cleared, and all the living seeped to the eastern side of the Long Tan rubber.

In the centre, equally carefully, the Australians prepared for their move west. B Company was to lead, followed by A; D and the casualties were to ride out on the APCs. In the pitchblack darkness, trust and discipline would be needed if order was to be maintained and the move was not to collapse into a herd-like scramble. The APCs jockeyed into position, one behind the other, the dead and wounded were put inside, and the survivors of D Company boarded. No one knew if they would have to fight their way out, but the VC had not made any offensive moves for some hours.

Ross Smith and his section 'formed a sort of daisy-chain, led by B Company, moving to the rear, visibility zilch. If somebody stumbled, or lost contact, you would have been wandering around. Rain was still falling.'

Adrian Roberts 'put Ian Savage in front, with the dead, and we drove out, with headlights on, straight out there'. Savage was a little surprised to find that, in the dark, with the unlighted vehicles juggling into their order of march, his had become the leader for the drive out — as second-in-command, he would normally be at the rear. But there was no way to alter the arrangement. Before they started, Savage had said to his driver: 'Boy, this is the drive of your life.'

They would have no way of knowing where the enemy was.

Ian Savage and the others waited for 'the word "Go", we all turned on our engines, and on the word "Go" again we all turned on our headlights and went flat strap'.

The sudden roar of engines briefly froze the nearby VC, who relaxed again when they saw the lights rolling off to the west. Moving as quickly as possible through the plantation, a runner took the news to

HQ: the foreigners were retreating in the direction of their base. Work went on faster, with less attention to noise and lights. Still the artillery slammed down on the routes east.

The gap between the trees in the rubber plantation was just larger than the width of an APC, and for Savage it was a frightening drive, in the rain and the dark, with the trees rushing back through the headlights, and the driver doing as he thought best, without direction from the vehicle commander. When they reached the edge of the plantation, Savage's driver forgot the irrigation ditch, and the APC went down on one side.

Savage called on the intercom: 'For Christ's sake, mate, get us out of this one, don't bog now!' With a brilliant piece of driving, Muir got them out of trouble.

When they had withdrawn from the D Company position, Peter Dinham's 2 Platoon had been the last out, with his small HQ preceding the last section. Travelling with him in the darkness was Lieutenant-Colonel Townsend's Battalion HQ party. In one of the vagaries of radio communication, Townsend lost contact with Mollison's HQ; and Dinham's platoon radio passed messages from the Battalion Commander to the Company Commander.

Arriving at the cleared area agreed on for the night position and helicopter evacuation, the APCs moved to the edges. Behind them, B and A Companies slogged along in the dark and wet.

Adrian Roberts positioned the M113s so that they 'formed a big square, and I had this idea of leaving the lights on inside the carriers, so that from the air you'd see the squares of light making a big rectangle, and I'd stand out in the middle, with a couple of torches, guiding the helicopters in'.

Back towards the battlefield, A and B Companies were walking, like a long centipede, through the blackness. Peter Dinham's 2 Platoon was last, and the rearmost man was Trevor Atkinson, hanging onto Rod Armstrong's webbing straps. Atkinson would often release his grip and walk along on his own, until Armstrong would say 'Where *are* you?' and Atkinson would catch up again.

As an extra aid, those with compasses opened them and held them up in such a way that the luminous faces were visible to those following.

Around the silent APCs in the dark — around the landing-zone — the soldiers watched the helicopters arrive. Brian Halls thought the American medical evacuation helicopter, the Dust-off, 'very professional and fast', whereas the Australian helicopters 'came, circled round, no lights, and seemed to be a long time before landing'.

122

Indeed, 9 Squadron did take longer than the US Dust-off. When they were told to follow the lone American machine in, and Scott asked if lights could be used, they were informed that because the enemy situation was unknown, and landing-lights would flood the entire area, no illumination was to be used.

Our guys had to go in with no landing-lamps whatsoever, and try to get their depth-perception, their position, and so forth, from the lights of an APC. And that's extremely difficult. You could get virtually no depth-perception whatever. I went in first — to be quite frank, went the last hundred feet with great trepidation. I didn't know what was on the ground, and it's extremely difficult at that speed.

So we were very slow because somebody gave us bad advice. There would have been little chance of the enemy doing anything.

Geoff Banfield was flying as co-pilot to Wing Commander Scott, and knew some of the men of D Company from training activities in Australia as well as from various meetings in Vietnam. Thankful that the foul weather had cleared, he looked down at the landing area, big enough for only one helicopter at a time.

It was an eerie feeling as we approached slowly to land, with the stench of cordite strong even with the rotors beating the air. We were in constant communication with the ground on FM radio. I felt rather vulnerable sitting in this slowly descending machine, my armoured seat and a flak jacket my only protection. All aircraft got in and out safely with their loads of wounded Diggers.

For Cliff Dohle,

this part of the mission was certainly the most difficult action I can remember during my Vietnam tour. We assembled over the Dust-off area at 4000 feet [1200 m], all milling about in the same piece of airspace, not being able to see each other, waiting for a radio call directing us one by one to make our approach to the helipad.

As each unlighted helicopter approached the dim glow of Roberts's APCs, and of his torch, the pilot in command had to make the gradual descent into the unknown blackness below. Bill Shepherd later joked that as he was descending, his mind kept telling his left hand to go down (on the cyclic control, to lower the machine) but the hand kept coming up all the time.

As soon as a helicopter rose from the darkness with its load of casualties, the next was called in.

Ian Savage watched the helicopters, admiring the flying of the US pilot.

Marvellous: came in without light so they would not pinpoint our position, flew in very low at tree-level, and at the last minute switched on the searchlight, straight into the ground, loaded on the wounded, and straight off again. The Australians were a little more hesitant, they were not used to this sort of thing.

I had a problem, as nobody would take the dead out of my vehicle [the living had priority] but we finally got them out and loaded onto a helicopter.

The Riley and Dohle crews had been at Nui Dat the longest, so they were allocated the last places in the queue, to go in only if needed. Cliff Dohle was called down:

Far below there was one small dull light which marked the touchdown point in the middle of the battle. Reference to the single light did not provide any depth-perception, and the height of the ground was unknown. I set up a fairly gentle descent rate and just flew down into the blackness until the skids touched the ground.

A soldier immediately appeared at my window, advising that our cargo would be three wounded and two KIA. We lifted off as soon as possible and flew on instruments back to Vung Tau. I assumed the battle had gone against our troops, and it was not until next day that we learnt the real results.

It was now early a.m. and after being on duty for more than 18 hours I had a strong feeling of relief to be back.

Frank Riley and Bob Grandin decided to work together, Riley flying on instruments and Grandin keeping a lookout and giving instructions, as if for a ground-controlled approach. They knew that aircraft before them had experienced trouble in trying to land, some having to make two or three approaches.

Arriving on the ground near Roberts's torch — the last aircraft to do so — they were told that there were no more wounded, and were about to be sent away. But they asked if there was not anything else to be taken, so the bodies were brought across from Ian Savage's APC, and stacked in the back, wrapped in their ponchos.

Riley began the ascent, up out of the plantation, with Bob Grandin as lookout:

and we just got to the top of the trees, when the whole hill in front of us erupted with a huge red fireball. This turned out to be bombs from an aircraft which had been given Nui Dat [East] as a secondary target...

It was less than a kilometre in front of us. I thought it was the artillery opened up again and I called, 'Stop the artillery, we're still there'. Wing Commander Scott was just getting back from dropping the first load of injured in at Vung Tau, and he called out to us if we were all right, thinking we had crashed, and we notified him we were OK, headed back to Nui Dat and Vung Tau. Then they started up the artillery again.

It was ten minutes to one on the morning of 19 August before the helicopter flights were completed. The guns had ceased firing while the choppers were going to and fro, but, as Ray Scott maintains, if the RAAF had been able to use their lamps they would have 'been in there and out again at three-minute intervals. It's one of those things ... we were given wrong advice and the evacuation took a hell of a long time.'

Riley and Grandin flew to the Australian Hospital at Vung Tau, unloaded the bodies, then flew back to the pad and drove back to the villa, where, recalls Grandin,

we were pleased to see that the cooks had stayed up and cooked for us, had a beer and steak all waiting for us, to end up a very nerve-racking day: one in which there was lots to talk about, lots of experiences — and one in which the magnitude of the affair never really came out till later on, though I think we appreciated that things were very, very tense, and that the situation for those on the ground had become critical.

For 9 Squadron, this mission represented perhaps the final break with the peacetime flying regulations. Individually capable, and for the most part willing to take risks if the situation required it, they had come in through the deadly darkness to pick up fellow Australians. A feeling of respect was beginning to emerge among the Army ranks.

The men of 9 Squadron were feeling quite pleased with themselves. Without a great deal of night-flying experience, they had answered the call, successfully lifted out all the casualties, and learnt that they could cope with a demanding operational contingency. A barrier had been crossed, and a new sense of competence and participation was being felt.

Back in the Long Tan area, by 00.50 the evacuation missions were completed. The last helicopter had departed without incident and some of the wet, tired men could try to sleep before seeing what the coming day, 19 August, would bring.

Savage was left with a vehicle sloshing with rainwater, and with blood and other fluids that had drained from the bodies. He spent an uncomfortable night.

D Company tried to organize itself in the dark. A rollcall was held, but many names went unanswered. The platoon officers and NCOs tried to establish who was present, who was missing, and who was known to have been killed or wounded; but it was difficult.

Feelings among the men of D varied. Some were still alert with the exhilaration of battle, others were in a state of depression; some felt a deep sadness at the thought of lost friends, and others were just plain happy to have got out alive.

Bob Buick 'was still numb, on a high, but not tired. There was too much to do, and I was still thinking about the guys in the battle area. How many were still alive?'

Kev Branch was 'remorseful, shaken up, wet as a shag, and couldn't relax. Maybe I caught twenty minutes' or an hour's sleep, then it was daylight . . .'

'Yank' Akell does not remember much of the night. 'My mind was blown at what had happened . . . in too short a time to be able to think straight. It wasn't till days later that we knew what had happened. I appreciated a hot cup of coffee and a cigarette, followed by a cold can of meat and a packet of dog-biscuits.'

Perandis had no gear. 'Someone gave me a raincoat to sleep in, and in the morning I found I'd been sleeping in a thorn patch and didn't know. I was numb. Next day I was thankful we were so well trained.'

Halls was sitting in an APC near the helipad, 'pretty numb by that time, probably going into a bit of delayed shock . . . Buggered. Drained, but not ready for sleep. I *think* the Battalion Commander came around.'

And out there in the rain, mud and coal-black darkness were two wounded Australians, J.P. Richmond and Barry Meller. Around them the VC swarmed, collecting the wounded and the weapons, and then the dead.

At one point during the long night, Barry Meller looked up and saw standing over him, silhouetted against the sky, a VC with a grenade. Alone, still waiting for friends, Meller had run out of good humour. He shouted 'Fuck off!' — and the VC did just that. Meller crawled away, found a dead Vietcong and took his poncho. He wrapped himself in it and tried to get some sleep, but to no avail.

Slowly the plantation quietened, though to the east the ground still shook as air-strikes hit suspected locations and the tireless artillery went on and on. The stealthy movements, the soft calls, the moans, the slitherings in the mud — all grew fainter and less frequent.

Isolated in the darkness, Barry Meller decided *to hell with the VC* and tried to light a cigarette. His annoyance increased when he found his lighter saturated and unworkable. Furious, he waited out the endless hours.

Ross Smith did not know what time it was 'when we threw ourselves on the ground, in raincoats, hutchies, or whatever'.

'Pom' Rencher has no memories of the night, after the arrival of the relief force — apart from loading the wounded into the helicopters. He believes that this was part of 'the brain's own defences closing it down for protection'.

The gun positions at Nui Dat continued to be a centre of activity, for the ammunition had to be stored and prepared as long as fire missions were still being called. The Chinooks swooped in, rear ramps lowered, into an X-shaped area lit by Landrover headlights. Without stopping, the helicopters rolled across the ground, unloading the heavy ammunition as they went, then rose up into the night sky again. No one wanted to present a stationary target to any VC that might be about.

As it became clear that the crisis was past, tea and coffee were delivered and the helpers walked off, back to their units. Many of those who helped man the guns during the battle relate their entire experience in Vietnam to that night of 18–19 August. No rewards were given to these men.

Like a great wounded dragon, the bleeding VC regiment coiled upon itself and stretched out to the east. Moving as rapidly as possible, jogging down the wider trails, every man knew the supreme importance of getting well clear of the area before the sun rose.

The surviving commanders and political officers began to analyse their lack of success. The proud and confident battalions had been shredded in the storm, yet they had gone into the attacks time and again, seeking the enemy. There was fighting spirit, and that spirit could be allied to the thought of the martyrdom of those who had made the ultimate, heroic sacrifice — of dying for unification and independence — to produce a thirst for revenge.

Semi-conscious from multiple shrapnel wounds, Chau, leader of D445's Reconnaissance Platoon, was carried east in the long columns of agony and defeat. Vaguely, he wondered how his battalion had fared. They had never seen a battle such as this.

Behind was the noise of helicopters and artillery, ahead lay some sort of safety. Raindrops still pattered from the leaves, brushed or shaken by the men passing. The deep, velvety, tropical darkness pressed all around; overhead, a few stars peeped through the clouds. The morning would be fine.

Aftermath

A many of our bodies shall no doubt
Find native graves; upon the which, I trust,
Shall witness live in brass of this day's work...

King Henry V (IV. iii.)

EARLY IN THE MORNING of 19 August, the remainder of 6RAR, D/5RAR and the APCs prepared to move from Nui Dat to the final night position of A, B and D Companies. At 06.55, 2 Troop of 1 APC Squadron, with the 6RAR elements aboard, left Nui Dat and rolled east. At the same time, D/5RAR was lifted by US Army helicopters to a landing-zone at GR 462675, and came under command of 6RAR. Alan Hutchinson and Brian Wickens accompanied them.

Ross Smith, in A Company, was woken by the sound of the helicopters, and watched their arrival. 'A friend from D Company 5RAR, Bob Simpski, came up to me, and said, "God, mate, you look as if you've been through bloody hell. How are you?"'

Rod Armstrong, 2 Platoon, A Company, looked around at the harbour position in the morning sun. 'It was nothing like a textbook, blokes were just where they'd dropped. I saw Bob Buick standing on a carrier — they must have slept around them or in them.'

At 07.30, Lieutenant-Colonel Townsend gathered the officers and gave his orders for the assault back into the battle area. Fifteen Australians were still missing, and it was not known what the VC would do, or were intending to do.

Shortly afterwards, Brigadier Jackson flew into the position and spoke to Townsend and others, gaining information and an impression of the events.

When they were told that D and C Companies would lead the assault back into the rubber plantation, there was surprise and disbelief among some of Smith's men. Geoff Kendall thought, *'Bloody hell! They could have used A or one of the fresh companies.'* Now, older, he agrees that the decision was a wise one, and hopes that it was deliberate — which it was.

Brian Reilly, like many of the others, also found it hard to accept the assault role for D; but he too later realized that it had been needed 'to finish the job'.

Overlaying the men's apprehension of a second day of fighting was the worry that the missing members of D Company would not be found, or that they would be found mutilated.

The order came to remove camouflage twigs completely so as to avoid being mistaken for the enemy, who used them a lot. There were still people missing, and it was thought undesirable to risk confusing them by appearing among the trees with camouflage twigs on, like the VC.

Air-strikes were put onto the area into which the assault would advance, including the abandoned village of Long Tan itself and positions to the east. Something exploded at Long Tan, giving off intense black smoke: possibly oil or petrol in a cache.

At 08.45, the assault began. D/6RAR and D/5RAR led, in the APCs, followed by the other companies on foot. As the troops swept through the battle area, most of them saw sights they had never considered possible.

Adrian Roberts: 'When we came back, the first lot of dead were in greens, and it had rained; they were all face-down, as if they were asleep. It was a 60mm mortar crew, killed by artillery.'

Harry Esler and other D Company men were riding in the APCs. 'As soon as they let that back door down we bolted out. We looked around and didn't know what to expect. As I got down I accidentally stood on a bit of an arm — half an arm of a VC. I picked it up and said, "How would this go hanging up in the canteen?" And whoever it was nearby said, "Put that bloody thing down!"'

Brian Wickens had also begun walking through the rubber-trees.

It was pretty eerie going back onto the battlefield, with bodies everywhere. There were an awful lot. It wasn't raining. I was up close — in fact, right up front. You'd see a rifle, a man in a black uniform behind a tree, pointing at you ... you'd fire. It's the natural thing. I didn't fire a shot at anyone. The riflemen alongside me would give a burst. The VC were dead already, but propped against a tree they looked alive.

'Pom' Rencher, carrying Harry Smith's radio, was 'very surprised at the number of bodies and amazed at the devastation. The first body I saw was a VC whose clothes had been stripped away by blast and whose skull was half missing, and with an arm blown off. It was the first badly mutilated body I had ever seen, but it didn't touch me. I felt nothing for it.'

For Peter Dinham and his soldiers, the scene represented 'the biggest surprise of our life. The figure of enemy dead kept mounting and mounting. The previous night, we only knew we had 15 or 17 Australians missing in action.'

'Some very large Orientals' drew the attention of Rod Armstrong, 'two of them very large, five-ten or six foot, well fed, possibly Chinese advisers'.

The battle area reminded Peter Short, A Company's medic, of 'a rubbish tip'.

Ross Smith was absorbing a different sight. 'Where the tracks had moved through, their marks were everywhere. Bodies were everywhere. They'd started to blow up, flies were thick . . . bits and pieces of bodies.'

The number of enemy dead and the quantities of abandoned weapons 'amazed' Sergeant Frank Alcorta. And in Geoff Kendall's words:

> There was no firing and we met no opposition. Just walking through on this bright crystal morning, and seeing the absolute *carnage* that we'd caused the day before — it was a sight you couldn't imagine. An area as big as two or three football fields and several hundred bodies spread all over the place. Also, as we topped the first rise, we saw old 'Custard' Meller leaning against a rubber-tree, weakly waving his hand. That was pretty marvellous.

Meller, still angry at being left alone for so long, had finally decided to walk back, across the battlefield. Leaning against the trunk of a rubber-tree, he waited for them to come closer. There were yells and calls of greeting from the Australians, but Meller's reply was distilled from more than twelve hours alone out there: words to the effect of, 'You took your fuckin' time, didn't you!'

Adrian Roberts also saw 'this soldier, one of ours, standing up. He was wounded, in a state of shock, had somehow contrived to walk himself to the spot.'

As Meller was having his wounds attended to, and began to relax a little, 'Pom' Rencher walked past and said, 'G'day, Custard'.

Meller replied, 'G'day, you Pommy bastard'.

Rencher walked on, with lightened spirits. He had been in Australia for only 15 months, and in 6RAR for five, and regarded Meller's reply as 'the finest acceptance speech I had ever heard'.

Brian Wickens could not recall ever having seen so many bodies.

It took three days to bury them, with the constant hum of flies around. Burial was for humane reasons, and for hygiene. Captured VC documents later showed respect for the Australians because they buried the dead at Long Tan. The document said, 'They buried our dead, they are a true enemy'. That is, we didn't abuse them. Some Americans cut off hands or ears, or buried them with an ace of spades sticking up, that sort of stuff.

Wickens walked on ahead, alone, passing the lines of Diggers making their way more slowly across the scene. He was looking around, and noticed a group of soldiers in prone positions, ready to fire. He called, 'Soldier, any sign of movement on the left flank?'

No answer. He called again, louder. No answer. Thinking *What the hell. . .?* he walked over to them, and found that 'the platoon I thought were protecting me were all dead. I thought, *Crikey, where am I?* and looked around. Everybody else was way back!'

The thing that struck Wickens, not a stranger to combat, about the 11 Platoon site was that he had never seen a battle-field where 'every soldier was still in a firing position. They'd stuck to their guns, they really had. It was the bravest thing I'd ever seen, and I've been in seven theatres of war.'

As A Company came to the position where D Company had fought, Rod Armstrong thought it was 'virtually a nightmare. The bodies were torn to pieces from the artillery. They seemed to vary, from long hair down to their shoulders to very neat haircuts — perhaps Regulars were mixed in with them. You could see the difference.'

Also noticed among the dead were big men, with a different type of webbing and the older 'Chinese-type burp-gun'. They had stainless-steel tooth fillings, and for a time it was wondered who they were: North Vietnamese? Chinese advisers? They were eventually said to be North Vietnamese.

At one point, Peter Bennett saw three bodies:

I thought they were Vietcong, but looking again I saw a wristwatch. It had a cover on it, and I realized it was one of ours. I looked at Australians lying on their stomachs, with

131

their weapons at the ready, their heads lying along the rifles. I remember someone removing a weapon, but the man's finger was on the trigger and it went off.

Like the others, Bob Buick marvelled at the 'rubber-trees blown apart and lying in all directions [as if] a giant hand or foot had flattened an area for a couple of hundred metres square. How the hell did we get out? I still don't know — 5 per cent luck again?' Buick was

OK until I returned to where 11 Platoon fought for its life for about three and a half hours. There were my Diggers lying dead, still holding their loaded rifles. Grice, my radio-operator, shot dead when he stood up to withdraw. Sharp shot through the neck because he would not keep his head down. What a bloody mess.

Ian Savage 'came across a fellow who'd been wounded, and there all night; we came across mortar crews; but the most memorable was when we came to Gordon Sharp's platoon area':

We switched off the engines and it was an eerie situation, because all the dead were lying there in firing positions, and they looked as if they were alive except for the pools of blood underneath them. I remember Gordon Sharp, shot running from cover to cover. His radio-operator had been shot in the chest, was sitting upright, and the squelch sound was still coming through his handpiece. This upset everybody.

'Pom' Rencher had passed many VC and been left unmoved; but then,

I came to the 11 Platoon position. My mates lying in an arc, facing outwards, with rifles still in the shoulder as if they were frozen in a drill and it only needed a touch to bring them back to life again. They hadn't been touched by arty, thank goodness, and the rain had washed off any blood.

They looked very peaceful and dignified, dying in place, doing their duty. And that's when the tears started. I don't suppose anyone was dry-eyed. I know I wasn't.

Rencher saw the body of Gordon Sharp, 'the young, fun-loving National Service commander, not the most brilliant soldier in the world, but one of the nicest and most well-liked people in the company'.

Ross Smith remembers: 'Trees were cut off, lying all over the place. We came across some of our own blokes, that was the worst part of it.' And like many of the others, Kev Branch thought, *'This is the part I don't know if I can handle, but if I had been wounded they'd do the same for me.'*

Brian Reilly was one of the group who tried to remove the M16 from Sharp's hand, accidentally firing the rounds in the breech and magazine. The short burst was heard all around the area, taut nerves reacted, and soldiers prepared for a recurrence of the intense combat of the day before. *Christ, here we go again!* is what flickered through many minds.

Contrary to fears, the dead had not been interfered with by the VC, and were in fact just as they had been when left by the survivors the previous day. Only two weapons were missing, and one of these was found near the final D Company position. One M16 was not recovered. Because, during the latter stages of the fighting, it had not been known whether any of the missing were still alive in the 11 Platoon position, this had been avoided by the artillery and not fired on during the night. Washed by the rain, the men were untouched.

Captain Mike Wells, from the Province HQ, had been contacted by 1ATF and invited by Brigadier Jackson to bring Colonel Dat, the Province Chief, to discuss what had occurred. They drove to Nui Dat, and were briefed by Jackson and some of the staff. From there they flew by helicopter to the battlefield. Other visitors were also arriving, including General William Westmoreland.

Wells was stunned by the 'unbelievable devastation' and found it 'quite incredible what the artillery had done'. He thought that most of D Company seemed to be in shock, but understood why as he saw more of the battlefield. Other staff officers, from all arms, were brought in to see what had happened, and Wells noticed that some of them were 'upset' by the slaughter and the devastation.

Wells himself had been in-country for some six months and seen the ARVN suffer heavy casualties because of their poor methods; so he was inured to such scenes. He 'swallowed twice' and got on with his inspection. It appeared to him that most of the VC casualties had been caused by shells bursting in the trees, and by the flail of shrapnel from these. He had not seen 'what artillery could do, and it remained a horrific sight'.

Later, Wells was to receive information, from GVN sources, to the effect that the VC appreciated the burial of their dead by the Australians.

Peter Bennett saw 'numerous tracks, made when taking most of their dead, but there were quite a number of graves found'.

'Pom' Rencher had a 'heart-stopping moment when I went back to the rubber-tree I'd called home for a few hours, to find, not far away, a tripod-mounted 57mm RCL, loaded and cocked, pointed right at the CHQ position, the VC dead all around it'.

During the search of the D Company battlefield, Ian Savage took two other APCs and went back to the area where they had fought on the way in on the previous afternoon. They found the dead Vietnamese from that combat, as well as weapons, and the scene of Carter's exploit against the RCL crew. One prisoner, wounded in the leg, was taken. He waited in the long grass until it was obvious that he would be run over by the APC if he did not stand and surrender.

Frank Alcorta took another prisoner, 'a lone North Vietnamese Army soldier, a terrified young fellow of about 17, who had the fight knocked out of him altogether. In fact, about the only thing he wanted to do was to crouch and kiss my feet.'

Raised in an organized society that permitted no room for individual opinion or dissent; taken from his family and his home village; put into the Army, marched for months along the jungle trails, sent into the attack and deluged with high-explosive that obliterated his unit; probably alone all night among the rending salvoes; then, in the eerie quiet of the new sunlit morning, finding himself surrounded by the silent dead, the mutilated bodies and the parts of bodies; and finally seeing the foreigners appear, the ones who had caused it all: unsmiling, unfriendly... It is hard not to feel sympathy for a lone 17-year-old in the shattered Long Tan rubber plantation on that August morning.

Esler, walking through the scene, saw bodies everywhere: 'Bits of bodies, full bodies. I came across this little dugout, and there's this fellow lying in there, a VC with not a mark on him. He was dead all right, but unmarked. Maybe the concussion got him.'

'Wild Bill' Doolan created newspaper headlines when he addressed General Westmoreland in classic Digger's language. The General walked up to a group of Australians digging the graves, and said, 'You've done a good job, fellows, but this is the dirty part'.

Doolan replied, 'She'll be right, mate. We can handle it.'

Doyle, Deller and Esler at one point came across a small group of bodies, 'big in build compared with the VC: six-foot, chubby-faced fellows. Lieutenant Kendall, Major Smith and General Westmoreland came over. Deller said they looked like Chinese. A South Vietnamese interpreter arrived and, after some discussion, decided that the bodies were of North Vietnamese Regulars.'

Esler was dragging a noticeably young VC. As he bent over and pulled on the body, 'his face just caved in. He was full of maggots, I got a whiff of the smell and that was the only time I came close to being sick the whole time I was over there, except at the end when I was really sick.'

The sheer number of bodies was immediately evident to Chaplain Les Thompson.

Dead bodies everywhere. As you jumped off the chopper, they were there. There was a lot of activity. The guys from D Company were worn out, they were pretty edgy, they were sweaty-dirty, they had looks on their faces which showed quite clearly that they'd been through a horrendous ordeal and were still extremely toey.

It was a funny feeling as a Chaplain to be in that situation. My feeling for those who were dead, and who were being buried, is something that's too hard to explain, really. I had tremendous feeling for them. I was torn, in a sense, almost in loyalty.

Because suddenly I saw human beings and wondered what I was doing there. But I think this was the reaction of most people. And I could just imagine their families, I could see them receiving the letter; at the same time I could see our families receiving the letter about our men. And they seemed to be together, there didn't seem to be a distinction then of an enemy, and of us and them, it just seemed to be 'us' in this tragedy. It was a difficult situation.

I remember one burial ... I went and stood there, and I wanted to do something, I wanted to pray for the fellow and his family, and I most certainly did.

I went to another burial, a young fellow of 19 or 20, in a scrape-hole, and one person pushed the guy, just shoved him, and swore as he did, and I just had to remind him that this man was a soldier, he had fought hard, and was a part of the whole campaign. I still felt that idea of a oneness, of the lot of us together on this terrible stage, and asked would he bury him, and bury him with some military dignity.

The task of searching the many bodies was allocated to some of the men, and they were careful at first in case of possible booby-traps; but none were found. No one had yet comprehended the magnitude of the effort on the part of the VC in having searched the area in the dark for the wounded and the weapons. There had been no time left for such niceties as booby-trapping their own dead.

Naturally, the members of D Company tended to find their way to the various parts of the battlefield, and to the 11 Platoon area. The casualties from the main company position had been evacuated during the night, and now, in the sunlight, the young men had to look upon friends and fellow soldiers who lay dead in a foreign country.

Bob Buick, having shed a few tears at the sight of the dead men of the platoon and still under strain, reached boiling-point when the visitors began to crisscross the area making thoughtless remarks about the Australian casualties.

He was about to explode when the observant Jack Kirby materialized beside him. Kirby quietly pointed out an area of rubber-trees a short distance away: Buick was to be responsible for securing and searching it. This moved him away from the scene, gave him something to do, and allowed him to calm down.

At 10.00, Brigadier Jackson returned to 1ATF and signalled HQ AFV in Saigon:

> SITREP. Contact yesterday was with one to two battalions. All enemy dressed in greens with full web equipment. Weapons used by enemy were 82mm mortars from two separate baseplates, one to east, one to south, a large number of .50 and .30 MGs, M79 grenade-launchers, 57 and 75mm RCL. Enemy carrying large quantities of ammunition engaged us for approximately three and a half hours. Consider we inflicted very heavy casualties on the enemy. This is being checked out this morning. [Then followed details of the move to the site by D/5RAR and 6RAR.]
>
> Future plans — 6RAR to conduct search operations in three phases:
>
> Phase 1. D/5RAR and D/6RAR with 1 APC Sqn (31 APCs) advance from LZ GR 473674 to area of yesterday's battle, GR 483674. A/6RAR to follow APC force on foot. D/6RAR to search battle area. D/6RAR and C/6RAR to remain area of LZ.
>
> Phase 2. D/5RAR with APCs continue sweep east to the end of the rubber, then continue sweep west back to LZ, moving south of track from GR 494664 and GR 478673. B/6RAR in reserve for both phases to remain in location with Bn HQ.
>
> Phase 3. A/6RAR plus one Troop 1APC Sqn to sweep east through Long Tan GS 4866, then west to GR 489654. At the same time D/5RAR to sweep north-east to feature Nui Dat. B/6RAR and D/6RAR to remain in reserve for Phase 3.

Earlier, the 1ATF INTSUM for 18 August had briefly described the battle and other events of the day, stating that the VC forces were considered capable of inflicting heavy casualties on company- to battalion-size forces patrolling in the TAOR 'should these forces be deployed so as to present an attractive target'. The INTSUM concluded:

> It is not considered that the VC have the strength to launch a major attack against the Task Force Base area. They could possibly launch a raid in strength against one sector of the Task Force perimeter but will probably confine their activities to mortar attacks at night and quick battles with Task Force patrols. Unless forced to do otherwise the VC can be expected to initiate such quick attacks about 2−3 hours before last light.

Walking over the battlefield, Chaplain Les Thompson was becoming overwhelmed by it all, feeling that

> it was a pretty hopeless and helpless situation from my point of view. I was glad I was the Chaplain, I was sorry I was there. I wouldn't have wanted to be anywhere else, but I wished I was a thousand miles away.
>
> I went to the CO and asked why we couldn't extract the dead of the Vietnamese, back to a grave in Baria, so that we might bury them with some dignity. I remember making up reasons, and the first one was the only one that I thought legitimate: that we would bury them with some military dignity. To sort of substantiate that, I said it would mean that we've got some respect for the dead and [I brought up] a point I didn't care about, but I thought it might be a persuasive one: that it would prove to the Vietnamese that the battle was won and that we did inflict casualties.
>
> (It was only a few days later that we heard from Hanoi that the glorious D445 had wiped out the Sixth Royal Australian Regiment, and that they'd had light casualties themselves. Obviously, as we know, it was the reverse.)
>
> The CO rejected that, and he said we didn't have time, we had to keep moving. And move they did.

Peter Doyle, Esler and a few others were searching a group of corpses. When one body was pulled over onto its back, they found, underneath it, two pearl-handled Colt .45 pistols. The Diggers assumed that these had been taken by the VC from a dead American. One of the soldiers said, 'Look at this. This would be a good souvenir to take home.'

Behind them, a voice said, 'Aren't they beautiful?'

They turned, and it was Harry Smith. 'We spotted them first', a Digger told him.

Smith pointed to his rank badges. 'They're mine', he said.

Smith is also said to have acquired a Russian pistol, and can be seen wearing the belt in some of the Public Relations photos taken later.

At 11.05, 6RAR sent a situation report as follows:

Enemy. 113 enemy dead and two wounded recovered. Collection continues. Possibility that they are North Vietnamese.

Own troops. Two casualties recovered and evacuated. 13 dead recovered, which accounts for all missing in action. LOCSTAT [location statement, i.e. position] 6RAR GR 480672. Will commence Phase Two as approved by Commander 1ATF in ten minutes.

Adrian Roberts, sweeping out with his APCs, 'came across this most enormous dug-in position, pits that looked as if they'd been used for mortars'. The expanse of concentric pits was found by following telephone cable from the battlefield to this spot. Obviously, it was the VC battle HQ.

Peter Short, the medic, noticed that in some places where wounded VC had brushed against trees and bushes, the blood had not congealed. So many had congregated and passed along the evacuation routes that 'you could smell them'.

All over the scene, people were examining the bodies and the scattered weapons and equipment. Only a portion of what was littering the ground was handed in: mainly the larger weapons, plus what was left after enough had been appropriated as trophies and souvenirs — though D Company retained only a few.

At about midday, at GR 490665, Alan Hutchinson, with D/5RAR, came across the main trail made by the departing VC.

Through the bush, a three-metre-wide path had been trampled, with mud splattered up to head-height on the shrubs and trees along it. Here the struggling stretcher-bearers and wounded had slipped, fallen, grasped for handholds, forcing their way on through the night, the rain, the falling hammer-blows of artillery, among the moans of the wounded, the curses of the hurrying, the sharp commands of the unit leaders trying to maintain some order. . .

In Saigon, Captain John Dermody, on the Intelligence Staff at the Australian HQ there, was assigned the task of checking that all available information had been given to 1ATF in time for it to be of use; and if not, of recommending steps to be taken to ensure that, in future, it would be. After visits to the Australian and US units and HQs in the Saigon–Bien Hoa area, and to 1ATF, he confirmed that no information about the enemy had been lacking at 1ATF, and that none that could have alerted the Australians, or affected the battle, had been held elsewhere.

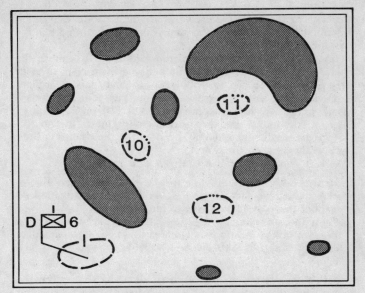

*The battle area: shaded patches indicate where bodies,
weapons and equipment were found after the battle*

Meanwhile, in the steaming heat of 19 August, the searching
and counting; the digging, collecting and tagging; the patrolling,
and the following of enemy trails — all of it continued. The
severity of the battle had attracted political attention, and in
order that a statement could be made in Parliament, some facts
and figures were required. A time deadline of 15.00 hours was
set for the completion of the count of bodies, to enable the figure
to be sent to Canberra.

By 20 August, 245 enemy were to be counted, and this figure
has gone into the records as the official number of enemy killed
in the battle. Scores of others were found later — where the
artillery had fallen on them in the assembly areas or reserve
positions, or in graves. Other parts of the field showed obvious
signs of having been cleared: bloody patches, bandages, clothes,
webbing and equipment, and pieces of bodies.

As late as four weeks after the battle, in patrols through the
area, decomposed bodies were still being discovered. These were
not included in the total.

Only three wounded enemy were found. This small number
attests to the conscientiousness of the VC evacuation teams, the

efficiency of the units themselves, and the personal dedication and morale of the soldiers. No others came in to surrender in the days following.

One of the prisoners was a member of D445 Battalion; the others were North Vietnamese who believed themselves to be in 45 Regiment, which had four 500-man battalions plus an artillery regiment. According to them, it was the guns and mortars of this regiment which had bombarded Nui Dat on 17 August. Later, it was found that these prisoners' regiment was in fact 275: apparently the men had not been told of the change in their unit's designation in the South.

At 12.15 on 19 August, 6RAR reported to 1ATF:

Enemy. Body count difficult to assess at this stage. Bodies been sighted as far east as GR 487667. Approximately 40 weapons have been recovered, including four LMGs, one 60mm mortar, one .50 MG, and three rocket-launchers of unknown origin. All tracks from area lead east. Own situation: A/6RAR and D/5RAR at GR 489669, remainder at GR 483674.

During the afternoon, patrols were allowed to sweep out no further than 1000 metres from the battle site. The trails were clear and easy to follow, but the unlocated enemy battalions were still around and could very easily have been waiting to maul any groups that wandered a little too far afield.

Brigadier Jackson visited 6RAR at 15.00, for further information on the results of the day's activities.

As things became more organized on the battlefield, Rod Armstrong began to feel the need for a shave. But A Company had left its packs at Nui Dat, bringing only basic webbing for the afternoon's action. All around him were Vietnamese enemy Regulars, whose packs had been searched. He 'went up to this North Vietnamese and went through his pack, found a couple of razorblades, French (you could tell by the wrapping), and it was just my luck: they were blunt. I wanted a drink, as our resupply had not come, so I opened up one of their bottles, and it had grass in it. I opened another one, and it had grass in it too. I never found out why they had grass in them.'

For two more days, 6RAR and the elements under its command continued the search, ending Operation Smithfield at 17.30 on 21 August, on their arrival back at the Nui Dat camp. More graves, food and ammunition caches, trails and small camps were found, but there was no further contact. However, a Corps-sized sweep through the region, named Operation Toledo, was mounted to maintain pressure on the VC.

Away to the east moved the columns of wounded, on stretchers or on the backs of a number of GMC trucks that the VC had positioned near the river known as the Song Rai, finally arriving at hospitals in the May Tao mountains, well out of the Australian area of operations.

Chau, leader of D445 Reconnaissance Platoon, was in one of these hospitals, together with about 100 other patients. His platoon had been annihilated in the battle with the APCs, and the 57mm RCL taken there had belonged to that platoon.

Talking among themselves, the wounded agreed that it had been a big battle, and were saddened by the heavy losses. The Northerners who had died and been buried were lost forever to their families, so far away to the north. The D445 casualties represented a concentration of grief in the Phuoc Tuy villages, as almost all were local men.

The Committee that had met to approve and plan the attack was now discussing the reasons for the lack of success, and what future methods of struggle should be adopted.

Weapons handed in at the battle site were:

33	AK47 rifles
7	RPD LMGs
5	SKS rifles
4	RPG-2 rocket-launchers
2	57mm recoilless rifles (RR or RCL)
2	M1 carbines
1	PPSh M1941 submachinegun
1	SGM heavy machinegun, on wheels
1	M1 'Garand' rifle
1	Thompson submachinegun
1	Browning Automatic Rifle (BAR light machinegun)

More than 10 500 rounds of ammunition for the rifles and machineguns were found, plus 300 hand-grenades, 40 mortar bombs for the 60mm mortar, 22 rounds for the 57mm RCLs and 28 rockets for the RPG-2s. Ammunition and magazines were also found for the old German MG34, though no weapon was located. No pistols or binoculars were recorded as being handed in.

The dead were all males of military age, dressed in green or khaki uniforms, or a mixture of blue, green, grey, black or khaki trousers and shirts. All had packs, belts, waterbottles and magazine-carriers, and either sandals or the 'Ho chi Minh' foot-wear made from old tyres. When the men were going into the attack, the sandals were often removed and tucked into the waistbelt. In the packs were hammocks, sewing kits, small lamps made of bottles with a wick threaded through the neck, ricebowls and aluminium food-containers, and spare clothing. Headwear was pith helmets or floppy cloth hats similar to those worn by the Australians. A piece of twine netting was often draped over the pack and back of the soldier, for camouflage purposes.

In the evening, the searching companies returned to the battle position, weary after a day of waiting and anticipating further combat, tired from following the trails and bloodstains, wary of the mauled VC units as the hunter is wary of the wounded tiger or buffalo.

On the evening of 19 August, returning to the central position, A Company was a little disgruntled to find that their shallow diggings had been used in their absence by the burial parties, thus turning the site into a cemetery.

During that night, the corpses in the graves stiffened or altered position as after-death changes took place in them, and next morning a further macabre touch was added to the scene when the Australians awoke to see parts of bodies protruding from the graves.

Despite sweeps during the following days to try to locate the retreating enemy, the Battle of Long Tan was effectively over.

Beyond Long Tan

If we are mark'd to die, we are enow
To do our country loss; and if to live,
The fewer men the greater share of honour.

King Henry V (IV. iii.)

WITH THE HUNDREDS of bodies now buried, the area thoroughly searched and the VC clearly suffering a set-back, the tired men of D Company returned to Nui Dat. For some, reaction set in only then.

Confronted with the rows of empty tents in 11 Platoon, Neil Rankin burst into tears, thinking of the boys he had trained and brought to Vietnam, wondering if he might have been able to save some of them had he been with them.

He was not the only one. But perhaps he did feel the loss of so many men more keenly than any other member of D Company.

Chaplain Les Thompson had flown back to Nui Dat on the morning of 20 August. He first visited the wounded in hospital, then went back to write to the families of all the casualties. He still has the names and addresses.

A memorial service was held in the tent lines of D Company, and Chaplain Thompson was 'happy to be there, just to share'.

D Company was sent *en masse* to the coastal town of Vung Tau, used as a rest centre by the Allied units — and allegedly by the VC as well. There, they found that they had little in common with outsiders, and clung together in D Company groups, alone in the crowds — reliving the battle, the many incidents, the loss of friends; laughing, crying, releasing the pressures of close combat. Like soldiers down the thirty centuries of recorded history, they were young men who had learnt that they could die.

143

The government of South Vietnam realized that this battle was significant and wished to award decorations to the Australians involved. But at almost the last moment, with the ceremony already arranged and those attending it already in place, word was received from Australia that the traditional policy of non-acceptance of foreign awards was to be observed.

This was embarrassing both to the Vietnamese and to the Australians, and a compromise was reached. The Australians paraded and were presented with dolls in Vietnamese national dress, and also cigarette-cases and lighters.

When those who had been selected for awards returned to their units, there were some hilarious scenes as they tried to convince their fellows that they really had been presented with dolls.

It says much for the often-maligned Vietnamese that they went ahead with the ceremony, persisting in observing the spirit of honouring their allies. Many another nation would have reacted to the last-minute decree by officially seeing it as an insult.

It also says much for the sense of humour of the Australian soldier that the incident was borne and accepted without much rancour, though once again he had been treated shabbily by the people in Canberra.

Before and after Long Tan, many South Vietnamese decorations and awards were accepted by individuals and units. At least 622 awards are known to have been made by the US and GVN authorities to individual Australians, plus four unit awards. Two of the latter went to AATTV — the US Meritorious Unit Commendation and the GVN Cross of Gallantry with Palm Unit Citation — and the third, a similar GVN award, to 8RAR. The fourth was the Presidential Unit Citation awarded to D Company for the Battle of Long Tan.

Only the unit awards are officially recognized by the Australian authorities and allowed to be worn. Because of the confusion over policy at the time, individual awards are not recognized. There are arguments for and against acceptance of such awards, but that debate is outside the scope of this book.

Messages of congratulation streamed into 1ATF from the Australian and US hierarchy. From Harold Holt, Prime Minister of Australia:

Our forces in their latest engagement have acquitted themselves in the best Australian tradition. Please tell them that Australia is proud of them. I have publicly expressed my sympathy to the bereaved. My sympathy goes also to the wounded. I send them best wishes for speedy recovery.

From General William Westmoreland:

Your troops have won a spectacular victory over the enemy. Aggressiveness, quick reaction, good use of firepower, and old-fashioned Australian courage have produced outstanding results. Congratulations.

From General Jonathan Seaman, Commanding IIFFV:

Please pass on to the Sixth Battalion, Royal Australian Regiment, my heartiest congratulations for the outstanding results obtained during Operation Smithfield. The large number of enemy killed as compared to the light casualties on the Australians is indicative of the professionalism of your Task Force. I especially want to congratulate D Company for its outstanding performance during this operation.

And from General Cao van Vien, Chief of Staff, Republic of Vietnam Armed Forces:

I wish to express the gratitude of the people and the Armed Forces of Vietnam for the successful performance of the men of the Australian Task Force during Operation Smithfield. Their action demonstrated to our enemies and the world the professional competence of your troops and their determination to help our nation in the preservation of its freedom. We share the pride of your people in the accomplishments of your brave soldiers! We also share the grief of the families of those who lost their lives in this action and other actions. We hope for the speedy recovery of those who suffered wounds.

However, the affair was seen in a different light by the opposing side. On 27 August, Radio Hanoi reported:

The Australian mercenaries, who are no less husky and beefy than their allies, the US aggressors, have proved as good fresh targets for the South Vietnam Liberation Fighters. According to Liberation Press Agency (LPA), in two days ending 18 August, the Liberation Armed Forces (LAF) wiped out 500 Australian mercenaries in Baria Province.

On 18 August, in the coastal province of Baria, east of Saigon, the LAF wiped out almost completely one battalion of Australian mercenaries in an ambush in Long Tan village. At 15.00 hours that day, an Australian mercenary battalion and a column of armoured cars fell into an ambush. Within the first few minutes the LAF attacked fiercely and made short work of two companies, set fire to three M113 armoured cars and drove the remnants into a corner of the battlefield. The LAF then concentrated their fire on them and heavily decimated the remaining company.

The LAF also shot down one of the US aircraft which went to the aid of the battered Australians.

According to first reports, in this battle the LAF put out of action 400 Australian mercenaries, thus annihilating two full-sized companies, heavily decimated another, set afire three M113 armoured cars, downed one US jet fighter and captured a large quantity of arms and munitions.

The day before, 17 August, the LAF in the same province wiped out 100 Australian mercenaries.

For these victories, the South Vietnamese LAF Command has decided to award a Liberation Military Exploit Order Third Class to the victorious units.

Next day, Radio Peking repeated the gist of the Hanoi report.

Closer to the scene, word of the Australian victory spread through the province. Banners congratulating the Task Force were made and quickly hung from trees and buildings in local towns and villages. VC propaganda tried to reverse this trend, but the tremendous artillery fire had been heard for kilometres around, and the Australians were as active after the action as before. To a people who had watched military units for decades, it was obvious that the Australians were not members of a defeated formation.

In addition, no captured Australians, or their equipment, were paraded or produced by the VC.

Despite all the talk by their military and political leaders, it was obvious to the survivors of D445 Battalion and 275 Regiment that their own losses had been heavy. However, they did believe that their adversaries had also suffered considerable losses in men and material. The sheer intensity of the fighting made it easy to assume that severe damage had been inflicted on the Australians.

Later, when members of D445 began to surrender, they found it hard to accept that Australian casualties had been so slight by comparison.

The VC did not award medals but rather Certificates of Commendation: either a general commendation or a class of hero, such as a 'Determined-to-Win Hero' or 'Brave Destroyer of Armoured Vehicles'.

Tran van Tranh, C2 Company, D445, received a Commendation for his part in the battle. Awarded on 12 November 1966, the citation stated that 'during the battle with the Australians on 18 August 1966 he fought courageously, kept control of his men during the battle, and organized the evacuation of all the wounded'. Tranh was later killed in action.

As usual, after-action reports were written by the commanders of the various elements involved in the battle. None from the VC side is known to have come to light, and it would be very interesting to see the VC version of the events.

Part of Lieutenant-Colonel Townsend's analysis of the action is reproduced in the paragraphs that follow. The extract has been edited slightly.

D Company's action, which precipitated Operation Smithfield, again proves the value of patrolling in depth and patrolling in strength. By its contact and subsequent developments, D Company completely disrupted what are believed to have been the enemy's preparations for an attack in regimental strength on 1ATF area. While these types of patrols are operating well outside the perimeter, they reduce significantly the enemy's capacity to securely deploy in strength and launch an attack. The chances of detection are very high, and it must be upsetting for the enemy *not* to know when or where he will run into a large patrol, ready to fight and capable of being of far more than nuisance value.

There were valuable lessons learnt in this operation:

(a) While a company patrol is out, another company plus a command element of the TOC [Tactical Operations Centre] must be on no more than 30 minutes' notice to move, for assistance or reinforcement. This must include the RMO [Regimental Medical Officer]. The reaction force must have its first-line holding [i.e. immediate supplies] of ammunition, and at least two days' [extra] ready for immediate issue. It must constantly keep up with the tactical situation and be able to move, by air, APC or foot, with minimum briefing and orders.

(b) Ammunition for SLRs should be in magazines and resupply should also be in magazines. Under the conditions, which could easily recur, it was impractical to load more than five rounds into SLR magazines, because mud clogged them. Similarly, a suitable ammunition container which can be carried (preferably slung), and which can be attached to the gun, is needed.

(c) While such large contacts are always possible, at least 140 rounds of ammunition should be carried by each rifleman.

(d) The aspect of command when APCs are included in the force has already been dealt with [in an earlier part of the report]. It is essential that the infantry commander have overall command and have the final decision in any matter; naturally he will be guided by the APC commander.

It was initially the intention to locate the enemy's withdrawal route and to follow up quickly with the aim of destroying the withdrawing elements. However, it took some time to positively establish the general direction of withdrawal, and by this time the battalion was almost out of effective gun range and was not balanced adequately for a sustained pursuit. A Company had completed a three-day patrol only about two hours before they were called out again, and they were beginning to get tired. B Company was in an even worse state. This company had left the Base at first light on 17 August to locate the enemy mortar baseplate and RR [Recoilless Rifle] position of that morning's bombardment, and had gone out in patrol order only, with no rations or personal equipment. Although rations were resupplied by porter, it still had no bedding or spare clothing. In addition, almost two-thirds of the company was absent on R and C leave, and did not return to the company, in the field, until 16.00 hours, 20 August. D Company had suffered heavy casualties and had effective only two platoons, and even these were at much reduced strength.

A further restricting factor to a quick follow-up was the enemy strength, which was believed still to be about two battalions. Although the enemy had suffered heavy casualties, and was probably carrying a lot more, it was believed he still had the capacity to interfere with our pursuit, by at least company-sized groups and maybe by battalion, probably using ambushes. It would have been unwise to have thrown caution to the wind, despite the temptation.

The enemy almost certainly withdrew to a base area or areas in the east or north-east, where he will reorganize. It is believed his reorganization and regrouping will take at least a month, during which the effectiveness of the regiment will be at a very reduced level.

The enemy met was very well organized and equipped, and showed very skilful battle drills at company level with control by visual signals and bugles. It is almost certain at least an NVA battalion was included in the force, and that 6RAR's previous enemy, D445 Battalion, provided guides in strength and probably some support elements.

The performance of D Company was admirable, and overall command and control good.

There is no doubt that our training, organization and equipment are generally adequate, though improvements are needed and will be made or sought. There is no need to change the pattern of our operations, but the meeting of such a large force emphasizes the need to keep the battalion balanced; and, when operating as a battalion, the need to keep companies reasonably close together to provide mutual help when the need arises. While this magnitude of engagement exists, forces must move in a minimum of company strength to ensure adequate security. Platoon patrols are acceptable, but their operations must be limited in distance, depending on terrain, so that they can at all times be supported quickly by the remainder of the company.

6RAR has achieved a great victory, [and] the lessons and experiences gained have provided the soundest of bases for successful further operations.

The Company Commanders and Adrian Roberts also wrote reports, which included the usual conclusions and recommendations.

Most of the comments by Captain Mollison, who commanded A Company, concerned communications and the problem of command when infantry were being transported in APCs. Obviously, he believed that while the APC commander was 'the best man to manoeuvre the vehicles and conduct a running firefight', it was the infantry commander who 'must have the power of veto if he is to retain control of his troops and the overall battle'.

Lieutenant-Colonel Townsend supported Mollison, while Roberts naturally had the view of the Armoured Corps: that 'Infantry must realize that they are under command for movement till I can get them no further, and that these vehicles must be fought with secure tactics, especially when the enemy has RR'.

Roberts also pointed out that improved communications equipment for the APCs was needed, as were personal weapons for the APC crews (instead of the pistols on general issue) and a third crew-member in each vehicle to take over in the event of one of the others being hit in action.

Harry Smith, in his report, devoted some space to commenting on the performance of the weapons with which D Company was equipped. The M60 machinegun

failed in the extreme conditions of mud, dirt and wet. There were no mechanical failures, but the ammunition could not be kept clean. The ammunition pouch issued with the M60 is useless, as it shrinks, and folds in, stopping the feed [of the ammunition-belt]. All belts should be in light metal magazines, carried in a canvas bag which can be slung. With the present system it is impossible to prevent the belts dragging in the mud. It should be noted that all enemy LMG [light machine-gun] ammo is in cylindrical metal magazines, and their LMGs remained firing. [Recommendation followed for metal magazine.]

M60 ammunition containing one-in-five 1960 tracer failed on every tracer round. Gun fired four rounds then stopped, etc.

Smith saw the SLR as 'the outstanding weapon of the action, with only two broken firing-pins'. Recommendations were then made for more magazines to be carried, for refilling apparatus for them, and for acquisition of plastic magazines.

The Owen gun was 'not effective', and it was recommended that it be replaced with the SLR or M16. The M16 'performed well', but some stoppages could not be cleared without the cleaning-rods that were not then available in sufficient numbers. Smith also commented that the use of tracer ammunition 'was invaluable':

The D Company policy of the initial five rounds [in the] rifle and 25 rounds [in the] machinegun, followed by normal one-in-five tracer, proved successful in the poor conditions of visibility and lack of background to show the fall of shot. I recommend that even more tracer be used. Although small-arms accuracy has been questioned, there is no doubt that 50 per cent of the dead around the D Company area were killed by small-arms fire, and the use of tracer was a main factor.

Other observations, comments and recommendations were made in the various reports, and it was generally agreed that patrolling well out from the Nui Dat base should continue, to keep the VC at a disadvantage. One report did argue for strong defence works and minefields to counter future attacks, but was rejected because of the defensive mentality that can arise from such measures.

Further writings on the action tended to give the impression that 1ATF as a formation had been involved in the battle, but it was in fact fought by A and D Companies, plus the APC Troop, with artillery support. Within D Company, several platoon actions were fought. The number of Australians actually involved in combat was relatively small. Most of 1ATF, including the HQ, was 'there', in the sense of being present at Nui Dat, but had little idea of what was really happening.

There was no Task Force battle, in the sense of a pre-planned reaction to events. The fighting developed as it did from a basic lack of knowledge of enemy strength, locations, capabilities and intentions.

Brigadier Jackson had to consider the security of 1ATF at Nui Dat; Lieutenant-Colonel Townsend was more concerned with D Company, and argued strongly for the dispatch of another company to assist and relieve D. Relatively inexperienced but well trained, 1st Field Regiment had provided the shield against which the VC had expended themselves. D Company, also relatively inexperienced but well trained, had kept its nerve and held on. A Company and the APCs had fought their way through. All these things had happened, but not as part of a plan to deal with a foreseen situation.

After the battle, the Australian units continued to push on out into the further reaches of their area of operations, and the VC never again posed as great a threat to 1ATF as they had on the afternoon and night of 18 August.

The artillery, who had performed so magnificently, went back to 'normal routine'. It should be remembered that the guns were either in action or on call for 24 hours of every day. Gun-crews normally comprised a Sergeant, a Bombardier and five men; and regardless of leave, sickness, casualties and the endless work necessary in military units, the guns had to be available. The effort required of the individual Gunner was heavy and constant for the 365 days of his tour of duty in Vietnam.

For the remainder of its twelve-month tour of duty, 6RAR continued its patrolling, ambushing, and participation in larger-scale operations. Sadly, Jack Kirby was killed in February 1967 by an artillery salvo misdirected by an inexperienced officer.

On its return to Australia, the battalion in its 1966 form dissolved as the National Servicemen re-entered civilian life (to be replaced by a fresh draft of men) and the Regulars that remained began training for future tours of duty in Vietnam.

In the months and years following the battle, D445 and the lesser units in the province continued to operate against the Australians, but were gradually worn down by operations mounted by 1ATF against their base areas, their resupply systems, and the local guerrillas and Party organizations.

Gradually, 274 and 275 Regiments found they were unable to exist in the area. They moved away to the north and east, though they returned now and again for forays into Phuoc Tuy. In February 1967, and again in February 1968, D445 was in heavy contact with the Task Force. It was badly damaged on each occasion.

In 1967, another battalion was formed — D440. Instead of

being recruited from the local population, it was composed mainly of groups of Northerners. Internal trouble began almost at once, since the NVA regarded allocation to a local unit as a lowering of status. They had come south to join their own formations, to take part in decisive battles.

The age-old bickering between Northerners and Southerners raged in the platoons and companies. Captured documents, prisoners and 'ralliers' (defectors from the VC) told of arguments, orders and counter-orders, and of general dissatisfaction.

D440's combat exploits were few and it was eventually disbanded, in late 1970.

By early 1971, the once-proud D445 had been reduced to a total strength of 80. These split into five groups of about 15, which dispersed to the far corners of the province — to grow food, avoid contact and wait until the Australians left.

Entire VC units and village organizations had ceased to exist, and no recruits could be enticed to join. The local population had seen the repeated success of 1ATF's patrolling and ambushing operations too often to consider a life in the VC as worthwhile.

Few D445 veterans of Long Tan survived the subsequent years of jungle life, the constant moving to avoid detection, the bombs and shells, the steady drainage of men in the patrol clashes, the ambushes, the few large battles, the illness, the lack of medicine, and the ever-increasing shortage of food and of recruits. Some surrendered to the South Vietnamese government, unable to wait out the long years with little beyond promises of success.

Some of the wounded were sent to units where their injuries were less of a liability — where they could still be of use to the Revolution.

Gradually, the elite fighting unit of Baria Province melted away, shrinking to a few bands of refugees subsisting on a mere strand of hope and few supplies, and incapable of anything more than pinprick operations against 1ATF.

Throughout the period 1966–72, the VC continued to make laughable claims of success, even towards the end of 1ATF's time in Vietnam. The HQ of NLF Military Region 7 issued documents stating that in the Campaign of Summer 1969, units had engaged in 206 battles, killing about 2000 Thais, 3000 ARVN and 95 Australians, as well as sinking 89 ships and destroying trucks, helicopters, artillery pieces, and so on. In all of 1969, 1143 battles had been fought, with 20 296 ARVN or Allied troops killed, 52 planes shot down and 540 vehicles destroyed. Outstanding units mentioned were C3 Company of

D445, the Dat Do Guerrilla Unit and the Long Dat District Unit.

It was claimed that 861 battles had been fought in Baria Province in 1970, resulting in 12 864 enemy put out of action. An outstanding unit mentioned was K8 Company (of D440, in reality disbanded), which supposedly killed 744 enemy in ten battles.

These claims are put in a different light when compared with other captured documents, which convey the reality of life in the local units. The Chau Duc Unit operated largely to the west of Nui Dat. Its own documents state that in 1970, of 137 people, it lost 28 killed, 32 missing, two captured and 22 deserted. In the last half of that year it suffered four killed, 21 missing, one captured and 12 deserted.

When 1ATF did leave, in late 1971 and early 1972, it was North Vietnamese units which were brought in to attack the ARVN in the province.

The Task Force had indeed taken over Phuoc Tuy.

* * *

In April 1975, South Vietnam fell to the military might of the North. It was not a VC or an NLF unit but a North Vietnamese tank, filmed by the late Australian combat cameraman Neil Davis, which crashed through the gates of the Independence Palace in Saigon.

The Provisional Revolutionary Government, the People's Revolutionary Party, the VC, the NLF — all vanished within days, if not overnight, as the North at last attained victory. Few Southerners came to hold positions of authority in the new regime, and the much-talked-of 'elections' of the 1954 Geneva agreements were not mentioned by Hanoi.

Since its victory, the Hanoi regime has occupied Laos and Kampuchea, the latter only after Pol Pot had murdered almost everyone in the country with even a smattering of education. The potential for the emergence of an effective anti-Vietnamese resistance was thus destroyed.

The old dream of the Vietnamese — possession of the giant rice-paddy of Kampuchea — is now reality. And their march 'Southward!' (*Nam Tien!*) has taken them to the borders of yet another neighbour.

Myths and Memories

Old men forget; yet all shall be forgot,
But he'll remember with advantages
What feats he did that day...

King Henry V (IV. iii.)

A S WITH ANY EVENT of major importance, rumours, half-truths, cases of wishful thinking and outright myths surround the Battle of Long Tan. Some of these sprang into existence almost before the smoke had cleared. Like certain religious tales and traditions, the Long Tan myths have, with time, taken on a plating of truth. A number of the rumours and myths are discussed below; followed by a brief review of what some of the men most vividly remember about Long Tan.

1ATF knew of the enemy, but sent D/6RAR out uninformed

The first and most obvious of the rumours is that a great amount of information was available to the Task Force staff and commander about the approaching regiments, but that this was ignored and D Company was sent out with no warning.

There is no evidence for such a view in any of the material gathered for this book, including off-the-record talks with people in the Intelligence community. After the event, it was easy to sit down with all the information received by 1ATF over the preceding days and weeks, and to select items that, together, *may* have added up to a forecast of enemy strengths and intentions.

But no one could do so convincingly before the event. Also, the infantry had become very tired of fruitless patrolling, of sweeping through patches of country said by Intelligence to contain enemy. The SAS had just swept the area to the north and east, finding nothing. The Intelligence people could well have been regarded as 'crying Wolf'.

The Task Force had a mission — 'Take over Phuoc Tuy' — and to accomplish this, 1ATF had to move out of the base and assert itself in the province. To remain in camp, strengthening it for a possible attack, would have been exactly what the enemy wanted. Risks had to be taken.

Another suggestion is that D/6RAR should have been warned of the presence of large numbers of enemy in the area. But dozens, if not hundreds, of patrols had covered the area close to the Task Force base, just as D Company was to do, with no contact or only fleeting exchanges of fire with small groups of Main Force or local enemy. It had to be accepted that the VC would continually be trying to reconnoitre the Nui Dat environs, and that they would continually try to move through the area to the villages.

Also, the VC would try to move battalions into, through and around the area to launch their own operations, to test 1ATF reaction, or for training purposes. Not every concentration of VC within a certain distance of Nui Dat meant that they were about to attack 1ATF.

The heavy weapons used in the bombardment of Nui Dat on 17 August were obviously not part of the equipment of local village guerrillas; but it was accepted by D Company, no less than by A and B, that the VC responsible would be long gone by the afternoon of 18 August. More than 36 hours elapsed between the time of the mortaring and the departure of D Company; and only bloodstains and after-action litter had been located by B Company.

Although some may have felt uneasy about enemy intentions, the fact remains that before the action no one could assemble items of accurate, confirmed information based on known enemy movements to show convincingly that a large-scale attack was imminent.

In this respect, the VC achieved surprise.

However, Long Tan surely vindicated the Australian insistence on patrolling and dominating no-man's-land — in this case, the approaches to 1ATF.

It was still early days in the life of 1ATF in Phuoc Tuy. The Intelligence base, its reservoir of knowledge, was still narrow, and its system was still smoothing and perfecting itself. Later, the Intelligence files would contain information on the VC which included names, ranks, unit positions held, types of weapon carried, personal weaknesses, marital status, and so on.

The SAS had seen the enemy approaching

Several people, including some D Company veterans, believed that the SAS had located, followed and reported the advance of the VC regiments towards Nui Dat. Colonel (then Major) John Murphy commanded the SAS Squadron at the time, and refutes the story. His men had patrolled in very bad conditions and had found no signs of large formations in the area. The SAS was preparing to operate to the west, where 1ATF intended to move against the Nui Dinh—Nui Thi Vai massifs. Later, the SAS did locate large numbers of enemy and their camps, but this had nothing to do with the battle in the Long Tan rubber plantation.

D Company daydreamed their way into an ambush

A widely held version of the battle is that D Company, with the proverbial 'thumb in bum' and 'mind in neutral', walked into an ambush, and were then saved by the artillery.

The history of the war from 1963 to 1966 contains numerous examples of VC expertise in setting such ambushes, and of executing them very well indeed. To the north, at Binh Gia, and to the south, at Dat Do, the VC had done this and inflicted severe defeats on the ARVN. But if D Company had fallen into an ambush, it is unlikely that it would have faced, as platoons and later as a company, the succession of outflanking moves and the waves of attacks. There were no prepared ambush positions found at the scene. Such diggings as were located at the actual battle site had been carried out for protection against the artillery, not in order to catch a company (or battalion) in a murderous fire.

Instead, it seems obvious that the VC were as surprised by the meeting as D Company was. Why else the flanking attacks and the wave-assaults, exposing men to small-arms and artillery fire? The length of time it took the VC to ascertain the location of the D Company HQ and final position indicates unpreparedness.

These patterns are hardly characteristic or suggestive of the VC ambush, especially at that stage of the war. Slaughtered ARVN units testified to VC expertise in the annihilation ambush.

The VC fell into 1ATF's trap

This has also been mentioned by some people, but does not bear much scrutiny. It is hard to envisage a 'trap' — one that would be expected to involve heavy fighting — in which a company goes out with 60 rounds per man; in which the APC relief force lacks gunshields and intercom; in which the Infantry and Armour elements have not decided who is in charge; and so forth.

Vung Tau, the VC capital

It has also been stated, quite seriously, that the assault force was intended not only to exterminate 1ATF but to roll south, eliminating the GVN–Allied presence all the way to and including Vung Tau. There, a Revolutionary Liberated Zone Capital was to be declared.

This (such a scenario continues) was all planned by Hanoi, to the extent that the administration cadres for the new government were dispatched by sampan from further east along the coast, following a timetable that put them ashore at Vung Tau during the night of 18 August. But instead of being met by the victorious VC, they were collected by the alert Australian sentries.

Research for this book located no documentary evidence for such an assertion, nor could anyone on the staff or in units either in Saigon or at Vung Tau recall any such events.

The basis for this belief may be the numerous reported sightings of VC resupply traffic by sampan along the coast, with a focal point in the Long Hai area, among the old villas there. Many night flights along this strip, without lights, were conducted by 161 Recce Flight and provided a great amount of information on this activity.

The APCs took too long to get to D Company

The APCs were beset with technical problems from the beginning — they had already done a year of operations with 1RAR and 1ATF. In the Long Tan action, they lacked radios, lacked a clear idea of D Company's location, had to complete a river-crossing, and had to fight their way through the enemy — and all this in torrential rain, over muddy ground, in close country. In addition, past VC successes from deliberately creating such a tactical situation in order to ambush the relief force were very well known.

To those who understand something of armoured operations, the APC Troop did well that day.

The APCs killed and wounded some of D/6RAR

One claim was that the APCs caused casualties to D Company by charging blindly over them. This has already been refuted earlier in the text.

12 Platoon fired on 11 Platoon, and lives were lost

Dave Sabben's account (not contradicted by any other member of the platoon) of the care with which he advanced, and his claim that, before long, he knew 11 Platoon's position by observing the areas from which fire was or was not received, must cast doubt on such an accusation.

11 Platoon buried their weapons

The members of 11 Platoon were said to have been so determined, that when they thought they were about to be overrun (which they never were) they calmly buried their weapons to deny them to the enemy; the weapons were found the next morning by an engineer using a minesweeper. The relevant accounts, quoted earlier, by survivors from 11 Platoon and by those who found the bodies the following day, give the truth.

11 Platoon was overrun

Casualties with head wounds were seen in the morning, and it was assumed that the soldiers had been killed as the VC swept over the position. In fact, the enemy did not occupy the position until the survivors had withdrawn.

As related in the text, these men were killed by VC firing from the trees.

Prisoners were killed

On 19 August, it has been said, prisoners were killed. It is true that at least one very badly wounded VC, almost dead, was shot as an act of mercy. Other enemy in the area refused to surrender, though wounded, and were killed when they tried to fire an RCL at the advancing Australians. Shooting also occurred when VC already dead were thought to be pointing weapons.

There were a few minor contacts with small groups of VC around the edges of the battlefield; and in one of these, two VC who would not surrender were killed.

In no other instances were VC fired at on 19 August. In no account by anyone from any of the sub-units involved in the sweep through the battlefield, on or off the record, was reference made to wanton killing. The atmosphere in the plantation that morning was not depicted by anyone as being conducive to revenge-shootings. The Australians were advancing, at first in expectation of another fierce clash, then in general amazement at the scene. The VC had obviously taken a severe beating, their casualties far outnumbering those of the Australians. This is not, historically, a setting for the killing of prisoners by Western armies.

At the scene of 11 Platoon's battle, almost everyone was affected by the sight. Some emotional words were uttered, but that was all.

(In the early 1970s, a National Serviceman from 1 APC

Squadron, who had been at the battlefield on 19 August, alleged that prisoners were shot, and that he had heard the firing. He received some media attention, but no proof could be found of the shootings.)

In addition, officers and NCOs were present, controlling their men in anticipation of a further battle. In such a situation, shooting of any kind requires immediate explanatory reports. Close behind came the staff officers from 1ATF, the ARVN, and the media. Killing of prisoners could not be hidden from all of these people, many of them trained observers and some always alert for the whiff of sensation.

Artillery inflicted by far the heaviest VC casualties

What annoys most D Company veterans interviewed is the claim that they inflicted few casualties with their personal weapons, and that most VC were killed by the artillery. Despite the artillery, many VC were managing to close on D Company, and had to be shot down with 7.62 or 5.56mm weapons, if not with the old 9mm Owens. Maury Stanley could not see the fall of shot for most of the time he was assisting Buick, and although the artillery support for 11 Platoon was first-class, it did not do all the work there.

As David Sabben points out, the entire battlefield was raked by artillery, during and after the actual battle involving the infantry. Throughout the night, concentrations fell right across the location. Many enemy killed or wounded in the afternoon were further mutilated in the later bombardments.

The VC were drugged

Yet another story is that the VC were drugged, and advanced like zombies. No one who was there believes that the men who laboured all afternoon to exterminate the Australians were under the influence of drugs. Except for normal medical supplies, no drugs were reported found after the fighting, when the field was searched.

The RAAF refused to fly

It was also alleged that the RAAF refused to fly to assist D/6RAR and had to be threatened with expulsion from Vietnam before the ammunition resupply was flown; and that the pilots concerned had to be spoken to forcefully by Group Captain Raw, and ordered to make the flight.

'Frank Riley had his faults, but lack of bravery was not one of them', was the comment by (Air Commodore) Ray Scott when he was told of this allegation. Other pilots also spoke of Riley in the same terms. Riley and Bruce Lane were prepared to fly in alone, orders or no. The others were less keen, mainly because of the abysmal flying conditions; but they flew.

There is some difference between (on the one hand) wanting to know details of the D Company location, arranging for the artillery to be halted, and discussing the best way to execute the mission, and (on the other) refusing to fly.

The story was related by several people of different ranks, but no one was prepared to state that he was an eyewitness, or was able to recall the words.

The case of 'Custard's' boots

Finally, the widely reported encounter between 'Custard' Meller and the VC, in the night on the battlefield, when the VC were said to have been trying to steal Meller's boots. Meller himself denies this. Why the VC would want a pair of heavy, size 9 or 10, Australian Army boots for their own smaller feet was ignored by the media, but the tale was spread by them. What the VC may have been feeling for, in the dark, around Meller's calves and ankles, was the cane-loops worn by many of them — to facilitate their own removal from the scene of action in the event of being wounded or killed.

Assumptions, misconceptions, remarks taken out of context, and things said in jest or sarcastically — these attach themselves to most events of note, and battles are no exception.

What is factual about the Battle of Long Tan is that, on 18 August 1966, young Australians in the rubber plantation and at Nui Dat reacted to their training and leadership to snatch victory from a brave and determined enemy.

Around this rock, the discoloured swirls of rumour and myth continue to eddy.

* * *

Memories of the action are as varied as the men who participated, and illustrate the wide range of mental outlooks among them. D Company veterans have vivid, photograph-clear images of moments during that long, wet afternoon and night: a friend firing; a VC running; an artillery salvo falling into a line of enemy; a wounded Digger, unconscious, with his tongue fastened to his lower lip by safety-pin (the medic's way of preventing accidental choking); Harry Smith calmly directing his platoons; Jack Kirby looming through the rain, throwing down a handful of rounds; the incredible mass of coloured tracer that streamed out and around the Australians; 'Paddy' Todd's return; the ammunition resupply by helicopter; the rain and mud; the APCs lurching up, with headlights blazing and machineguns firing; the friendly shapes and voices of A Company; and friends — friends alive, friends wounded, friends dead.

Peter Ainslie, 11 Platoon, will always remember 'those first few seconds. The enemy were on the run, we were after them, and then the tracer. The hail of fire was enormous, intense. Besides the noise of the enemy fire I remember the *lights* — it was just unbelievable! There was so much tracer, just zipping straight through the rubber-trees, you simply, absolutely, couldn't conceive it, and I still sort of can't.'

When he hears the words 'Long Tan', the image invoked for Maury Stanley is that of the painting by Bruce Fletcher in the Australian War Memorial. For him, it *is* Long Tan.

Peter Bennett, machinegunner in A Company, has as his most vivid memory their driving into D445. He 'could not believe my eyes as we pushed on through the VC running everywhere'.

For Ross Smith, Section Commander in A Company, it was 'the comradeship, the valour, and the amount of artillery; the legend of Anzac upheld'.

To Alan Hutchinson, Forward Observation Officer with D/5RAR, the most vivid memory of the day is the rain, the mud, and being very apprehensive — for he had already done his 'last' operation of that tour of duty.

Brian Wickens was profoundly affected by the battle. 'Prior to Long Tan, I had always refused to change my nationality to Australian. The battalion was 45 per cent NS — kids. I had really despaired, as a professional soldier, that we should take this battalion to Vietnam. They were not ready for it, I felt. They were just National Servicemen. I found them to be the bravest soldiers I had ever seen and I came back and changed my nationality to Australian because of it.'

Though he later commanded an artillery regiment, for Ian Darlington the Battle of Long Tan encapsulated 'everything I had trained for and knew about artillery. Nothing else compared with it.'

The very bad weather remains the single most vivid memory of that day for Group Captain (later Air Commodore) Peter Raw, closely followed by 'thankfulness that I was not an Army guy, but an airman; the apprehension that I had about what hung on the success or otherwise of the RAAF resupply operation to D Company; and the pride I had for all concerned after the battle'.

The speed of the entire event, the quickness of the afternoon and night, is what remains as Rod Armstrong's chief impression of the battle.

The crews that flew into the rain to supply D Company hold the weather as their most vivid memory of the day. And for Bruce Lane, there is also the frightening leap by that 'something' in the bushes as the helicopter drummed over.

What made the deepest impression on Bob Grandin was 'the intensity of the day: it was amazing that so much was happening, you were almost working in a void, not being able to see any of the action, to see the results of what you did, [knowing only] that something quite desperate was going on'.

Phil Cooke, 9 Squadron duty-pilot that day, still clearly recalls the feeling of relief and pride when word arrived that the small force of soldiers had inflicted 'Don Bradman's highest score' on the enemy.

Adrian Roberts cannot bear to be in places such as pine plantations at around dusk.

Brigadier Jackson still has nightmares about Long Tan.

For one member of D Company that day, the memories are of more than a battle. 'Pom' Rencher 'was on the company's strength from March '66 to February '67, when I was casevacked [casualty-evacuated] out after getting wounded when Jack Kirby was killed. Since then I've served with BHQ, a language course at Point Cook, three years in Australian Intelligence Corps, and thirteen years in the Brit Int Corps, but my spiritual home was, is and always will be D Company, 6RAR. I have never really left them.'

APPENDIX 1

The Artillery

Extract from the Operations Log, 1st Field Regiment RAA, listing the regimental fire missions for 18 August 1966:

Time	Mission
16.19	Fire Mission Regiment (FM Regt) grid 487674 called by callsign (cs) 34 (Stanley)
16.22	FM Regt grid 487676 A 400 (490672) D 300 (488670) D 200 (487668)
16.28	FM Regt 490672 called by cs 34 — suspected VC company area D 200 (488672) R 200 D 200 (486670) D 200 (484670) L 200 (484674) A 400 (488674) D 100 (487674) R 200 (487672)
16.32	FM Bty fired cs 4 (US 155mm) 485660
16.46	FM Regt called by cs 34 grid 487669 A 100 (478670) R 200 (479668) R 200 (481667) D 100 (480666)
17.06	FM Regt called by cs 34 grid 480678 A 400 (484677) L 200 (484679) R 100 A 100 (485678) R 200 (485676)
17.28	FM Regt called cs 34 grid 481669; not cleared as air-strike in progress
17.35	FM Regt called cs 39 (Honner) during enemy assault grid 481664 R 200 D 100 (479665)

            D 100 (479666)
            D 100 (479667)
            D 100 (479668)
17.37   FM Bty (US 155mm) called cs 39 (Honner)
            A 100 (488659)
            R 100 D 100 (487658)
            R 400 (486654)
            R 400 (486650)
18.06   cs 34 told cs 39 after helicopter resupply that
        nothing must be allowed to interrupt the fire of the
        guns
        (18.00 to 18.15: firing was halted to allow the heli-
        copter resupply)
18.32   FM Regt called cs 34: VC attacking grid 482671
            L 200 (483672)
            D 100 (482673)
            A 400 L 200 (487672)
            D 200 (485673)
            L 200 (484675)
18.36   FM Bty (US 155mm) called cs 39 grid 485654
            A 200 (487652)
            L 200 (487655)
            L 200 (488658)
18.58   FM Regt called cs 34 grid 484675
            D 100 (483675)
19.15   FM Regt called cs 39 grid 493671
            R 300 (493668)
            R 200 (493666)
            R 300 (493663)
19.55   FM Bty called cs 39 grid 510662
            R 200 (510660)
            L 400 (510664)
21.15   FM Regt called cs 39 grid 493671
            L 200 (493673)
            R 400 (493669)
23.25   FM Regt as for at 21.15
02.54   FM Bty called cs 39 grid 487671
            D 200 (485671) fired 8 times in early morning.

Total rounds expended in the period were 2639 rounds of
105mm and 155 rounds of 155mm. This is an official figure, and
some who were present believe that another 1000 rounds or
more may have been fired.

When the position of D Company had been established
beyond doubt, Ian Darlington ordered 'continuous fire' — that
is, the guns would continue to fire at about three rounds per

minute, consistent with accuracy and safety on the gun line, until ordered to cease.

George Bindley believes that 'the artillery can proudly claim success'.

But success for a gunner is measured by ability to provide fire support to the supported arm — that is our role. In this case 6RAR was magnificently supported, and, because of it, survived and prevailed.

There has always been a healthy professional disdain (and respect, though never acknowledged) between fighting arms and there was plenty before and after Long Tan. The 'grunts' always look askance at the 'drop shorts' and 'tankies', and that will always be the case. But after Long Tan there was respect for the guns and it was shown. Whenever we came in contact with infantry of either battalion after Long Tan, we got the thumbs up, and that said it all.

Bindley thinks highly of his gunners of 1966–67:

Throughout the whole of my tour in Vietnam, I never had any cause to doubt, or to fear, any one of my soldiers. I hope they felt the same about me. I believe that it is important to communicate the need to be good to soldiers, to demonstrate that there is an expectation of achievement in how well the job is done; that is, beyond what their training ensured, more than just efficiently or ably.

The Battery was good. Not that they were angels, or even ambassadors, which some pompous and sometimes silly senior officers sometimes expected them to be. They were just a well-trained team, who liked and respected one another and wanted to win and survive.

I was lucky, and so was 103 Battery, because we had it, the 'goodness'. It had always been there. It was there in Malaya in 1961 and it just seemed to get better. I personally doubt that there was a better sub-unit in which to be a member by the time we left Vietnam in May 1967.

Harry Smith, when asked in 1984 what single factor had the greatest effect on the outcome of the Battle of Long Tan, replied with one word: 'Artillery'.

The RAAF

The aircraft and crews of 9 Squadron listed for the medical evacuation flight on the night of 18 August are:

A2-1019 Shepherd, Middleton
A2-1020 Riley, Grandin, Collins, Stirling
A2-1021 Macintosh, Sharpley, Taylor
A2-1022 Dohle, Lane, Harrington, Hill
A2-1023 Hayes, Munday, Buttriss, Rowe
A2-1024 Hindley, Champion, Williams
A2-1025 Scott, Banfield, Roche

The aircraft are listed in numerical sequence, not in actual sequence of flight or in sequence into the landing-zone. The first two in each crew are pilots, the others machinegunners.

* * *

Following is Wing Commander Scott's letter to Group Captain Raw, 16 August 1966, refuting the claim by Brigadier Jackson that 9 Squadron was not adequately supporting 1ATF. It indicates fault on the part of both the Army and the RAAF in not ensuring a clear mutual understanding of the problems faced in operating, and is perhaps best viewed as a letter brought about by the manner in which the separate Services were employed after 1945, with each developing its own techniques and procedures while paying lip-service to the need for cooperation, joint planning and understanding.

TASKING OF NO. 9 SQUADRON AIRCRAFT

1. During the visit of the CAS on 14 August 1966, the Commander 1ATF apparently stated that No. 9 Squadron was not producing the support he desired, and that as a result he wanted the unit to be based in the vicinity of the Task Force Headquarters during the daylight hours to decrease the reaction time to tasks. Whilst I agree that during the initial two weeks

after the Squadron became operational, aircraft were frequently on target after the time requested by 1ATF, I do not accept that this was the fault of No. 9 Squadron. Basically, the small number of delays which did occur were beyond the control of this Squadron and can be attributed to:—

    (a) difficulties in communications between the ATOC and RAAF Operations Vung Tau,

    (b) the Ground Liaison Section at Vung Tau having insufficient knowledge of the intelligence situation in the TAOR,

    (c) the Army component of the ATF ignoring the principle of joint planning, and being reluctant or refusing to give details for air planning when requested,

    (d) the Army units concerned rarely pre-planning tasks, and

    (e) adverse weather.

2. Initially, communications between the ATOC and the RAAF Operations Room were very poor. Loss of communications was frequent, and details of tasks were delayed during transit. At times these communications delays were reflected in aircraft arriving for tasks after the Army-nominated TOT. Improvements to the communications network have been made, and the reliability and transmit/receive times of the nets are estimated to be:—

Duplex T/P	Hot Line T/Phone	Normal T/Phone
95.8%	94%	85%
9.1 mins	instant	instant

In addition to the above communications equipment, HF and VHF FM links are being installed, and VHF AM and UHF links to aircraft in the TAOR are operating efficiently. No aircraft has been delayed through poor communications between the controlling authorities during the past week.

3. Until recently, the only intelligence information available for the briefing of aircrew was supplied by a daily Situation Report (SITREP) and Intelligence Summary (INTSUM) supplied to No. 67 GL Section at the Vung Tau Operations Room. These SITREPs and INTSUMs were up to forty-eight (48) hours old when received, and consequently were of very little use for the briefing of aircrew on the tactical situation. The obvious inherent danger in this situation was that crews could have been, and were, subjected to high and unnecessary risks through ignorance of the latest tactical situation. To obviate this risk, the Vung Tau Operations Room staff frequently had to make special requests to the ATOC for the latest situation pertaining to a

particular area where aircraft were to be committed. At times this caused slight delays in the briefing of the crews and subsequent departure of the aircraft. Although the requesting of this additional information obviously was justified, it was not the most efficient. Consequently, on 1 August I requested the Commanding Officer No. 67 GL Section to obtain constant updating of the intelligence information. His request for this, plus the reply from HQ ATF, are attached. [Not released for this book.] For comparison with HQ ATF's reply, precis No. 67 of Air Support Units 'Transport Air Support' is interesting.

4. As No. 67 GL Section's approach for more information received no cooperation from HQ ATF, I requested that the ATOC attempt to supply updated intelligence reports. Since 3 August intelligence information has been supplied on an hourly basis by the ATOC, and this information is adequate for the briefing of aircrews. No future delays of aircraft through insufficient intelligence information are anticipated.

5. There has been little, if any, joint planning of operations at the ATF HQ. Sqn Ldr Ramsey has stated frequently that although he is trying to correct the situation, in most cases the first he is aware of the impending operation is when the completed operation order is received at his desk. Although the ATOC is not a JOC, it has representatives of the RAAF transport squadrons, US Army Aviation, and USAF FAC and ground-attack aircraft units. From observation and bitter experience I am sure that there are no Australian Army air experts at the ATF HQ. I would therefore deem it prudent, in fact necessary, that the RAAF, US Army and USAF experts should attend the commander's conference every evening and they should also be present when plans for projected operations are being formulated.

6. No. 9 Squadron frequently does not receive pre-planned tasks until very late at night. In addition, these tasks are usually for tasks which are to take place early (0630–0800) hours of the following day. From a study of tasks carried out to date, there appears to be no reason why the majority of tasks could not have been pre-planned well in advance of the required TOT and consequently avoided last-minute 'panic' requests, which, apart from demanding an almost impossible TOT, allow little time for correct and efficient crew briefing and flight planning. There is no doubt in my mind that the impression has been gained that since the Squadron is in direct support of the Army component of the Task Force, they are on call much the same as a radio cab. To agree to this type of tasking inevitably will lead to

inefficiency, aircrew fatigue, a lowering of aircraft serviceability, and eventually the totally unnecessary loss of aircraft and crews.

7. Frequently the US Army is quoted as the experts in the use of helicopters in the tactical field, and some Australian Army officers who have had liaison with US Army helicopter units tend to ridicule procedures and techniques which No. 9 Squadron uses. The US Army 1st Aviation Brigade 'Operations Manual' dated 1 June 1966 is the US Army 'bible' for helicopter operations. A comparison of this manual with the RAAF Vung Tau Iroquois Standard Operating Procedure C/1/1 Appendix (dated 1 November 1965) indicates there is close agreement between RAAF and US Army procedures. [Some sentences here following were deleted from the document when it was released for inclusion in this book, as they were quotations from the US manual.] We cannot compare the effort of six RAAF Iroquois with the forces available to the US Army. Nevertheless, it is obvious that the principles stated in the US Army manual, and to which the RAAF has subscribed during and since WW2, apply to any size force.

8. A study of the Translands and operational briefing forms for the last week indicates that eighty-two (82) missions were flown by the Squadron. On six (6) missions the aircraft did not meet the TOT. A summary of these missions and the reasons for not meeting the TOT are:—
[The missions were tabulated, and reasons for lateness given. For brevity, the full explanation is not included. Lateness was caused by weather in two cases, diversion to a more urgent task in two others, inability to make radio contact with the ground in one, and lack of time between request and an aircraft becoming available in the sixth case.]

9. The majority of the Squadron aircrew have been flying Iroquois in the Army support role for the last four (4) years. They have an excellent understanding of the ground-support mission requirement, and have done their utmost to meet the Army requirements under adverse tasking and operational conditions. Consequently it is a bitter experience to hear criticism which is unjustified, and not supported by facts. I believe that while we have a poor working relationship and are not trusted by certain elements of the Army component of the Task Force Headquarters, we do have an excellent reputation with the man in the field. In this regard a quote from a letter received from the Commanding Officer No. 3 SAS Squadron (who certainly would suffer if this Squadron was not carrying out operations efficiently) is appropriate: '. . . my blokes think your blokes are

doing a tremendous job for them. The joy at seeing the aircraft coming in to pick them up really has to be experienced to be fully appreciated.'

10. I do not believe that the criticisms levelled at No. 9 Squadron have any bearing on present operations. I believe that the desire to have the Squadron operate from the HQ ATF area is designed to weaken RAAF control of air operations, and ultimately pave the way for incorporation of the Iroquois force into the new Army Aviation Regiment. Advance warning of this aspect was given by the RAAF team which visited Vietnam during March 1966 to organize the deployment of the RAAF element of the Australian Task Force.

11. To gain maximum efficiency from the RAAF Iroquois force, the following actions should be taken:—

   (a) issue a clear directive as to what communication links are required between the ATOC and Vung Tau Operations Room, stipulating the transmission and security delays acceptable in each link,
   (b) insist on the Army component of the Task Force accepting its responsibility for providing information to No. 67 GL Section so that it can discharge its duties effectively,
   (c) insist on the principle of joint planning of operations,
   (d) insist on adequate pre-planning of tasks, dissemination of information, and nomination of TOTs, and,
   (e) the fostering of a better understanding and mutual respect between the two Services.

(R.A. SCOTT)
Wing Commander
Commanding Officer

The Vietcong in Phuoc Tuy

The image of the VC as a ragged patriot fighting with little but bare hands and a dream of independence was probably nurtured by the more naive in countries outside Vietnam. In reality, the individual VC was a member of a highly organized and tightly controlled political structure.

An outline of the complex politico-civilian structure (as distinct from the military formations) in the VC province of Ba Long may be of interest.

The insurgency was supported by a complex of organizations managed by political cadre, and this supporting complex was known as the *Vietcong Infrastructure* (VCI). The VCI existed to fulfil two main tasks:

(a) to provide an administrative and governmental structure that could assume control of the country in the event of a Communist victory;

(b) to provide support, such as food, intelligence, money, refuge, labour and medical supplies, to VC/NVA military units — essential for their very survival.

The administrative and governmental structure was provided by organizations such as those listed below. Their roles and functions are only sketchily described.

The *Civilian Proselyting Section* recruited and gathered people belonging to particular groups — farmers, women, youth and so on — into an Association. Nominally, the Association would be part of the NLF, but Party members would control it.

The *Civil Health Section* attempted to meet civil health needs with dispensaries and medical services.

The *Propaganda and Training Section* spread Party policies and propaganda by way of clubs, live entertainment and films, all emphasizing the righteousness of the NLF and the wickedness of the GVN.

The *Court and Detention System* of the *Security Section* in theory resolved civil disputes but actually suppressed opposition and deviation.

The *Organization Section* kept detailed records of all VCI personnel, including Party members. When People's Liberation Committee members were needed, this Section judged candidates according to Party standards.

People's Liberation Committees served as transitory organs of control, more sophisticated than the NLF mass organizations. Representatives were chosen first at hamlet level, and then upwards through villages to region level, but candidates were strictly controlled by the Party.

With the Party directing all of the above organizations, it was able to control the areas from which the South Vietnamese government was excluded by VC/NVA military force.

To support the military, the following Sections were needed and created:

The *Finance and Economy Section* supervised the collection of money and food, and their allocation — a large undertaking. The Section also arranged when and where collection was to take place, as well as determining the quantities involved.

The *Military Proselyting Section* conducted operations to subvert enemy personnel, an important task that needs no further explanation.

The *Security Section* was responsible for intelligence, counter-intelligence, counter-subversion and reconnaissance.

The *Forward Supply Council* coordinated activities between the Finance and Economy and the Rear Services (logistics) elements, for the purpose of passing supplies to military units. It managed all civilian labourers supplied through the VCI and Front Associations (see below). The Council was jointly staffed by civilians from the Finance and Economy Section and the Security Section, and by military from the Rear Services staffs.

The *Propaganda and Training Section* recruited for the military units. It was paralleled by a civilian equivalent, as we have seen, and was so important that recruiting was closely supervised by Party Executive Committees at all levels.

Front Associations provided the manpower base for recruitment into military, paramilitary and VCI organizations.

All these worked closely together, and were coordinated by *Executive Committees* at province and district levels.

As long as the VCI was allowed to function, the insurgency would flourish. And as long as the abovementioned organizations existed and operated with little or no interference, the armed units and formations of the VC and NVA would be well supported, and able to live and operate outside the urban areas.

But if the armed units could be isolated, or their support seriously reduced, they would find it impossible to carry on.

Even with such a widespread VCI organization, the VC/NVA units required massive supplies of Communist-bloc weapons. Two of the best-known are the AK47 rifle and the RPG launcher. Also provided were mortars, artillery, AA guns, rockets, radios, medical supplies and vehicles.

The Vietcong soldier was personally well-equipped, with a supply-line reaching back to Hanoi, and also to the factories of the USSR and the People's Republic of China. The patriot in ragged clothes, armed with little more than a bolt-action rifle, existed only in propaganda messages and credulous minds.

APPENDIX 4

The Vietcong Ambush

A Vietcong document describing in detail their concept of the ambush, and the ways to go about it, was captured and circulated among the Allied forces. Composed of five parts, the document covered every aspect of ambushing as seen by the Vietcong.

Part I described basic principles and stated that ambushes were either *static* or *mobile and manoeuvre*. In a static ambush, the attackers were already in the chosen area, camouflaged, awaiting their prey. If, because of terrain and regular enemy activity, a static ambush was not possible, the attack forces would gather close by and manoeuvre around and onto the enemy according to a plan.

The fundamentals necessary for success were listed as preservation of secrecy, maintenance of the initiative, careful preparation, rapid attack, rapid action and rapid withdrawal. The last four were often included in other reports as the '*Four Quicks and One Slow*': quick advance, quick attack, quick reorganization, quick withdrawal, but slow preparation.

A section described the selection of sites for an ambush, and the conditions required were:

(a) good terrain features for disposition of the VC, concealment of their weapons, and observation of the enemy;

(b) suitable routes for fast advance, contact, assault and development of firepower;

(c) convenient withdrawal routes, and the more of them the better;

(d) lack of good terrain features for use by the enemy; and

(e) terrain features that would not attract enemy attention, while enabling ambushes to be laid against them.

In the section describing employment and disposition of the ambush, it was stated that the VC were not to spread their forces but to concentrate them, so that they could envelop and split the enemy for destruction by segments. The VC force was to be organized into elements responsible for blocking the front and rear of the enemy, blocking any other movements, holding off any enemy reinforcements, and assaulting the ambushed unit. If the enemy were too numerous to be ambushed in total, then a part of their force was to be selected and destroyed.

Part II contained instructions on organizing and preparing for combat. Naturally, the first requirement was for a thorough *Reconnaissance*, comprised of information on enemy, terrain and local situation.

Information required on the enemy included type, weapons, morale, usual routes, formations used, concept of operations, command and control, reinforcements available and routes these would follow, fire support available, and locations from which it would come.

The terrain study was to be carefully carried out, to determine the advantages and disadvantages to both sides.

Information on the local situation included contacting and working with the local Vietcong Infrastructure to gather information on both the enemy and the population, as well as to obtain support from the various VC organizations.

Combat Planning would begin only after the reconnaissance phase had been carried out thoroughly. All the gathered information was consolidated and a view of the situation was gained.

Based on a knowledge of the situation and of the combat potential of the VC force, a *Combat Objective* would be determined. Would an entire enemy force or only a part of it be destroyed? Political purposes would also be included.

A *Force Employment Plan* would be decided, and would include strengths of personnel and weapons, combat potential, command personnel and the mission of each element of the ambush force in each combat phase. Responsibilities of each element were to be clearly determined.

Political Activities involved informing all who were to take part as to the purpose of the ambush, the advantages enjoyed by the VC and the difficulties to be mastered to gain success. Political officers were to talk to units about not underestimating the enemy, and about not 'entertaining pessimistic opinions'. All members of all units were to be lectured about evacuation of casualties, handling of prisoners, removal of captured enemy equipment and the opportunities for propaganda among the enemy.

Suitable *Equipment* was to be acquired for the mission, and it was noted that leaders 'must personally conduct thorough inspections of every element down to every man'.

The *Command and Communications* section stated that observation posts were to be placed at many locations, to watch for approaching enemy and inform command personnel at once.

Commanders 'must be located where they can observe the enemy, control their main elements and observe the overall combat situation'. Communications across the battlefield were to be simple and easily used, with messengers or telephone relied upon.

Part III described the conduct of the ambush. *Before the Operation*, command personnel were to carry out a final check of the situation and the ambush area. Travelling-time to the location was to be carefully controlled to avoid early or late arrival. Routes were to be away from populated areas, and while on the move the VC units were to maintain strict discipline as to noise and camouflage. If enemy 'spies' or patrols were encountered, they were to be avoided or totally destroyed. Depending on the outcome of such action, a further decision was to be made as to whether the operation was to continue or be abandoned.

The *Battlefield Occupation* phase followed, the advance party maintaining constant contact with the commanders. When in location, observation and guard posts would be organized, fire plans arranged, assault and withdrawal routes selected, fortifications constructed if necessary, then camouflaged, and liaison and communications established.

If a mobile ambush was intended, commanders of all elements were personally to inspect the battlefield so as to know the routes for advance and assault, as well as those leading to fire-support positions. It was emphasized that secrecy was of paramount importance during this phase.

The *Combat* phase was to be executed with aggressive attack, assault and pursuit. The critical aspects of this phase were the time to open fire, the time to assault, and the controlled use of maximum firepower against the enemy.

If the ambush did not go as planned, the force would 'rapidly move out of the area', using terrain and small diversionary groups to allow the main elements to escape.

After a successful ambush, the *Battlefield Recovery* phase began. During this time, the location would be guarded and enemy reinforcements prevented from arriving; while casualties and prisoners were moved away, the area was searched for routed enemy trying to escape, and all weapons, documents and ammunition were carried off or destroyed.

Withdrawal was 'a "must" in the combat plan'; and, whether successful or not, the following principles were to be obeyed:

Personnel were not to vie with each other in withdrawing; all casualties were to be evacuated, with the seriously injured going first; commanders were to control the rear element to deal with unforeseen events; enemy situation and conditions of the route were to be considered; mutual support was to be provided so that all elements could move in good order; deliberate withdrawal without orders was forbidden; diversions to deceive the enemy were to be used; and command personnel were to 'remain calm, display bravery and set an example to the combat morale of their unit'.

Post-combat Activities, after both successful and unsuccessful actions, were to include: determining the lessons learnt; interrogating prisoners and then handing them on to higher HQ; obeying policy on equipment seized from the enemy; deciding which individuals should be commended; 'instituting good patterns of thinking to eliminate subjectivism and pessimism'; collecting and consolidating reports of enemy attainments and forwarding them to higher HQ for study; working out plans for the strengthening of the units for the next operation; under the leadership of senior cadre, conducting propaganda activities in organized groups; and visiting the families of casualties.

Part IV discussed various types of ambush — against small numbers of enemy; against patrols on regular routes; against vehicles, whether alone, in small groups or in large convoys; against enemy on rivers; against encircling movements; and against withdrawing enemy.

These ambushes had evolved from actions against the French and the ARVN — both would often move at regular times and along the same routes, a habit branded by more than one observer as 'an ambush looking for a place to happen'.

One paragraph, relevant to this book, describes *Attack of Motorized Enemy Reinforcements*, and states:

Regardless of the number of vehicles, attack must be conducted on the first vehicle. If assault forces are available, rapid assault must be conducted to prevent enemy reaction. If the enemy uses grenades during our assault, we must rapidly take cover on the sides of the vehicles and continue assaulting after the grenades have exploded. To attack motorized enemy reinforcements, it is best to use mines together with an assault element and sabotage teams.

It is obvious from this paragraph, and from the VC reaction to Adrian Roberts's APC Troop, that the VC had not considered the possibility of a quick ambush against a force of vehicles moving in formation but *off* the road.

Part V of the document referred to enemy reactions to ambushes — such as increased use of aircraft flying low ahead of convoys to search the sides of roads and the banks of waterways — and made other observations not relevant to 1ATF operations in Phuoc Tuy, or to this book.

Readers may be interested enough to consider the principles of ambush outlined in this VC document, and to decide for themselves whether D Company 6RAR was ambushed, and whether an ambush in the Long Tan rubber plantation had in fact been the VC intention.

Decorations and Awards

Decorations and awards for the battle were supplemented by the US Presidential Unit Citation. The list below sets out the decorations and awards bestowed under the Commonwealth system.

Distinguished Service Order (DSO)
> Brigadier O.D. Jackson
> Lieutenant-Colonel C. Townsend

Member of the Order of the British Empire (MBE)
> Captain M. Stanley (NZ)

Military Cross (MC)
> Major H.A. Smith

Distinguished Conduct Medal (DCM)
> Warrant Officer 2 J.W. Kirby
> Corporal J. Carter

Military Medal (MM)
> Sergeant R.S. Buick
> Private R.M. Eglinton

Mentioned in Dispatches (MID)
> Lieutenant F.A. Roberts
> Second Lieutenant G.M. Kendall
> Second Lieutenant D.R. Sabben
> Warrant Officer 2 J.W. Roughley
> Corporal P.N. Dobson
> Corporal W.R. Moore
> Private W.A. Akell

The text of the award of the Presidential Unit Citation reads:

D Company, Sixth Battalion, Royal Australian Regiment, distinguished itself by extraordinary heroism while engaged in military operations against an opposing armed force in Vietnam on 18 August 1966. While searching for Viet Cong in a rubber plantation north-east of Ba Ria, Phuoc Tuy Province, Republic of Vietnam, D Company met and immediately became engaged in heavy contact. As the battle developed, it became apparent that the men of D Company were facing a numerically superior force. The platoons of D Company were surrounded and attacked on all sides by an estimated reinforced enemy battalion using automatic weapons, small arms, and mortars. Fighting courageously against a well armed and determined foe, the men of D Company maintained their formations in a common perimeter defence and inflicted heavy casualties upon the Viet Cong. The enemy maintained a continuous, intense volume of fire and attacked repeatedly from all directions. Each successive assault was repulsed by the courageous Australians. Heavy rainfall and a low ceiling prevented any friendly close air support during the battle. After three hours of savage attacks, having failed to penetrate the Australian lines, the enemy withdrew from the battlefield carrying many dead and wounded, and leaving 245 Viet Cong dead forward of the defence position of D Company. The conspicuous gallantry, intrepidity and indomitable courage of D Company were in the highest tradition of military valor and reflect great credit upon D Company, Sixth Battalion, The Royal Australian Regiment and The Australian Army.

Australians eligible to wear the emblem of the PUC awarded for Long Tan are:

Maj.	H.A. Smith	Cpl	K.T. Miller
Capt.	H.I. McLean-Williams	Cpl	D.R. Mogg
2Lt	G.M. Kendall	Cpl	W.R. Moore
2Lt	D.R. Sabben	LCpl	G.J. Ballinger
2Lt	G.C. Sharp[†]	LCpl	M.G. Campbell
WO2	J.W. Kirby	LCpl	G.K. Crowther
SSgt	R. Gildersleeve	LCpl	J. Jewry[†]
Sgt	R.S. Buick	LCpl	C.T. Lithgow
Sgt	W. O'Donnell	LCpl	W.T. Luther
Sgt	N.J. Rankin	LCpl	B.E. Magnussen[*]
Sgt	D.A. Thomson	LCpl	G.R. Richardson
Sgt	J. Todd[*]	LCpl	J.C. Robbins[*]
Cpl	P.N. Dobson	LCpl	P. Slack-Smith
Cpl	L. Drinkwater	LCpl	G.R. Smith
Cpl	J.M. Duroux	LCpl	D.A. Spencer[*]
Cpl	M.W. Green	Pte	P.T. Ainslie
Cpl	J.W. Harris	Pte	W.A. Akell
Cpl	T.H. Lea[*]	Pte	R.A. Aldersea[†]
Cpl	M.V. McCullough	Pte	A.G. Bartlett
Cpl	I.E. McDonald	Pte	D.F. Beahan[*]
Cpl	C.M. Marchant	Pte	J.E. Beere[*]

Pte	S.R. Belford	Pte	P.R. Hunt
Pte	N.R. Bextrum	Pte	P.W. Jameson
Pte	K.D. Branch	Pte	G.D. Langlands
Pte	C.W. Brown*	Pte	P.A. Large†
Pte	R.D. Brown	Pte	A.J. May*
Pte	W.R. Buckland	Pte	A.F. McCormack†
Pte	R.T. Burstall	Pte	D.J. McCormack†
Pte	V.M. Cameron	Pte	I.J. McGrath*
Pte	I.M. Campbell	Pte	B.C. Meller*
Pte	R.C. Carne*	Pte	D.I. Mitchell
Pte	J.C. Cash*	Pte	W.D. Mitchell†
Pte	A.R. Collins*	Pte	D.B. Montgomery
Pte	G.R. Davis*	Pte	R.C. Moss
Pte	A.R. Deller	Pte	I.D. Munro
Pte	P.H. Dettman	Pte	P. Nash
Pte	I. Dixon	Pte	T. Newall
Pte	P.R. Dixon	Pte	A.L. Parr
Pte	K.P. Doolan	Pte	R.V. Perandis
Pte	P.J. Doyle	Pte	G.M. Peters
Pte	G.A. Drabble†	Pte	J.H. Quincey
Pte	R.M. Eglinton*	Pte	B.R. Reilly
Pte	H.T. Esler	Pte	R.L. Rencher
Pte	D.P. Fabian*	Pte	J.P. Richmond*
Pte	B.D. Firth*	Pte	J.E. Riley
Pte	B.D. Forsyth*	Pte	W.A. Roche
Pte	A.R. Fraser	Pte	T.P. Ryan*
Pte	K.H. Gant†	Pte	D.J. Salveron†
Pte	D.A. Graham	Pte	V.W. Simon
Pte	K.W. Graham*	Pte	A.M. Stepney
Pte	E.F. Grant†	Pte	R.N. Stewart
Pte	V.R. Grice†	Pte	D.J. Thomas†
Pte	N.J. Grimes	Pte	F.B. Topp†
Pte	B. Halls	Pte	K.J. Tronk
Pte	J.E. Haslewood	Pte	B.F. Vassella
Pte	R.C. Healey	Pte	L.S. Vine
Pte	S. Hodder	Pte	M.R. Wales†
Pte	J.R. Holmes	Pte	G.C. Warrell
Pte	W.F. Hornett	Pte	T.W. Watts
Pte	B.G. Hornung*	Pte	H.P. Webb*
Pte	J. Houston†	Pte	C.J. Whiston†
Pte	T.R. Humphries	Pte	S.R. Williams

New Zealanders:

Capt. M. Stanley
LBdr W. Walker
LBdr M. Broomhall

† Killed in action at Long Tan
* Wounded in action at Long Tan

List of Abbreviations

AA	Anti-aircraft
AAFV	Australian Army Force Vietnam (later AFV: Australian Force Vietnam)
AATTV	Australian Army Training Team Vietnam
AIF	Australian Imperial Force
ALSG	Australian Logistic Support Group
APC	Armoured Personnel Carrier
ARA	Australian Regular Army
ARVN	Army of the Republic of Vietnam
ATF	Australian Task Force (1ATF = First Australian Task Force)
ATOC	Air Tactical Operations Centre
BAR	Browning Automatic Rifle
BC	Battery Commander (in Artillery)
BHQ	Battalion Headquarters (also Bn HQ)
BK	Battery Captain (in Artillery)
Bn	Battalion
Bty	Battery
CAS	Chief of Air Staff
CHQ	Company Headquarters
CO	Commanding Officer
COSVN	Central Office for South Vietnam (the Hanoi-controlled HQ for waging the war in the South)
Coy	Company
CP	Command Post
CSM	Company Sergeant-Major
DCM	Distinguished Conduct Medal

FAC	Forward Air Controller (a pilot who flies a small aircraft into the battle area to guide fighters or bombers onto targets)
FFV	Field Force Vietnam
FOO	Forward Observation Officer (an Artillery officer trained to adjust the fall of artillery by observing from a frontline position)
FSCC	Fire Support Coordination Centre
GL	Ground Liaison
GMC	General Motors Corporation
GR	Grid Reference
GS	Grid Square
GS02	General Staff Officer Grade 2 (of the rank of Major); also GS01 (Lieutenant-Colonel) and GS03 (Captain)
GVN	Government of Vietnam (the Saigon regime)
H & I	Harassing and Interdiction
HMG	Heavy Machinegun
HQ	Headquarters
INTSUM	Intelligence summary
JOC	Joint Operations Centre
KIA	Killed in Action
LAC	Leading Aircraftman (RAAF rank)
LMG	Light Machinegun
LOCSTAT	Location statement (present location)
LZ	Landing-zone
MC	Military Cross
MFC	Mortar Fire Controller
MG	Machinegun
MM	Military Medal
MORTREP	Mortaring report
NCO	Non-commissioned Officer (i.e. below the rank of Second Lieutenant)
NLF	National Liberation Front
NS	National Service
NVA	North Vietnamese Army
OC	Officer Commanding
OSS	Office of Strategic Services

PRP	People's Revolutionary Party
R & C	Rest and Convalescence
RAA	Royal Australian Artillery
RAAF	Royal Australian Air Force
RAAMC	Royal Australian Army Medical Corps
RAASC	Royal Australian Army Service Corps
RAR	Royal Australian Regiment (6RAR = Sixth Battalion, RAR; D/6RAR = D Company, 6RAR)
RCL	Recoilless Launcher
Recce	Reconnaissance
Regt	Regiment
RMC	Royal Military College (Duntroon)
RMO	Regimental Medical Officer (the Battalion doctor)
RPG	Communist-bloc squad-level rocket-launcher (often wrongly assumed to stand for 'Rocket-propelled Grenade')
RR	Recoilless Rifle
RSM	Regimental Sergeant-Major (the senior NCO in the unit)
RVN	Republic of Vietnam
SAS	Special Air Service
SEATO	South-East Asia Treaty Organization
SITREP	Situation report
SLR	Self-loading Rifle (Australian 7.62mm rifle)
SP	Self-propelled (gun)
Sqn	Squadron (Sqn Ldr = Squadron Leader)
TAOR	Tactical Area of Operational Responsibility
TOC	Tactical Operations Centre
TOT	Time on Target
Tpr	Trooper
UH	Utility Helicopter (UH1 = 'Huey')
USAF	United States Air Force
VC	Vietcong

Index of Names

Bestselling War Fiction and Non-Fiction

☐ Passage to Mutiny	Alexander Kent	£2.50
☐ The Flag Captain	Alexander Kent	£2.50
☐ Badge of Glory	Douglas Reeman	£2.50
☐ Winged Escort	Douglas Reeman	£2.50
☐ Army of Shadows	John Harris	£2.50
☐ Up for Grabs	John Harris	£2.50
☐ Decoy	Dudley Pope	£1.95
☐ Curse of the Death's Head	Rupert Butler	£2.25
☐ Gestapo	Rupert Butler	£2.75
☐ Auschwitz and the Allies	Martin Gilbert	£4.95
☐ Tumult in the Clouds	James A. Goodson	£2.95
☐ Sigh for a Merlin	Alex Henshaw	£2.50
☐ Morning Glory	Stephen Howarth	£4.95
☐ The Doodlebugs	Norman Longmate	£4.95
☐ Colditz – The Full Story	Major P. Reid	£2.95

ARROW BOOKS, BOOKSERVICE BY POST, PO BOX 29, DOUGLAS, ISLE OF MAN, BRITISH ISLES

NAME ....

ADDRESS ....

....

....

Please enclose a cheque or postal order made out to Arrow Books Ltd. for the amount due and allow the following for postage and packing.

U.K. CUSTOMERS: Please allow 22p per book to a maximum of £3.00.

B.F.P.O. & EIRE: Please allow 22p per book to a maximum of £3.00.

OVERSEAS CUSTOMERS: Please allow 22p per book.

Whilst every effort is made to keep prices low it is sometimes necessary to increase cover prices at short notice. Arrow Books reserve the right to show new retail prices on covers which may differ from those previously advertised in the text or elsewhere.

Bestselling Non-Fiction

☐ The Alexander Principle	Wilfred Barlow	£2.95
☐ The Complete Book of Exercises	Diagram Group	£4.95
☐ Everything is Negotiable	Gavin Kennedy	£2.95
☐ Health on Your Plate	Janet Pleshette	£2.50
☐ The Cheiro Book of Fate and Fortune	Cheiro	£2.95
☐ The Handbook of Chinese Horoscopes	Theodora Lau	£2.50
☐ Hollywood Babylon	Kenneth Anger	£7.95
☐ Hollywood Babylon II	Kenneth Anger	£7.95
☐ The Domesday Heritage	Ed. Elizabeth Hallam	£3.95
☐ Historic Railway Disasters	O. S. Nock	£2.50
☐ Wildlife of the Domestic Cat	Roger Tabor	£4.50
☐ Elvis and Me	Priscilla Presley	£2.95
☐ Maria Callas	Arianna Stassinopoulos	£2.50
☐ The Brendan Voyage	Tim Severin	£3.50

ARROW BOOKS, BOOKSERVICE BY POST, PO BOX 29, DOUGLAS, ISLE OF MAN, BRITISH ISLES

NAME ....

ADDRESS ....

....

....

Please enclose a cheque or postal order made out to Arrow Books Ltd. for the amount due and allow the following for postage and packing.

U.K. CUSTOMERS: Please allow 22p per book to a maximum of £3.00.

B.F.P.O. & EIRE: Please allow 22p per book to a maximum of £3.00.

OVERSEAS CUSTOMERS: Please allow 22p per book.

Whilst every effort is made to keep prices low it is sometimes necessary to increase cover prices at short notice. Arrow Books reserve the right to show new retail prices on covers which may differ from those previously advertised in the text or elsewhere.

Bestselling Non-Fiction

☐ The Gradual Vegetarian	Lisa Tracy	£2.95
☐ The Food Scandal	Caroline Walker & Geoffrey Cannon	£3.95
☐ Harmony Rules	Gary Butt & Frena Bloomfield	£2.25
☐ Everything is Negotiable	Gavin Kennedy	£2.95
☐ Hollywood Babylon	Kevin Anger	£7.95
☐ Red Watch	Gordon Honeycombe	£2.75
☐ Wildlife of the Domestic Cat	Roger Tabor	£4.50
☐ The World of Placido Domingo	Daniel Snowman	£4.95
☐ The Sinbad Voyage	Tim Severin	£2.75
☐ The Hills is Lonely	Lillian Beckwith	£1.95
☐ English Country Cottage	R. J. Brown	£3.50
☐ Raw Energy	Leslie & Susannah Kenton	£2.95

ARROW BOOKS, BOOKSERVICE BY POST, PO BOX 29, DOUGLAS, ISLE OF MAN, BRITISH ISLES

NAME ....

ADDRESS ....

....

....

Please enclose a cheque or postal order made out to Arrow Books Ltd. for the amount due and allow the following for postage and packing.

U.K. CUSTOMERS: Please allow 22p per book to a maximum of £3.00.

B.F.P.O. & EIRE: Please allow 22p per book to a maximum of £3.00.

OVERSEAS CUSTOMERS: Please allow 22p per book.

Whilst every effort is made to keep prices low it is sometimes necessary to increase cover prices at short notice. Arrow Books reserve the right to show new retail prices on covers which may differ from those previously advertised in the text or elsewhere.

Bestselling Fiction

☐ Dancing Bear	Chaim Bermant	£2.95
☐ Hiroshima Joe	Martin Booth	£2.95
☐ 1985	Anthony Burgess	£1.95
☐ The Other Woman	Colette	£1.95
☐ The Manchurian Candidate	Richard Condon	£2.25
☐ Letter to a Child Never Born	Oriana Fallaci	£1.25
☐ Duncton Wood	William Horwood	£3.50
☐ Aztec	Gary Jennings	£3.95
☐ The Journeyer	Gary Jennings	£3.50
☐ The Executioner's Song	Norman Mailer	£3.50
☐ Strumpet City	James Plunkett	£3.50
☐ Admiral	Dudley Pope	£1.95
☐ The Second Lady	Irving Wallace	£2.50
☐ An Unkindness of Ravens	Ruth Rendell	£1.95
☐ The History Man	Malcolm Bradbury	£2.95

ARROW BOOKS, BOOKSERVICE BY POST, PO BOX 29, DOUGLAS, ISLE OF MAN, BRITISH ISLES

NAME ....

ADDRESS ....

....

....

Please enclose a cheque or postal order made out to Arrow Books Ltd. for the amount due and allow the following for postage and packing.

U.K. CUSTOMERS: Please allow 22p per book to a maximum of £3.00.

B.F.P.O. & EIRE: Please allow 22p per book to a maximum of £3.00.

OVERSEAS CUSTOMERS: Please allow 22p per book.

Whilst every effort is made to keep prices low it is sometimes necessary to increase cover prices at short notice. Arrow Books reserve the right to show new retail prices on covers which may differ from those previously advertised in the text or elsewhere.

Bestselling Fiction

☐ Toll for the Brave	Jack Higgins	£1.75
☐ Basikasingo	John Matthews	£2.95
☐ Where No Man Cries	Emma Blair	£1.95
☐ Saudi	Laurie Devine	£2.95
☐ The Clogger's Child	Marie Joseph	£2.50
☐ The Gooding Girl	Pamela Oldfield	£2.75
☐ The Running Years	Claire Rayner	£2.75
☐ Duncton Wood	William Horwood	£3.50
☐ Aztec	Gary Jennings	£3.95
☐ Enemy in Sight	Alexander Kent	£2.50
☐ Strumpet City	James Plunkett	£3.50
☐ The Volunteers	Douglas Reeman	£2.50
☐ The Second Lady	Irving Wallace	£2.50
☐ The Assassin	Evelyn Anthony	£2.50
☐ The Pride	Judith Saxton	£2.50

ARROW BOOKS, BOOKSERVICE BY POST, PO BOX 29, DOUGLAS, ISLE OF MAN, BRITISH ISLES

NAME ....

ADDRESS ....

....

....

Please enclose a cheque or postal order made out to Arrow Books Ltd. for the amount due and allow the following for postage and packing.

U.K. CUSTOMERS: Please allow 22p per book to a maximum of £3.00.

B.F.P.O. & EIRE: Please allow 22p per book to a maximum of £3.00.

OVERSEAS CUSTOMERS: Please allow 22p per book.

Whilst every effort is made to keep prices low it is sometimes necessary to increase cover prices at short notice. Arrow Books reserve the right to show new retail prices on covers which may differ from those previously advertised in the text or elsewhere.

Bestselling Thriller/Suspense

☐ Voices on the Wind	Evelyn Anthony	£2.50
☐ See You Later, Alligator	William F. Buckley	£2.50
☐ Hell is Always Today	Jack Higgins	£1.75
☐ Brought in Dead	Harry Patterson	£1.95
☐ The Graveyard Shift	Harry Patterson	£1.95
☐ Maxwell's Train	Christopher Hyde	£2.50
☐ Russian Spring	Dennis Jones	£2.50
☐ Nightbloom	Herbert Lieberman	£2.50
☐ Basikasingo	John Matthews	£2.95
☐ The Secret Lovers	Charles McCarry	£2.50
☐ Fletch	Gregory Mcdonald	£1.95
☐ Green Monday	Michael M. Thomas	£2.95
☐ Someone Else's Money	Michael M. Thomas	£2.50
☐ Albatross	Evelyn Anthony	£2.50
☐ The Avenue of the Dead	Evelyn Anthony	£2.50

Bestselling SF/Horror

☐ The Brain Eaters	Gary Brandner	£1.95
☐ Family Portrait	Graham Masterton	£2.50
☐ Satan's Snowdrop	Guy N. Smith	£1.95
☐ Malleus Maleficarum	Montague Summers	£4.95
☐ The Devil Rides Out	Dennis Wheatley	£2.95
☐ Cities in Flight	James Blish	£2.95
☐ Stand on Zanzibar	John Brunner	£2.95
☐ 2001: A Space Odyssey	Arthur C. Clarke	£1.95
☐ Elric of Melnibone	Michael Moorcock	£1.95
☐ Gene Wolfe's Book of Days	Gene Wolfe	£2.25
☐ The Shadow of the Torturer	Gene Wolfe	£2.50
☐ Sharra's Exile	Marion Zimmer Bradley	£1.95
☐ The Blackcollar	Timothy Zahn	£1.95

ARROW BOOKS, BOOKSERVICE BY POST, PO BOX 29, DOUGLAS, ISLE OF MAN, BRITISH ISLES

NAME ....

ADDRESS ....

....

....

Please enclose a cheque or postal order made out to Arrow Books Ltd. for the amount due and allow the following for postage and packing.

U.K. CUSTOMERS: Please allow 22p per book to a maximum of £3.00.

B.F.P.O. & EIRE: Please allow 22p per book to a maximum of £3.00.

OVERSEAS CUSTOMERS: Please allow 22p per book.

Whilst every effort is made to keep prices low it is sometimes necessary to increase cover prices at short notice. Arrow Books reserve the right to show new retail prices on covers which may differ from those previously advertised in the text or elsewhere.

A Selection of Arrow Bestsellers

☐ Voices on the Wind	Evelyn Anthony	£2.50
☐ Someone Else's Money	Michael M. Thomas	£2.50
☐ The Executioner's Song	Norman Mailer	£3.50
☐ The Alexander Principle	Wilfred Barlow	£2.95
☐ Everything is Negotiable	Gavin Kennedy	£2.95
☐ The New Girlfriend & other stories	Ruth Rendell	£1.95
☐ An Unkindness of Ravens	Ruth Rendell	£1.95
☐ Dead in the Morning	Margaret Yorke	£1.75
☐ The Domesday Heritage	Ed. Elizabeth Hallam	£3.95
☐ Elvis and Me	Priscilla Presley	£2.95
☐ The World of Placido Domingo	Daniel Snowman	£4.95
☐ Maria Callas	Arianna Stassinopoulos	£2.50
☐ The Brendan Voyage	Tim Severin	£3.50
☐ A Shine of Rainbows	Lillian Beckwith	£1.95
☐ Rates of Exchange	Malcolm Bradbury	£2.95
☐ Thy Tears Might Cease	Michael Farrell	£2.95
☐ Pudding and Pie (Nancy Mitford Omnibus)	Nancy Mitford	£3.95

ARROW BOOKS, BOOKSERVICE BY POST, PO BOX 29, DOUGLAS, ISLE OF MAN, BRITISH ISLES

NAME ....

ADDRESS ....

....

....

Please enclose a cheque or postal order made out to Arrow Books Ltd. for the amount due and allow the following for postage and packing.

U.K. CUSTOMERS: Please allow 22p per book to a maximum of £3.00.

B.F.P.O. & EIRE: Please allow 22p per book to a maximum of £3.00.

OVERSEAS CUSTOMERS: Please allow 22p per book.

Whilst every effort is made to keep prices low it is sometimes necessary to increase cover prices at short notice. Arrow Books reserve the right to show new retail prices on covers which may differ from those previously advertised in the text or elsewhere.

A Selection of Arrow Bestsellers